# OPEN THE CAGE, MURPHY

www.**transworldbooks**.co.uk

*Also by Paul O'Grady*

AT MY MOTHER'S KNEE . . .
AND OTHER LOW JOINTS

THE DEVIL RIDES OUT

STILL STANDING

# OPEN THE CAGE, MURPHY

## MURPHY

Paul O'Grady

BANTAM PRESS

LONDON • TORONTO • SYDNEY • AUCKLAND • JOHANNESBURG

TRANSWORLD PUBLISHERS
61–63 Uxbridge Road, London W5 5SA
www.transworldbooks.co.uk

Transworld is part of the Penguin Random House group of companies
whose addresses can be found at global.penguinrandomhouse.com

First published in Great Britain in 2015 by Bantam Press
an imprint of Transworld Publishers

A CIP catalogue record for this book
is available from the British Library.

ISBNs 9780593072592 (cased)
9780593072608 (tpb)

Typeset in 11½/15½pt Sabon by Falcon Oast Graphic Art Ltd.
Printed and bound by Clays Ltd, Bungay, Suffolk.

Penguin Random House is committed to a sustainable
future for our business, our readers and our planet. This book
is made from Forest Stewardship Council® certified paper.

1 3 5 7 9 10 8 6 4 2

For Brendan Murphy,
who said I'd never write a book

# OPEN THE CAGE, MURPHY

# OPENING

As I write this, sitting up in bed, the overhead lights have started flickering and an old leather captain's chair on castors that lives in the bathroom has just casually rolled into my bedroom. There's an ominous rumbling sound and my heavy brass bed is starting to shake, doing a damn good impression of the one in *The Exorcist*. The dogs are going berserk at this unexpected disturbance at a quarter to three in the morning, set off by the noise that makes it sound as if an express train is running through the middle of the house, as Alma Cogan was wont to sing.

Naturally I immediately put this unusual occurrence down to paranormal activity, having just watched a series about the Enfield Poltergeist on the telly. Leaping out of bed and on to the landing, my suspicions are confirmed as I witness the light suspended over the stairwell swaying gently back and forth of its own volition.

Yes, I tell myself with the authority of Yvette Fielding, this can only mean one thing and that's poltergeist activity and any second now a child with no eyeballs and wild hair, wearing a dirty nightie and baring a set of yellow fangs with claws to match, is going to come tear-arsing down that lobby and leap on me.

However, the racket and shaking is over as soon as it began. Since there's no sign of the demon-child apparition I go back to bed and turn the radio on to see if BBC Kent has any information to impart on what might have been the cause of this palaver.

Unfortunately there's nothing to report. It all seems very laid-back at Radio Kent and since there's no newsflash to tell us that

A.  We've been invaded by aliens,
B.  There's been an earthquake,
C.  Dungeness power station is under attack from terrorists and has exploded,

I go back to my original deduction that the fuss was down to a visit from something unholy from the Other Side and that I now live in a house inhabited by a violent poltergeist, which means that I'll have to move.

If I were on Twitter or Facebook then I could check to see if anybody else in Kent had felt anything similar but as I'm not I have a quick shufti around the internet and, finding nothing of any help, call it a day. Telling myself that the dead can't hurt you I leave the landing light on and try to go to sleep, half expecting the duvet to be pulled off me at any moment and a pair of invisible hands to seize me by the ankles and drag me around the bedroom floor.

Turns out it was an earthquake after all, 4.3 on the Richter scale. Not that I fully understand what that means but I've been assured that although it's nowhere near the strength of the one that hit Nepal, thank God, it's enough to ruffle the feathers of the residents in our part of Kent and give us something to talk about.

You wouldn't expect earthquakes in Kent but this is the second in the fifteen years that I've lived here. The first one brought houses down in Folkestone but thankfully the only casualty incurred during last night's episode was a pottery garden gnome, who has been neatly decapitated.

I like the wee small hours of the morning when apart, from the occasional earthquake, the house is silent and peace descends. This is the best time to write, undisturbed by the phone and free from the daily hassle, with just a pack of snoring dogs and the radio for company. I tap away with two fingers on a laptop so old that if the nerds at the Apple Store clapped eyes on it they'd probably fall about laughing, like those aliens used to do in the Cadbury's Smash advert when encountering a real spud.

At this hour of the morning I'm at peace with both myself and the world. You could casually drop into the conversation that the banks had gone bust and that as a result I'd have to sell my home and return to some scuzzy flat, and I'd probably take it on the chin and resignedly start packing my bags. Then I'd see if Channel Five are thinking of adding a show called *Celebrities on the Dole* to their already growing roster of programmes about folk claiming benefits.

Lying in bed before I drift off to sleep, curious thoughts occupy my mind. For instance, if Hitler had been accepted by that Viennese art academy would the Second World War never have happened? And what is the point of Kim Kardashian? At first I'd always believed that the Kardashians were either a species from *Star Trek* or some fundamentalist group of religious fanatics. I'm still none the wiser about what they do apart from the bitter fact that it's hard to escape this family of American oddballs even if, like me, you don't share the media's obsession with them and are completely, totally and utterly underwhelmed by this ragbag of reality TV narcissists. One thing I have learned is that Our Kim has made her vast fortune out of a low-rent home video of her getting shagged and exposing her gargantuan arse to all and sundry. Oh and then there's the boyfriend/husband/partner whatever-he-is who gets up at awards and abuses those who've had the temerity to win one. It doesn't take a lot these days to become a celebrity. Forget years of study at drama school or trawling the pub and club circuit, just get your arse out and give someone a ham-shank on YouTube and the world's your oyster.

It's a different story though when the alarm goes off and I have to get up as that's the time when evil lurks, for festering underneath that duvet is malevolence personified. If ever I was to murder someone then undoubtedly it would be at seven a.m. I'm not a jump-out-of-bed-and-greet-the-dawn-with-a-song-in-my-heart kind of person; on the contrary, grumpy and resentful at having to leave the comfort of my bed, I lie there contemplating all the trivialities of life and enjoy myself for 'just ten more minutes'.

At the moment it's Operation Stack and the closure of a large section of the M20, turning the Garden of England into a lorry park courtesy of the striking French dock workers in Calais. I'm off the French at the moment and won't even buy their butter as they've made life hell for our local businesses and, thanks to the gridlocked side roads, getting into North Korea would be easier than getting home from London.

Our current government and their treatment of all our public services are guaranteed to get me going, as is the Inland Revenue, who hammer the little guys while turning a blind eye to the huge corporations with their offshore dealings who bla-tantly disregard our tax laws while the majority of us are forced to toe the line under the threat of imprisonment. Every time I walk past a Starbucks or Topshop I'm tempted to pop my head round the door and shout, 'Pay your bloody taxes!'

I relish my loathing for people who describe anything they find pleasurable as 'to die for'. Is it really worth sacrificing your life for a cream cake or a pair of ridiculously expensive shoes? No, of course it isn't, so drop the stupid Americanism if you don't mind and revert to adjectives such as 'wonderful', 'magnificent' or just plain 'nice'. Oh, and while I'm at it, give it up with the 'awesome', will you, and don't ever call me 'dude' if you want to go home with a full complement of teeth.

As you have probably gathered by now, I'm foul of a morning but after a mug of tea and two Weetabix consumed in a Trappist monk-style silence without the aid of telly or radio to shatter the nerves I'm relatively human again and trustworthy enough to be allowed on to the streets without a muzzle.

As I said, I'm not on Twitter, Facebook or Instagram. I simply haven't got the time and besides, I've no wish to invite the twisted nutters who seemingly troll social networking sites into my life. And while we're on the subject and if you want my opinion, which you probably don't but I'll give it to you anyway, I also believe that those who take photographs of their dinner and post them on such sites for the world to marvel at need psychiatric help.

Although I probably sound like a Luddite, I'm not. On the contrary, I embrace the age of the internet but I draw the line at texting a friend who is sitting directly opposite me in a restaurant, as some people frequently do. Soon we'll lose the power of speech and over the years the mouth and tongue will become smaller while the finger and thumb will extend to E.T. proportions.

Predictive text can get you into a lot of embarrassing situations, as I've frequently discovered.

At the after-the-ceremony dinner at the Baftas I replied to a friend who'd texted me wanting to know what we were having to eat, which, as it happens, was something called edible soil as a starter, followed by duck for the main course. Predictive text translated my message as 'Edwards Boil followed by Dick', adding for good measure 'You know how I could never touch Dick'.

I'm sixty now and have been told by friends that I've 'calmed down', which is a little worrying. Does that mean I'm finally settling into old age and will those endless brochures that I've started receiving from companies flogging walk-in baths, stairlifts, and a chance to plan for my funeral now, thus saving my grieving family unnecessary distress, suddenly start catching my full attention?

I'm even getting brochures advertising cruises for the over-sixties with the promise of meeting 'like-minded people' as I sail around the Treasures of the Mediterranean. I wouldn't want to go on a cruise, full stop, particularly not one with people who had minds like mine.

I hardly ever drink now, apart from that vinegar they serve up as wine at awards dos or a long, cool glass of a local Bavarian beer if I'm on holiday in that neck of the woods. That is a bevvy worth travelling for.

As for my clubbing days, I'm very happy to say that they're well and truly over. Nothing, not even a yellow mongoose or my very own baby elephant, would induce me to hit the West End and go clubbing on a Saturday night, or any other night come to think of it. I've done all that, had a ball but have no wish to try to recreate the glory days, thank you. I take quite a lot of drugs though. Unfortunately all of them are on prescription, for boring things like blood pressure and other elderly ailments, with not an upper in sight. Even the dogs are on tablets.

As for sleeping around, well, just like the clubs, my days waking up the next morning to someone whose name I can't remember have long been relegated to history.

Do I miss any of this hectic former life? No, I bloody well don't. Life is complicated enough as it is without raging hangovers and one-night stands to deal with.

I'm even seriously contemplating retirement as there's not a lot left that I want to do, although I doubt that the cost of keeping my menagerie would allow it. Even so, I wonder if it's time to turn the page, as Cilla was fond of saying, and move on to another chapter in my life. My trouble is that I get bored very easily and I'm always on the lookout for a project that I can completely immerse myself in. That's how it is with me, there are no half measures – it's all or nothing. So if there are any bright sparks out there in television or theatreland with an interesting and, more importantly, original project that doesn't involve the ubiquitous celebrity judges or eating a kangaroo's arsehole for the amusement of the Great British Public, then get in touch. Otherwise I'm going to start making my own chutney and going to Zumba classes in the village hall.

Writing these books, I've discovered that I've actually worked hard to get where I am, as opportunity certainly wasn't handed to me on a plate. I always believed that it would be impossible for me to give up a career I fought so hard to achieve and I'd continue battling on like an old trouper until I eventually dropped dead in some provincial dressing room like Old Mother Riley.

Nowadays, older and wiser, I'm of a different opinion and

the idea of turning my back on a career that I loved is no longer to be feared but to be accepted gracefully instead. It's best to make that difficult decision to get off the stage while they're still showing an interest.

It never ceases to amaze me that I've been able to support myself on and off for the last thirty-five years or so in this game of 'showbiz'. Personally I think it's been a bloody miracle and if I was an *X-Factor* contestant with whom the judges have finally come clean and admitted I was crap all along and booted me off, then I'd say it's been an incredible journey, but without the gushing.

'Going on the stage' was out of the question when I left school and any aspirations that I might have secretly harboured were quickly dampened by lack of opportunity and my own insecurities. I didn't think I had what it takes.

To scratch the acting itch I joined the Carlton Players in Birkenhead, an amateur group with an excellent reputation who performed in a converted church known as the Little Theatre. During my brief time with them I appeared in a non-speaking role in a Christmas production for a few nights and couldn't have been happier if I'd been at the Old Vic. Later, I joined the Everyman Youth Theatre in Liverpool and that's when the acting bug really stuck its teeth into me. Giddy with the idea of moving to London and becoming an actor, I had the fantasy forming in my mind and I convinced myself that I was capable of becoming the greatest star, just as Streisand sang in *Funny Girl*. Of course, Barbra didn't have my mother to deal with.

'You see, you can't stick at anything, can you?' I could just hear my mother say if she was around to listen to that declaration, pointedly ignoring the fact that I've managed to support myself in this game for over thirty-five years now, something I still can't quite comprehend.

I can remember my ma's reaction when I first suggested, albeit half-heartedly, that I'd like to go into show business.

'Show business? What sort of show business?' my mother asked incredulously.

'I dunno,' I replied, suddenly embarrassed and regretting even mentioning the subject in the first place. 'Acting, on the stage, I suppose.'

'This is all because you're doing that play over in Liverpool, isn't it?' she rightfully surmised, putting down the *Liverpool Echo* where she'd been spending a happy few minutes scanning the obituary column to see if anyone she knew had recently died.

'Just because you're enjoying yourself messing about with amateur dramatics doesn't mean to say you're the next Olivier, Paul,' she went on. 'And it's not a job with regular hours and a regular pay packet on the table each Friday, you know. They can go months without any jobs, actors can, years even and you don't want to end up dying penniless in a garret, do you?'

I could see from the library book lying open on the sofa next to her that she was reading a Georgette Heyer. Some of the more dramatic dialogue had obviously rubbed off on her.

'But it's something I really like doing . . . acting and stuff and being on the stage.' I was squirming by now.

'Look, the only stage you'll see is the landing stage when you're getting the ferry home from a proper job in an office or something, that's if you don't chuck it in after a week like you normally do,' she sniffed. 'Acting indeed, acting the bloody goat more like. Honestly, Paul, it wasn't that long ago you wanted to be a spy for MI5, then you wanted to be a chemist and a reporter and God knows what else. You live in a fantasy land, son, always looking for the unattainable and unable to stick at anything for very long. I don't know what's to become of you, honestly I don't,' she added, giving the *Echo* a quick flick to straighten it out.

'That's why I don't last long in these jobs,' I tried to explain. 'It's so boring doing the same thing day in day out and I hate working in that sodding abattoir. Talk about a dead-end job,' I added, referring to my current place of employment as a clerk for F.M.C. Meat, an abattoir on the Old Chester Road.

'You get half-price meat, don't you?' she said, as if it was a perk of the job up there with an expense account, company car and a yearly bonus. 'That leg of lamb last week would've cost a fortune in the butcher's.'

'Mother,' I said, sitting down beside her to plead my case. 'There's more to a job than coming home with cheap meat each week.'

'Well, you wouldn't get that on the stage,' she said finally, 'unless of course they chucked it at you,' and indicating that she'd had enough of this discussion she picked up her newspaper and began perusing the deaths again.

We sat in silence; me thinking about a life upon the wicked stage which in retrospect was as unrealistic as it was fanciful, while my mother continued her search for the recently bereaved.

'I wonder if this is one of the Kellys from Back Menai Street,' she said, having come across a name she vaguely recognized from the past. 'I'm sure it is. She had a sister who was a bit daft, a big, tall girl built like a Mullingar heifer with a cross eye, d'you remember her? She was a breach birth,' she went on, warming to her theme. 'Breach of the peace more like as she used to get violent in drink. She got arrested outside the Lord Ecky one Christmas Eve. You must remember.'

'No,' I said, bored with this nightly ritual of 'Spot the Stiff'.

'She always wore a green coat, the brother got shot in Burma during the war and got pensioned off with an artificial knee . . . Are you sure you don't remember them?'

'I never met them, Mother,' I told her. 'I'd have remembered them if I had, I mean how could I forget a seven-foot, gozzy-eyed violent drunk of a woman in a green coat ambling down Back Menai Street with a limping war hero in tow?'

'No, I don't suppose you would as you were only a tot at the time. I'll ask our Annie, she's like the Grim Reaper that one, she knows who's dead before they do.'

'I could go to drama school in London,' I pressed on. 'Angela Walsh is, she's going to Drama Centre.'

'Oh I see,' she said, turning her attentions away from the obits and back to me. 'Angela Walsh is going to drama school in London and now you want to go. Where are you going to live? Flats don't grow on trees, and what are you going to live on, eh? Those grants them poor students get don't go very far, that's if they give you one. I'm only being realistic.'

'I know,' I sighed in agreement. 'But I'm sure I'd manage somehow. I'd get a part-time job.'

'You don't want to end up as one of them rent boys hanging around amusement arcades, my lad,' she warned. 'London is a big unfriendly city, as you've found out to your cost in the past. Let's not forget the fiasco in that pub with the police on your tail as you came running home . . .'

'How do you know about rent boys?' I asked, keen to get her off the subject of my stint as a trainee manager/slave in a pub in Virginia Water that resulted in me getting nicked for 'borrowing' a bottle of Campari to take to a party.

'Saw them on the telly,' she replied disapprovingly. 'Scruffy buggers they were, going off with dirty old men.'

'And how come you're so knowledgeable about London considering you've never been?' I carried on trying to needle her.

'I do read, you know,' she pronounced grandly. 'And I listen to the news and keep up with current affairs in the papers.'

'You mean the deaths in the back of the *Echo*?' I laughed.

'Listen, mate,' she replied, waving the said paper at me and laughing herself, 'I'll stick to what I do best and you stick to what you do.'

'Which is?' I asked.

'God knows, son, but I'd give the acting lark up if I were you. What are you going to do? Can you act? You can't sing, son, let's face it, I've heard you – you've got a voice like a lump of coal caught under a cellar door. Now if you had a voice like Kathleen Ferrier it would be different.' Here she broke off to give her impersonation of that great Lancashire contralto whom she so admired by 'singing' in a thin, reedy, tuneless voice 'Blow The Wind Southerly', which set us both off laughing.

'Listen,' she said, attempting fake indignation at the amusement she'd just caused. 'Fame doesn't always lead to success, no matter how talented you are. Just look at Laurel and Hardy, all those wonderful films they made and yet they died unemployable and virtually penniless, the poor sods. So think on.'

I let out another sigh. She wasn't quashing ambition; she was in fact being kind, as this was her way of showing that she worried and wished that for my sake I'd get my life sorted out and settle down in a safe, secure job.

'I know you're right,' I was able to admit cheerfully as I knew it was only a daft dream, one of many, and this week's fad. 'But even so, it must be the best thing in the world to be acting in the theatre and I'd kill to be on the telly.'

'Well, that's the only way you'll ever get on it, love,' she said, folding the paper and getting up off the sofa.

'How do you mean?' I asked her.

'You'll have to kill someone, that way you'd be plastered all over the BBC news. Now let me go and ring Our Annie to see if this is the same Kelly from Menai Street that I think it is.'

Why then, a lifetime later, sitting in a very comfortable business-class seat on a flight to the Maldives, did that same person who all those years ago had claimed he was more than prepared to commit murder to get on TV feel slightly rankled at being asked by the charming flight attendant if I was a television presenter? Isn't that what he'd always secretly wanted?

Of course I am a television presenter, having fronted many shows over the years, and yet it feels wrong being pigeonholed as just a presenter. I believe there's a bit more to me than reading an autocue and being told what to do via an earpiece to the gallery, which, by the way, I've never done.

I'd have preferred it if the cabin-crew member had asked me, 'Weren't you once that notorious drag queen, Lily Savage? The Deadly White Flower of the Wirral?' I'd have been made up at that.

I can fire-eat, blow a bugle with my head between my legs while wearing four-inch heels and a gladiator's helmet, I've acted in plays, telly and film, written books, been a chat-show host, starred in musicals, presented endless documentaries ranging from strippers to rhinos, travelled South East Asia and America for a series of travelogues, can deliver piglets and lambs, bake cakes, brew medicinal potions out of the extensive range of herbs that I grow, make my own soap, perfumes and candles and just now, apart from hosting my own radio show on Radio 2, I'm probably best known for working with all those unwanted dogs at Battersea Dogs and Cats Home. Those animals never fail to break my heart on a daily basis.

Even with all this under my belt I still feel like a Jack of all trades but master of none and I never quite know, in all honesty, what to put down on official forms that ask me what my profession is.

When I took over from Paula Yates on *The Big Breakfast*, one of my favourite actresses of all time, the great Dora Bryan, would occasionally make a guest appearance as an agony aunt and she was a hoot, getting away with the most outrageous remarks by feigning complete innocence. We were having a cup of tea together one morning in my dressing room, moaning about the ungodly hour we had to get up, when one of the young runners came in to ask me if I'd read the script he'd written for a play he hoped to put on in the back room of a pub. I didn't fancy it in the least as it was pretty awful but I let him down gently by lying through my teeth and telling him that although it was a great part I wasn't right for it.

'It'll look good on your CV,' he said hopefully.

'Oooh, do you have to have one of those now?' Dora piped up.

'Everyone needs one,' the young runner said importantly. 'Otherwise how are casting directors supposed to know what you've done?'

'I don't think you need one, Dora,' I told her. 'You're one of the most celebrated actresses in the country,' I added as a gentle prod to remind our young friend that this funny little blonde lady supping tea was a genuine star.

'Just as well really as I wouldn't have a clue what to put in it,' she said, thinking for a moment before announcing mournfully, 'Specializes in playing women in plastic macs and high-heeled shoes who stand in doorways saying, "Hello, dearie." ' She sighed. 'I've made a living playing tarts.'

'You're not the only one, Dora,' I told her, opening my leopard-print coat to reveal a lurid pink top with half a yard of patent leather that called itself a miniskirt. 'And to think I used to be a good Catholic boy.'

'Oh dear,' Dora giggled. 'What would your mother say?'

Indeed, what would my mother say? When I'd briefly toyed with the idea of becoming a 'theatrical' way back in the 1970s it seemed so highly improbable, I might as well have declared my ambition to become the first man on Mars. As far as I was concerned, a life on the stage was a pipe dream that I consigned to the scrap heap and reluctantly got on with my life.

'What'll you do? How would you even get a foot in the door?' my mother had asked at the time when I was truly fired up with the acting bug but to which I had no answer. Little did I know that the foot that eventually kicked the door in for me would be wearing a leopard-print shoe with a stiletto heel. Life really is a joke.

I hope you enjoy this book. It's the fourth in the saga of my life and to be honest I'm ashamed at dragging it out for so long, as originally I only intended to write one. My trouble is I don't know the meaning of the word 'brevity'; I love detail and can take two pages to describe getting on a bus if I allow myself to be so self-indulgent.

Since writing this I've lost my good friend Cilla Black. She's not in this book, as a chapter or so wouldn't be adequate to describe our relationship. Our time together would take at least a couple of volumes to do her justice.

Anyway, enough of this for now. Let's go back a few years

to the Royal Vauxhall Tavern where a working girl called Lily Savage is sitting on the corner of the stage trying to earn an honest bob . . .

# CHAPTER 1

I SAT IN MY CHAIR IN THE CORNER OF THE STAGE AT SOUTH
London's premier palace of entertainment, the Royal
Vauxhall Tavern, bored stiff. Thursday nights was 'Stars of the
Future', an amateur talent night where anyone could throw on
a frock and get up and mime to their favourite record if they
fancied it. It wasn't just drag, there were male and female
singers, dancers and, once, a poet who, poor earnest little bard
that he was, died on his arse and never came back.

I was the compère of this weekly burlesque and had been for
over six years now and for me the joke was beginning to wear
a bit thin.

It was 1.15 in the morning and I still had three-quarters of
an hour to go before I could crawl upstairs to the bathroom
that Pat McConnon, the landlord, had let me use as a dressing
room, scrape off the slap and go home to another sleepless
night.

I took a slurp from my pint of cider and shivered, cursing
the doorman for keeping the pub door open as he knew full
well that the cold draught blew straight across the pub and on
to my bare back and shoulders.

'You want to borrow my cardigan, Lily?' old Irish Peggy
asked from her stool by the bar.

'No thanks, Peggy,' I replied. 'Crimplene always brings me out in a rash and anyway, love, I'm fine.'

I wasn't. I was freezing and wished I'd worn something less revealing. I'll have words with that bloody doorman when I finish, I promised myself.

Peggy, standing just under five feet tall in her stocking feet and built like a hamster, offered the cardy again.

'Are you sure, Lily?' she asked. 'You look feckin blue with the cold sat up there half naked.'

I thanked her again but declined her offer. I wasn't going to wear a little old lady's embroidered turquoise cardigan in public even if hypothermia and severe frostbite threatened to kick in and besides, I doubted if I'd be able to get my hand in Peggy's tiny cardy, never mind the rest of me.

It was February and outside the weather was typically foul. It takes a lot to come between a pub-going gay man and woman and their nightly beverage but tonight's deluge had obviously kept all but the most hardy from leaving the comfort of their sofas as the pub was only half full.

The door of the ladies' lav, which was situated at the side of the stage, was suddenly flung open and a drunken woman I'd never seen before launched herself into the bar. She stopped short by the stage to stare up at me myopically as she rearranged her clothing.

'You're supposed to pull your drawers up before you come out the lav,' I remarked. 'It's not very ladylike behaviour to adjust your clothes in public.'

Giving me a lopsided grin she popped her right tit out by way of response, holding it in her hand as if it were a balloon filled with water. This was a first for me in the Vauxhall Tavern, I'd had a few willies waved at me in my time but never a full-blown mammary gland. The prostitutes who frequented a pub called the Queens on Bradford's notorious Lumb Lane, a place where Vera and I once performed on a coffin lid of a stage, would frequently sit back on the bench in front of us, pull their skirts up and their knickers back and 'flash the gash' as they'd say, but I didn't expect a female flasher in here, not in the Royal Vauxhall Tavern on the Rue de la South Lambert on London's Barbary Coast.

'It looks like you've got the head of a baby Cyclops in yer hand,' I said, neither appalled nor amused as I gave the big fleshy boob with a nipple the size of an earthenware dinner-plate the once-over. 'Don't drop it for Christ's sake, you'll probably get splinters in it.'

She grinned again, popped her boob back inside her top and thankfully moved on. There were some weirdos in here tonight and 2 a.m. couldn't come quickly enough.

I suppressed a yawn as I watched a drunk weave across the empty floor around the stage as he made his way to the lav. The ladies' lavs were pretty much unisex, albeit unofficially, and those shy fellahs who didn't want to go to the gents and stand up against the stalls and pee snuck into the ladies to use the lock-up.

The drunk skidded in a puddle on the floor that was composed of 90 per cent spilt beer and 10 per cent pee from the overflow of the ladies' lav. It sent him reeling towards the front of the stage to steady himself.

'You wanna get a fucking mop and clear this up,' he slurred, one eye looking at the bar and the other at the ceiling. 'I nearly broke my neck then.'

'Shame you didn't,' I said, leaning forward. 'Now why don't you go to the bar and tell that skinny blond queen with the big specs called Vera to get out here and mop this floor? Oh and another thing,' I couldn't help adding maliciously, 'don't forget to demand a drink on the house as compensation for what could've been a very nasty accident. Go on, off you pop.'

He studied me for a moment before muttering something that sounded like 'I will.' Pushing himself away from the stage, he lurched towards the bar and the unsuspecting Vera. I sat back and waited for the fun and games to begin. 'And get that dog off the stage,' he shouted up at me as an afterthought. 'It wants fucking shootin'.'

I hadn't started appearing with a dog at this point. The canine in question was our ingénue, a Glaswegian wannabe drag queen, a twin called Sabrina who was busy enjoying herself slaughtering 'New York, New York'.

'It's up tae yae, NOOO YARK NOOOO YAAAARK,' Sabrina screeched, kicking her legs in the air as everyone invariably does when they either dance or sing karaoke to this popular number.

'Give it up,' the drunk heckled. 'Shoot the fucker.'

'I'm gonna make a brand . . .' Sabrina continued, totally unabashed by the catcalls from the punters. She broke off momentarily from her caterwauling for a quick swig of her pint and a drag of her fag before resuming her assault on the ears, ten beats behind her backing track and in a completely different key.

'Gerroff!' the drunk roared. He'd obviously forgotten that his mission was to get to the bar and annoy Vera and not to heckle the 'turns'.

'A brand new start . . . Aye, an fuck yae, dear . . . of it,' the Piaf of the Midden chanted, with her fag and the mike in one hand and a pint of lager in the other.

Out of drag, Sabrina was a perfectly respectable ordinary young alcoholic but done up in her Oxfam frock with hair courtesy of Ken Dodd and eye make-up that could've been applied by a very shaky Claudia Winkleman, Sabrina looked like roadkill.

'Stars of the Future' was one classy cabaret.

Sabrina finished her 'act' and, sticking two fingers up to what was left of the crowd, staggered off the stage and into the tiny dressing room, leaving her public with a heartfelt 'Fuck the lot o' yae.' Frank and Liza would've been proud.

'Thank you, Sabrina,' I announced without a jot of enthusiasm in my voice. 'You don't hear a sound like that come from someone's mouth every day of the week, do you? Well, not unless you work in A&E on a busy Saturday night.'

'Would you like a Tina Marina, Lily?' Peggy piped up. I understood her to mean a Tia Maria.

'The next act,' I said, shaking my head at Peggy, 'looks remarkably like the last act, which is unsurprising considering that they're twins.'

'Oh fuck me, there's two of them,' the drunk moaned, emulating the audience member at the Glasgow Empire on discovering that Mike Winters had a partner called Bernie. 'How do we know it's not the same one, eh? How can we tell the difference?'

'Sabrina's the one with two dents in her head. She was a forceps birth, now shurrup before I tell everyone you've got a piss stain down your trousers.'

The drunk started fiddling with his fly, muttering to himself as he swayed back and forth.

'They spent their formative years joined at the hip,' I went on, wishing the drunk would drink somewhere else, like the bottom of the Thames. 'What choice did these poor waifs have? Their mother was destitute and as times were hard and friends were few they shared the same nappy until they were four so, without further ado, as I can smell the anticipation over the Jeyes Fluid and piss that's wafting up from these lavs, ladies and gents, I give you twin number two, a little lady that's full of charm, wit and Tennent's Extra. Please welcome on to the illuminated runway of joy, a skittish little songbird, the lovely . . .'

On it went, week in week out, introducing the same old 'acts' while my brain slowly atrophied from the sheer monotony and tat of it all. So this was my fate then? Was I doomed to spend my days as a clapped-out drag queen in a south London pub presiding over a chorus of deeply untalented trannies who either mimed or squawked their way through the same tired routines every stinking bloody Thursday night? The good acts, the ones with talent, had moved on, poached by rival pubs with the promise of a paid spot of their own.

I didn't begrudge them flying the coop, they deserved it, but it left me with the dregs. No new acts seemed to be coming along and if they were they certainly weren't going to tarnish a reputation before it had begun to shine by appearing alongside my circus of horrors.

I still had my favourites. There was Tilly, a class act and a guaranteed crowd pleaser who charged around the stage to 'The Lonely Goatherd' regardless of the calipers he was hiding under his skirt, and Bunny Graham, who spun like an elderly whirling dervish to Bonnie Tyler's 'Total Eclipse Of The Heart'.

'Stars of the Future' had once been the night that everyone wanted to go to, but looking out from the stage at the dwindling audiences as twin number two murdered 'Puppet On A String' I was beginning to think that it was time to call 'Time'.

Having finally remembered what he was supposed to be doing, the drunk had made it to the bar and was busy berating an apoplectic Vera and demanding free drink.

'A couple more minutes,' I told myself, 'and Vera will be out from behind that bar and chucking this bum out.'

Sure as eggs are eggs, Vera, tea towel hanging out of the back pocket of his jeans, didn't waste much time in man-handling the drunk out of the door. Well, it was one way of getting rid of the undesirables.

It had been six months since my mother had died and I'd descended into a state where I wandered aimlessly through life, detached and apathetic as if mildly anaesthetized.

My dead eyes saw the world in monochrome and although normally fairly resilient and able to talk myself out of a grim mood, this time I'd allowed myself to become completely absorbed by the darkness. I felt as if I'd faded into the shadows until I became one myself.

Murphy, my partner, while not entirely unsympathetic, was growing impatient with this perpetual state of mourning that I was wallowing in and kept telling me to snap out of it. I would if I could work out what 'it' was, but I couldn't. I just knew that no matter how hard I tried, I couldn't shake off this lethargy and the permanent numbness that dulled my senses, shutting down those parts of my brain that controlled opti-mism, enthusiasm and drive.

I just didn't seem to care any more. Although I went through the daily grind as normally as possible, I was completely detached from what was going on around me, watching myself silently as I filled the kettle through the spout or sat in the launderette staring at the machine as my washing went round and round. It was as if my life was trapped in one of those Radio 4 afternoon plays, one that's slow, dreary and bleak.

I was still doing the rounds of pubs and clubs all over the country, switching it on for the forty-five minutes expected of me and then reverting to Misery riding on Poverty's back as soon as I'd scraped the last of the slap off, packed up and gone home.

Jonathan Ross had a show on at the time called *The Last Resort* and an episode of this was going out live from the London Palladium. I was asked if I'd like to be one of the guests, which, to be honest, I didn't want to do. But Murphy, who at my request had taken up the mantle of manager, sorting out my bookings and arranging the fees over the phone (a job I absolutely hated), wore me down until finally I gave in. As I couldn't drive, it was Murphy who drove me to the various venues up and down the country, covering thousands of miles in my pride and joy, a red Citroën DS which I'd convinced myself was the next best thing to a Lotus Europa.

*The Last Resort* was aptly named, at least it was for me as my appearance on that damned show turned out to be a total disaster.

On the night of transmission, filled with a mixture of terror and delight at actually getting the chance to set foot on the stage of the London Palladium, let alone appear on live television, I sailed out in front of the audience in all my glory to meet mine host.

Sadly, from the word go it was obvious that we weren't on the same wavelength. I was in full Lily mode but Jonathan wasn't interviewing me as the character, more as a genuine transvestite who dressed and lived as a woman for real. He simply didn't get it. Matters went from bad to worse until Jonathan crumpled up the questions mid-interview and the whole miserable affair dwindled to a damp, embarrassing squib. I felt my appearance on *The Last Resort* had done me no favours at all professionally and the experience seriously dented my self-confidence, making me wary of chat shows and Mr Ross, although happily I've long since changed my opinion of both of them.

For the umpteenth time I questioned this accidental career path and wondered if the life of a drag queen was really for me. Performing had been a hoot when I'd first taken up the call to leopardskin and platinum blonde wigs. It had been fun back when it was a part-time job but now I was totally dependent on it as this was the way I earned my living. After years of trawling around the country night after night, I was sick to death of it all and began to wonder if it was time to seriously consider another, less challenging occupation before it was too late. Wiping arses and dealing with severely disturbed kids was a doddle compared to the life of a drag queen.

Sleep had never evaded me. I could kip on a razor blade if I had to, but lately I'd taken to getting home from work at night and staying up until the late morning watching videos until I fell asleep.

Vera had finally moved out at my request. I enjoyed living with him and he'd been working behind the bar of the Vauxhall and sleeping on my floor for years now, even though he was only supposed to be staying the weekend, but in my present state of mind I seriously 'vanted to be alone'. He moved in with Chrissie, who had a flat in the next block.

The three of us had known each other for years now. Vera had known Chrissie longer than me, from the clubs in Liverpool. I had been vaguely aware of him but it was only when he was on the run from the police and took refuge with us in our flat in Crouch End that I really got to know him.

Chrissie was a character, to say the least. After a chip-pan fire one night that gutted his flat, instead of redecorating

Chrissie decided to strip the walls down to the bare brick, remove all the carpets and doors, apart from the front door, and go 'bohemian'. He'd always been eccentric but now his eccentricity was bordering on lunacy, and when the council declared the place uninhabitable he was evicted.

Undeterred, and conveniently still having the keys to an empty studio flat that we'd once lived in, Chrissie took up residence there. As he had no electricity his friend upstairs, who was also squatting and had an illegal supply, fed a lead down and inside via Chrissie's kitchen window. To it he attached every single electrical appliance that he needed to survive, most importantly his hairdryer. I'm surprised the place didn't blow up.

No electricity also meant no hot water, so when Chrissie wanted a bath he had to go upstairs to his neighbour, who in turn came downstairs to cook as he'd had his gas cut off. Chrissie said, 'As an arrangement it's very convenient . . . and more importantly it costs nothing.' Poor Vera moved into this shambles more than reluctantly, leaving me to my own devices.

A welcome diversion for me came in the form of a week's work on another episode of *The Bill* playing the same character as before, a beaten-up tranny called Roxanne who was copper's nark to DI Roache. I loved this change of scene and the chance to do something different, but come the end of the week it was business as usual. After a long day's filming that started when I woke at 5 a.m. it was off to Blackpool to work the Flamingo Club.

Due to my irregular sleeping pattern day had now become night, but this vampiric lifestyle was not helping my depression. To rectify this and to get my body clock back into some semblance of order, I'd spend the day following a sleepless night trying to stay awake by keeping myself occupied. Early one Sunday morning after another night watching endless taped episodes of *Prisoner Cell Block H* I set off for Hampton Court. I can't remember anything about it now, except rushing through the rooms of the palace wondering why I was there in the first place and buying a Margaret Tarrant print in a junk shop.

I took to going to morning mass at 6.30 in Westminster Cathedral. I was so desperate to shake the black dog off me and thought maybe a whiff of incense and candle wax might help. Even though I hadn't been to church and voluntarily sat through a mass in years, I found my heart was not so heavy when I was in that little chapel to the left of the main altar. Bathed in the warm light reflected from the racks of candles lit by the faithful and the desperate as an offering to the Virgin Mary, I found it reassuring to revisit a tradition from my childhood and for the forty minutes the mass lasted I felt at peace.

The congregation was made up mostly of nurses and staff from the nearby Westminster Hospital, shift workers, nuns and the devout who came every day and spent their time 'eating the altar rails', as my aunty Chris used to say of anyone she considered overtly pious.

I smiled as I found myself slipping back into the old routine and remembering the correct responses, although I wasn't prepared for all the handshaking that goes on now at the end of the mass. I'd assumed that the woman next to me was a little peculiar when she held out her hand for me to shake, until she quietly explained that this was the new order of things.

I didn't tell anyone I was taking myself off on the 2B bus at the crack of dawn to go to church each day. My bout of religious fervour didn't last very long but I can see that at the time it was a ritual that gave me much-needed solace.

11

When I wasn't chomping on the altar rails I took to travelling. We were all mad for the Channel 4 adaptations of E. F. Benson's Mapp and Lucia books, which I'd read time and time again. The fictional town of Tilling where the action takes place is based on Rye, a painfully picturesque town on the Sussex coast, and since I'd never been there I was on the first train out of Charing Cross.

I needed to think and I always find that a long solitary walk helps sort me out, so I set off for the station on foot. As I passed deep in thought through St James's Park, a woman ran towards me screaming for help. Apart from having a slightly mad eye and a wild mane of greying black hair that could do with a good brush, she seemed fairly normal at first glance. She was claiming in broken English that her companion was drowning in the lake, so I climbed over the railings to take a look. I couldn't see anyone, not that I'd have been much help if I had as I couldn't swim. Perhaps I could reach out to him with a branch and pull him in, I remember thinking. Even though there was no sign of this drowning man the woman kept pointing and screaming, 'There he is, right in front of you, drowning! Help him!' It soon became blatantly apparent that here was yet another dyed-in-the-wool crazy but vulnerable soul who shouldn't really be out on the streets of London alone.

I told her that there was nobody there and that she must be mistaken but she refused to be pacified, in fact she turned very nasty.

'I curse you,' she hissed, pointing her finger at me. 'Curse you to the ends of the earth, you semen of Satan.'

I've never forgotten 'semen of Satan'. I've been called some names in my time but that one definitely wins the cigar. I was shook up by the vehemence of her curse but had the presence of mind to play her at her own game. Forming a triangle with my thumbs and forefingers, I pushed my hands against my forehead to represent a protective pentacle and sent the curse back to her with a few well-chosen words.

She screamed long and loud and I was worried that a couple of coppers might come running and nick me.

'*Shuvihano!*' she shouted, running away from me. '*Shuvihano!*' I didn't have a clue what she meant at the time, just thought it was a swearword in some foreign language. It was only years later that I found out that *shuvihano* is Romany for a male witch.

A month or so before my encounter with the Witch of Endor in St James's Park I'd been to a pagan, psychic and holistic fair that was being held at the Battersea Arts Centre. I was on my way to buy a washing-up bowl in Arding and Hobbs, and for want of something better to do I went in. I've always been interested in alternative religions and during this odd period of my life I was searching for something spiritual to act as a crutch. Catholicism might have provided temporary comfort for forty minutes a day but it wasn't doing anything in the long term. That comfort came not from belief in what lay in the tabernacle but from reliving a ritual from a time when my life was uncomplicated, safe and innocent.

I'd leave the cathedral with a sense of peace but by the time I got home I was grimmer than any Reaper again. It was a sad realization for me to find that I'd simply grown out of Catholicism. It had once been a major part of my life, bred into me, but now what was left of my faith had died along with my mother. I could no longer blindly adhere to the rules of my formative indoctrination and as I was now supposedly an adult I could finally decide for myself what I chose to believe in.

I felt bitter as I recalled my schooldays, when religious instruction was drilled into me by the Christian Brothers by means of intimidation and brute force, and I'd long since come to the realization that the Catholic faith had its roots steeped in fear and guilt. Jesus died for our sins and for that we must not only pay dearly but do perpetual penance to boot.

'What sins?' I used to innocently ask the Christian Brothers. 'I wasn't born when Jesus was murdered.' For this I'd receive a smack across the ear for my impertinence and be told to learn two pages of the catechism by heart by the following morning.

I was looking for total fulfilment from whatever spiritual route I was going to go down and as I was at the crossroads and didn't know which way to turn, maybe witchcraft had something to offer?

Once I'd paid the admission fee for the fair to a jolly woman wearing an emerald green cloak and an arrangement of twigs, ivy and holly in her hair that made her look like she'd fallen into a hedgerow, I ventured inside and into another world.

Those of us dressed in everyday wear looked very much out of place at this gathering. I felt drab and boring as I mingled among druids, highly impressive in their flowing white robes, Gandalf lookalikes complete with genuine beards, witches of every shape, size and age, Goths, punks, shamans and pagans, heavy metal freaks, men dressed like extras from *Robin Hood* and a heavily tattooed young woman standing outside her stall, smiling cheerfully at passers-by and displaying her body art and piercings as proudly as Lydia the Tattooed Lady.

'Of course I've got lots of others but I daren't get them out in public,' she said coyly in a very posh voice that belied her appearance. 'My boyfriend does them,' she was telling a dwarf who was admiring the spike in her earlobe.

The man behind the stall looked up. He didn't seem to have a spare centimetre of flesh left to tattoo.

Maybe that was why his girlfriend was so inked up? He'd run out of space on his own body so he'd started doodling on her and had got carried away. God help the kids, I thought, and the dog and the budgie as no doubt they'd be next.

Mooching around the stalls I was amazed to see what was on offer. Diagon Alley had nothing on this place. If you were so inclined, you could try a bit of colour healing, crystal healing, psychic healing or even have your aura cleansed. Or maybe you were in search of a new cloak or ceremonial robe? It was all here, wands and cauldrons, amulets and altar cloths, incense and candles, spell books, grimoires and even a selection of very sturdy besoms to help you get your purchases home. It was wonderful and I went on a shopping spree, buying a selection of hand-turned wooden bowls and assorted amulets made out of shells and precious stones and covered in mystical runes. I've still got some of them hanging in the shed.

Browsing through some books, I was asked by the guy on the stall if I'd be interested in attending an introductory seminar on Wicca and Paganism.

'Oh, I'm not sure I've got time,' I lied, as I didn't fancy sitting through a lecture.

'It's only just under an hour,' he said, 'and very informative.'

'Oh, I'm not really sure . . .' I burbled nervously, wary in case he put a spell on me. 'I'm just browsing.'

'It's free of charge,' he said encouragingly.

'Go on then, I'll give it a go,' I heard myself saying and ten minutes later I found myself sat in a room listening to an extremely imposing self-confessed witch.

'I don't like the word "warlock",' he explained. 'The word "witch" is universal and should apply to both sexes. My name is Seth.'

A member of the audience got very heated during the lecture, particularly when Seth claimed that Catholicism was an invention of the Emperor Constantine in order to gain control over the masses and unite them under one religion by destroying the Roman gods and replacing them with the saints.

The punter declared that he was a Christian and he would not listen to this blasphemy any more.

'I know my Holy Bible inside out,' he ranted and proceeded to spout chunks of it at Seth.

'Then you'll be familiar with Revelation 13:13 and the true mark of the Beast?' Seth said, calmly interrupting him. 'The wound in the side?'

The punter stormed out, using some very un-Christian language and shouting, 'Don't listen to this man, his name is not Seth, it's Satan.' It was all very exciting and a lot livelier than going to church, but would probably have put my mother in hospital if she was still around and knew where I was.

'Satan is a Christian belief,' Seth called after him, 'and is not recognized by Wiccans.'

I surprised myself by sticking the lecture out. It was fascinating stuff and I even stayed behind to ask questions. After sifting the evidence I came to the conclusion that if everyone practised this old religion that pre-dated Christianity by thousands of years, observing the law of karma and showing respect for the planet and all its living creatures, then the world would be a better place.

Sounds a bit New Age hippy, I know, but when you think

about it, naive as it may sound, it's the only way to live your life.

Sadly, I can't see the maniacs swapping guns for elm wood wands in Syria. Nor can I visualize African poachers suddenly having a change of heart. Instead of slaughtering the rhinos and elephants to fund terrorism or to provide wealthy Vietnamese with the powdered rhino horn that these misguided fools believe has aphrodisiacal properties, would they begin to nurture and protect these magnificent animals? I don't think so.

There's no Rosemary's baby or Necromancy involved with Paganism, Witchcraft or whatever you choose to call it. Neither is there any cursing of enemies or casting evil spells on them, as the Three-fold Law forbids it. As my mother used to say, 'Curses, like chickens, come home to roost.' You know something? I've always wondered about her . . .

In the café area a young lad with badly dyed black hair and a T-shirt with the words 'I Bite' printed on it sat at my table. We started chatting and I asked him about the T-shirt.

'Oh, this,' he said, pulling his leather jacket back as he munched on his pitta bread and hummus. 'That's because I'm a werewolf and I believe it's only fair to warn people as there's been a few incidents in the past.'

'What sort of incidents?' I asked warily.

'Oh, I bit a girl,' he replied casually.

'Where did you bite her?'

'In college during media studies.'

'No, I mean whereabouts on her body did you bite her?'

'Oh,' he replied, revealing a set of beautiful white teeth. 'On the hand.'

'Did she need stitches?' I asked him, trying to sound as if a conversation with a werewolf in a café was the most natural thing in the world.

'Nah, it was only a nip but I couldn't resist it. She's got big fat hands, see, and I had an uncontrollable urge for flesh, which is not like me 'cos I'm veggie although I'll eat bacon.'

Now what do I do if he suddenly starts growling and flashing those choppers at me, I thought. I'd left my silver bullets and crucifix at home so it looked like I'd have to hit him over the head with one of the wooden bowls I'd bought.

'Are you in a biting mood now?' I asked him. Forewarned is forearmed.

'Nah,' he said, 'the moon's waning and anyway with all this Aids going around it's not safe any more, so I'm trying to lay off for a while. It's a shame because I've only just discovered that I'm the way I am.'

We sat in silence as he ate his food and I drank my tea. For a werewolf he had impeccable table manners.

'How long have you been a lycanthrope then?' I asked him, feeling flash for using the correct terminology.

'I'm not one of those lycanny things, whatever that is,' he replied, finishing his tea. 'I'm just helping on one of the stalls. You into Wicca?'

For a moment I thought he might be flogging wicker furniture on his stall like Flo in Birkenhead Market used to, and I was tempted to say, 'No, it snags your tights.' Then I twigged he meant the religion.

'No, I'm not, I'm afraid,' I told him, 'but I find it all fascinating.'

'Are you one of them . . . ?' the werewolf puppy asked.

'One of what?' I replied, instantly on the defensive. 'D'you mean gay?'

'No, I didn't mean that,' he protested. 'I'm bisexual, although I haven't done it yet.'

'With a man?'

'With anything,' he said, laughing, not a bit abashed that he was telling a complete stranger he was a virgin. 'No, I mean one of those things you called me before.'

'What do you mean, a lycanthrope?' He wasn't the brightest cub in the litter but his youth and naivety excused him and besides, he was highly entertaining. 'No, I'm not one of those either, although I've bitten off more than I can chew in my time.'

'Flesh, you mean?' he asked, lowering his voice and suddenly all ears. 'Really?'

'Not at all, don't be so daft,' I corrected him immediately. 'Who do you think I am, Dennis Nilsen? No, it's just an idiom.'

He looked at me blankly. 'Are you a Pagan then?' He was relentless, but as I didn't want him telling everyone on his stall that there was a flesh-eating cannibal in the café I said I was.

'I thought you were,' he said, getting up to leave. 'I can always tell. See you around, or rather, "Merry meet, merry part and merry meet again."' He gave me a conspiratorial grin to show he was in the know and vanished into the hall – not literally, you understand, just into a crowd of people.

I suddenly wished I were a Pagan. It was like coming out, admitting to a complete stranger, bold as brass, that I was a pagan, even if I wasn't. It felt liberating, exciting and comfortable, like finding a coat, or in this instance a cloak, that fitted me beautifully. Maybe this was my true calling.

On my way out I made another purchase, reasoning with myself that if I was going to study the craft then this was a tool that no self-respecting witch should be without. I didn't feel quite so confident on the packed bus home though, standing on the lower deck holding on to a washing-up bowl and a five-foot broomstick with all eyes on the bus upon me.

I've read lots of books on the subject of paganism, as I have on other faiths. Many of the books are risible but there were a few that I found informative, totally absorbing and highly complex.

Did I ever convert? Well, as a committed practitioner of the craft once told me, 'Secrecy is everything,' and as I'm not out of the broom closet yet I'll leave you to sift the evidence and form your own conclusions.

It was around this time that my daughter Sharyn and her mother came to stay for the weekend. I'd wanted to put them off as I wasn't in the mood for visitors but I knew if I did that then my action would be misconstrued as me just wanting to avoid spending time with my daughter. Instead I reluctantly agreed.

Sharyn was growing up fast, your typical sulky, angry kid, and I got the impression that she trusted me as far as she could throw me. I approached with caution, unsure how to act with this surly young girl, and it wasn't what I'd call a successful weekend. I found that Sharyn communicated better with me by post. Her letters, handwritten on Hello Kitty notepaper, were charming, full of information about her day and with no trace of the anger and the need to punish this excuse for a father that welled up and erupted whenever we met in person. Things could only get better and it was going to be a long uphill struggle, but we got there in the end.

This state of detachment from a grey world that I was experiencing became the norm and I had little or no enthusiasm for most things. Work was for purely financial reasons now – I turned up, went through the motions and went home.

'Liven up, will you,' Murphy would say as he drove me to the various venues, but I couldn't. No matter how I hard I tried to inject some enthusiasm into this hollow husk, I simply couldn't.

It didn't help matters that I'd had a run of apathetic audiences. The club scene was changing and I was beginning to suspect that the crowds would rather get high and dance than listen to a patter act. Maybe, I thought, it was because I'd lost my mojo.

Acid House culture had arrived. I remember seeing a sticker of that smiley yellow face on a DJ's record case one night as I was leaving a club in Manchester and thinking it an omen signalling the death of drag queens who told jokes in the dance clubs.

Dave Lynn, a popular act on the circuit, rang me to ask if I'd like to guest on his Wednesday night show at Heaven (the London gay club, not the place you go to after you've died providing you've led a life above reproach, which means that apart from the Boss and his minions it must be comparatively empty). I liked Dave, we'd got together at the White Swan pub a few times and I'd really enjoyed myself. He was a quick-witted, generous performer who could get even the most complacent of audiences eating out of the palm of his hand.

Apart from Murphy, I hadn't admitted to anyone else just how bleak I was feeling. Now, here I was with the floodgates open, pouring out my woes to poor Dave who'd only rung up to offer me a booking. Dave's ear must've been like a piece of liver by the time I'd finished my rant but he was laughing like a drain.

'What are you laughing at?' I asked. 'I'm being serious.'

'Tell that story in Heaven on Wednesday night,' he said. 'Word for word. Please, do it for me.'

So I did. Lily's mother, Hell Cat Savage, the darling of the wrestling ring, had died after a particularly hefty bout with the Wigan Mauler, a formidable opponent who was later exposed as a man after a rigorous drugs test during which her penis popped out of her leotard at the Birmingham Finals.

The management at Heaven had transformed the dance floor into a cabaret setting with tables with lamps on and a small stage with keyboard and drums. It was a nice crowd and there was no pressure as it was Dave's show and I had a ball, wondering why I hadn't worked through my grief by means of comedy in the first place.

There were no similarities between my mother's funeral and Lily's ma's. For instance, I didn't have an elderly aunty who took her teeth out at the funeral tea to demonstrate why she was so popular with the Yanks during the war by deep-throating a jumbo sausage roll, nor did Vera throw herself on the coffin in a fit of hysteria just as it was sliding through the curtains to the strains of Johnny Cash singing 'Ring Of Fire'. She didn't get the buckle on one of her new Clarks sandals caught as she tried to throw her leg over the coffin either, nearly ending up in the flames herself until an altar boy with a Stanley knife bravely cut her free at the last minute, causing an irate Vera to belt him for destroying her new sandal.

However, the sentiment was there and I delivered it deadpan in full widow's weeds, as if explaining to a neighbour who'd just asked in her best pious voice, 'How was your mam's funeral?'

I finished off with a duet with Skippy, the mangy old fox fur I'd transformed into a ventriloquist's puppet one night. We gave them our version of 'Sonny Boy'.

The audience's response was just what I needed to shake me out of my catatonic state. For the first time in a long while I'd really enjoyed getting up there and 'giving out'.

'What happened?' Murphy asked, astonished, coming into the dressing room. 'Where in God's name did all that come from? It was brilliant.'

'And you're talking about giving up?' Dave said, smiling slyly as he left for the stage. 'I don't think so, love.'

That night after I got home I sat down and instead of watching videos I wrote reams of new material for Lily. As I did so, a little light went on somewhere inside as I slowly began to rejoin the living.

A few mornings later I went into the Halifax Building Society to deposit the week's earnings not exactly full of the joys of spring and emerged into Victoria Street a different person. The opening sequence of *The Wizard of Oz* is shot in sepia and it's only when Dorothy arrives in Oz that the film bursts into glorious Technicolor. Well, that's what it felt like for me that morning except there were no Munchkins, just a lot of men in suits.

This epiphany had nothing to do with the Halifax, they hadn't offered me a long-term interest-free loan or anything, it was simply as though the dark clouds had cleared, the sun had come out and I could see, hear and feel again. Exhilarated, I was desperate to tell someone that my period of hibernation was finally over.

The unfortunate person who got to bask in the full glare of the summer sun that Little Mary Sunshine was radiating was an elderly lady in the café of the Army and Navy Stores. I'd gone mad in the food hall and spent a fortune on luxury items that I didn't need and probably would never eat as I couldn't pronounce half of them, but flushed from this shopping spree I went for a cup of tea and a fag. The café was busy with the local ladies having morning coffee and the only seat available was at a table an old lady was already sitting at.

I've had some wonderfully offbeat conversations with people from all walks of life in cafés. I love cafés, proper sausage, beans and chips caffs that is. I prefer them to glamorous restaurants any day. For me, food is sustenance and nothing more. If I could take a pill that provides all the nourishment one needs to survive then I would, as long-drawn-out lunches or dinners with an interminable wait between courses is my idea of hell. That's why I'd as soon have your common-as-muck caff as there's no hanging about, you're in and out and back on the pavement in fifteen minutes, stuffed full of cottage pie or a spag bol that hasn't cost you the price of a decent second-hand car. I had a whole circle of friends in the New Piccadilly café before it closed down and scattered the regulars to the four winds or, God forbid, to one of those soulless corporate coffee houses with wi-fi and a menu on the wall informing you where all their produce was 'sourced'.

'Is anyone sitting here?' I asked the elegant old dear at the table, all eyes and teeth, exuding cheeriness.

Looking up from stirring her coffee, she gave me a cursory once-over. 'Well, my friend normally joins me for coffee,' she hesitated, 'but since she had that stroke . . .' She paused to take a sip. 'So yes, I suppose in theory that seat is vacant at the moment.'

'I'm sorry,' the Ray of Sunshine gushed, dumping his bags and sitting down. 'When did your friend have her stroke?'

'Just over five years ago.' She blew gently on the foam in her cup.

'Oh,' I said, understandably puzzled by this. 'So when did she last get the chance to join you for coffee then?'

'Just over five years ago, silly,' she replied scornfully, raising her eyebrows and brushing an imaginary crumb from her lap.

'Is she showing any signs of getting better?' I asked her in a manner that the late Claire Rayner would've been proud of.

'Of course she isn't,' she snapped, looking at me as if I were mad. 'She's dead.'

'Oh,' I said again, as it seemed the only possible reply. 'I expect you miss her.'

'Not really.' She sighed in a way that implied our conversation was getting on her nerves. 'She talked too much and asked far too many questions. Very annoying really, and she was always so ruddy cheerful, a little like you.'

I could've kissed the old girl and couldn't wait to get home to tell Murphy I'd been accused of being too cheerful.

It was just as well that my spirits had lifted and I was feeling ready for anything. With the curse of Aids the hospital wards were still sadly overflowing and the turnover of patients was frighteningly quick.

I had naively hoped that the worst of it was over. Instead, the deaths came in waves, endless funerals and hospital vigils for months on end and then suddenly a calm. Life would continue as normal for a while, this respite lulling us all into a false sense of security.

The subject of death was inevitably brought up in most conversations by the regulars of the Vauxhall Tavern, not surprising really considering that all of us had been affected by Aids in one way or another.

'Been to any funerals lately?'

'No, strangely enough I haven't been to any for months.'

'Well, let's hope that's that then.'

That ubiquitous slogan 'Keep Calm and Carry On' is exactly what we did. It was as if we'd stepped out of the shelter after another prolonged and heavy air raid and were cautiously

25

going about our daily business, convincing ourselves that there might just be a slim chance that that was indeed that – until of course the next unexpected hit and the resulting carnage.

As well as working solo I still teamed up with Adrella as part of an act called High Society and occasionally got together with Hush and David Dale as LSD (Lily, Sandra and Doris).

Hush was extremely busy working in four different acts and it was not unusual to find him performing at the same pub three or four times a week. By day he transformed Brixton market nylon wigs, brought to his door by various drag queens, into magnificent gravity-defying sculptures courtesy of a severe backcombing and a couple of cans of cheap, extra-hold lacquer.

As well as being a genius with wigs, he also made costumes and headdresses and kept house at his council flat on the fourteenth floor for himself and his partner, Roy. Out of drag, standing over six feet tall and weighing in at a solid fourteen stone, Hush looked remarkably butch and his choice of outfit for cruising the bars on his nights off was what he described as 'salacious': a pair of those pale yellow Timberland boots worn with pale, bleached denims that had more rips in them than they did jean, a white string vest in which a few strategic holes had been placed to reveal a hairy nipple, and all topped off by a leather biker's jacket.

He'd met Roy, who was training to be a Catholic priest until he saw the error of his ways and changed his cassock for a rubber vest, in a leather bar. The pair almost immediately set up home together. Roy was quite a reserved man. I never got to know him very well as he was painfully shy. We had little in common except for our love of books, of which he had hundreds, stacked up in orderly piles all around the flat.

Hush doted on him and ironed his shirts and cooked his meals like a 1950s housewife. 'Wouldn't do you any harm, Savage,' he said one afternoon as he ironed his way through a pile of shirts, 'to cook Murphy a bit of dinner when he comes home.' Such domestic bliss wasn't for me and besides, Murphy and I didn't live together and even if we did then many a dinner would've been ruined as I'd never have known if and when the old tom cat was coming home. When we met he'd been sharing a flat above the Union Tavern with his friend Joan as well as David Dale, but he'd since moved to a flat in Stockwell. Having him just up the road was close enough for both of us.

'Don't forget you're working in Manchester on Friday night at the Number 1,' Murphy said over the phone. 'You'll have to make your own way up on the train as I've arranged to go out.'

Have you now, I thought, putting the phone down. I wasn't looking forward to standing all the way up north on the over-crowded Manchester train and then having to stay overnight.

I sat on the end of the sofa and fumed. 'That bloody Murphy,' I said to Lucifer, one of my Persian cats, who sat warming her back in front of the two-bar electric fire with her right paw raised, yowling something in cat language that sounded disturbingly like 'Heil Hitler'.

'You zink ve should invade Stockvell,' I announced in *Hotspur* German to the cat, who rolled on her back in reply and stretched out luxuriantly before settling down for a nice kip. She couldn't care less.

The phone rang again. It was Hush pleading poverty as he'd spent the last of his money on four yards of black French sequin from Borovick's that he 'just couldn't leave'. Hush had lived from day to day ever since I'd known him and couldn't resist blowing his entire budget on fabric for new drag and worrying about the consequences later.

'Why don't you come up to Manchester with me?' I asked him. 'I'll do a bit of patter, you can do a few numbers and we'll do something together to finish.'

'Oh, I could do with a night out,' he said happily. 'And the handbag [money] will come in very handy, wench, as I've got nothing in the diary until next Wednesday.'

Problem solved. I rang Geoff, the manager of the club, to tell him, hoping he wouldn't mind but knowing that even if he did he was too nice to say anything. It was a great night with a lively crowd and I was on form and relaxed, knowing that if I ran out of something to say there was always Hush waiting to come on and take over. We had the usual lock-in after the club closed and returned to the hotel pissed as farts.

By the time the train pulled into Euston station the next day, two very hungover drag queens lugged their cases and bin liners containing wigs up the platform like death warmed up. Hush dropped me off in the taxi and the first thing I did when I got in the flat was plonk myself on the lav for a pee as I was in no state to stand up.

The phone rang but as I couldn't be bothered getting up I let the answerphone take it.

'Are you there, dahling?' I could hear the unmistakable drawl of Regina Fong asking. 'Pick up the phone if you are, it's urgent, can you hear me? You mustn't let Hush go home alone. Something terrible has happened.'

I dashed off the lav, shuffling like a geisha with my trousers around my ankles to get to the phone, wondering what the hell could've possibly gone off overnight. A burglary perhaps? Or maybe Roy had gone back to the priesthood?

I stood in shock as I listened to Regina's grim news. Roy had got up that morning, gone out and bought the *Guardian*, finished the crossword over breakfast as usual, washed up his cup and plate, tidied the flat and taken a chicken out of the freezer to defrost, then thrown himself out of the fourteenth-floor window to his death below.

Sitting in the car as Murphy drove me round to Hush's flat I started blaming myself. If only I hadn't suggested he came up to Manchester with me, this might never have happened. Why hadn't I just gone up there and done the job myself as I was supposed to do?

'Oh, give over, Savage,' Murphy snapped as he listened to my self-flagellation. 'Why does everything have to be about you?'

When we got to the flat Hush was in a state of complete shock, sitting quietly on his sofa surrounded by neighbours and a couple of coppers. He stared at me blankly as we entered the room and I paused to give a hug to Pearl, one of Hush's neighbours, who had had the unenviable task of identifying what was left of Roy. Pearl was tough as old boots but this had shaken her up badly and her normally stentorious voice was reduced to a whisper.

'Oh, my God,' she was saying, 'I can't believe it.'

Kneeling down beside Hush, I held his hand and tried to offer some words of comfort.

'Why?' Hush pleaded. 'Why did he do it? Why?' repeating these same words over and over. 'It's just a typical Saturday,' he was saying to Murphy. 'How can this happen? He took a bloody chicken out of the freezer, you don't do ordinary things like that and then commit suicide, do you, Murph?'

'Oh, Hush, if only you hadn't come to Manchester,' I wailed, completely eaten up with guilt, 'he might not have committed . . .'

'It would've happened anyway.' Hush stopped me, suddenly calm. 'He's obviously been planning this, waiting for a chance to be alone so he could jump when I was out of the way, the selfish bastard.'

His mood turned from grief to anger. Standing up, he thanked the police for their help in a manner conveying that if they didn't mind he was very busy and had to get on with the housework. Politely excusing himself, he went off to unpack the wigs and hang up the drag as if nothing had happened.

There were no hysterics, just the daily methodical search throughout every room for a suicide note. Carpets were taken up, books flicked through, cupboards, drawers and wardrobes emptied out, their contents examined with a fine-tooth comb. He even wanted to peel the wallpaper off to see if Roy had written anything on the wall until I talked him out of it. Eventually, exhausted, he gave up, resigning himself to the bitter fact that there was no note offering an explanation to ease Hush's pain.

'Anything would've done,' Hush said eventually after he'd sat in silence for a while deep in thought. '"I'm sorry" written on the back of an envelope, anything. He can't just leave me hanging like this, not knowing.'

'Maybe it was a spur-of-the-moment thing,' I offered. 'You know, he just acted on an insane impulse.'

'You mean after defrosting a chicken he said to himself, "What can I do now? I'm bored. I know! I'll jump out of the fuckin' window, that'll be a nice change,"' Hush replied bitterly. 'No, he'd been planning this for a while, I just wish I knew why.'

Hush carried on working. Even on the night of Roy's funeral he was up there on the stage of the Vauxhall giving his all to 'Put The Blame On Mame', the pain dulled by a litre of vodka and Coke and half a dozen pints of bitter.

He never got over Roy's death and I believe that it contributed to his own decline and eventual death.

Madame Jo-Jo's was a drag cabaret club in the heart of Soho, owned by Paul Raymond and run by the hostess with the mostest, Madame Jo-Jo herself. Jo-Jo didn't have an act, her personality was her talent. She never forgot a face or name, was diplomatic and composed at all times and never let the mask slip in public. The waiters were beautiful androgynous young men known as the Barbettes, who dressed in skimpy leotards and not much else. They dispensed drinks around the tables to punters while Ruby Venezuela, Issy van Randwyk, assorted drag queens and a bevy of semi-naked male dancers strutted their stuff. When the cast were due to take a well-earned three-week break, Jo-Jo asked Adrella if he could get a show together to fill in and would I be interested.

It was regular, well-paid work that wasn't very demanding and I agreed to do it even though Murphy wasn't keen on the idea. He considered the cabaret at Jo-Jo's too 'draggy'. What he actually meant was that the show was all-singing, all-dancing and the acts weren't required to tell jokes or do any patter, which was my forte, unlike singin' and dancin'.

Two other acts, Ebony and Charlotte, signed up for this epic and along with two hunky male dancers and a couple of the Barbettes we pooled our individual backing tracks and managed to get together two half-hour spots with a big splashy Disney finale.

Backstage was tiny, with two dressing rooms. The smaller one, no bigger than a cupboard, I shared with Adrella. The slightly bigger one, with the toilet and the shower that was full of costumes, housed the rest of our motley crew. Plenty of booze flowed, as did the spliffs, and on one occasion a couple of us were hammered by the time it came to the finale.

After Jo-Jo closed shop for the night, if we didn't want to go straight home – which of course we didn't – there were plenty of illegal drinking dens to go to if you knew the right people. Soho hadn't become the caffè-latte-on-the-pavement place it is today. It was still deliciously seedy with strip joints and cards pinned on door frames advertising the services of a young French model on the top floor who in all probability was really a middle-aged woman from Streatham. Ah, the days of the friendly old brass with her working flat and an ancient maid to answer the phone and deal with the clients are long gone only to have been replaced by extremely young eastern European girls, victims of human trafficking forced into prostitution.

Old Compton Street had yet to become known as the gay village. Long before the profusion of ultra-trendy eateries sprang up all over the place, we gathered in the Salt Beef Bar opposite the Windmill Theatre, the Stockpot and the New Piccadilly café and Lee Ho Fook's in Chinatown, who stayed open late and did the best hot and sour soup in London. It was usually daybreak when the cab pulled up outside Vicky Mansions and I staggered upstairs to feed the cats before falling into bed.

Jo-Jo's audience was a blend of hen nights, office parties, out-of-towners who thought they were being very daring, drag queens, transvestites, the odd rent boy and his punter – although these usually hung out in the piano bar next door – and a smattering of celebrities.

It was an unusual mix but because of Jo-Jo's people skills it worked, and each night we went out to an appreciative audience who were up for a good time. There was an odd couple who usually came in on a Saturday night and who always sent a bottle of champagne backstage asking me to join them for a drink, which eventually, egged on by Adrella, I did.

They turned out to be a German brother and sister. The brother was a stunner with deep blue eyes and blond hair who undoubtedly possessed the physique of an Olympian hiding underneath his perfectly tailored suit. The sister, equally handsome, reminded me of a woman who used to go round door to door collecting the money each week that was due on the Provident cheque.

'We like your show very much,' she said approvingly. 'Certain aspects in particular, the tango with the whip for instance, which I know my brother is very interested in.'

The brother smiled and I quickly necked a glass of champagne.

'Do you do anything else?' the sister asked, topping up my glass.

'What like?' I was curious to know what she meant although I had a good idea what was coming.

'My brother likes to be beaten,' she said calmly, 'restrained and then flogged hard.'

'OK,' I nodded casually, pretending to be nonplussed by this information.

'Good,' she said. 'So will you do it then?'

'Do what?' I said, uncomfortable at being put on the spot like this.

'Beat him,' she asked expectantly.

'I don't think I can,' I said apologetically. 'It's not really my thing, you see. This is just an act, I take it all off at the end of the night and go home and—'

'I'll give you five hundred pounds.'

'No problem.'

I went back to the dressing room and told Adrella about my business proposition.

'Get him in here now, strap him to that dress rail and let him have it with that whip. Go on, what are you waiting for?' he said. 'If you don't, I will.'

Together we got him in the tiny room, stripped him down and tied him to the dress rail with some old tights. Adrella was extremely businesslike and set me off into hysterics as I watched him, fag hanging out of his mouth, tying up this strapping German with a pair of badly laddered fishnets.

Ten minutes later we emerged from the dressing room five hundred quid better off, while the German limped back to his sister a sore but satisfied man.

'Well, that's the easiest money I've ever earned,' I told Adrella, who surprisingly became rather prudish.

'It's not something I care to get into, Savage,' he informed me primly as he shoved his share of the loot into his handbag. 'Easy money or not.'

'Well, I'm just adhering to the family motto,' I said.

'Which is?'

'Is it wrong if a lad takes pay for something he would do anyway?' I replied.

'Tart,' he said, getting changed into his costume for the second half. 'Just don't let the boss find out that he's running a whorehouse.'

The boss was Paul Raymond, better known to favoured employees as PR, and his first words on meeting me were 'So you're that gobby Scouser everyone's talking about then?'

I liked him immediately and instead of fawning all over him I was irreverent and cheeky, which he loved. Long after I'd left Jo-Jo's he'd take me to lunch at L'Escargot and send the gold Rolls round to Vicky Mansions to pick me up, which caused a bit of a stir among the neighbours and the folk at the bus stop. We had a lot in common as we both came from Merseyside, with similar mothers who had brought us up 'proper' and an education beaten into us by the Christian Brothers. Most importantly we shared a love of showbiz, burlesque and variety. Paul had toured the variety halls with a mindreading act, which by his own admission was not very successful. He'd nicked the entire routine from a performer he'd seen in an end-of-the-pier show and toured the number three Moss Empires circuit with it in fleapit theatres around the north of England. After acquiring enough savvy he bought an old ballroom in Soho, transforming it into the most elegant strip club in the UK, the Raymond Revue Bar.

PR, dubbed 'the King of Soho' by the press and wealthier than the Duke of Westminster, was the Billy Minsky of his day, for just as the Minsky brothers in New York had presented their burlesque shows in elegant surroundings so PR elevated striptease from sleazy clip joints to a slick, professional show in a chic night spot.

Tempest Storm, a bountiful American burlesque stripper, was brought over to perform the honours on opening night. A stripper on the bill who went by the imaginative name of Bonnie Bell the Ding Dong Girl caused outrage in the press by inviting members of the audience to ring the bells that dangled from her nipples and crotch.

PR was quite a shy man with a slight stutter that vanished as he became animated, recalling stories of the imperious Gypsy Rose Lee's arrival at Southampton docks, complete with son Erik, a menagerie of assorted animals, a mountain of luggage and a Rolls-Royce with her initials painted on the side. He explained how he'd tried to help the UK's very own Queen of the Striptease, Phyllis Dixey. She had gone out of fashion – not because PR had blatantly moved the goal posts under the Lord Chamberlain's nose with his raunchy strip shows, as she claimed in the press – but simply because a prim middle-aged lady performing a twee little fan dance as she intoned 'Christopher Robin Is Saying His Prayers' belonged to another era. A huge star in her day, Phyllis had boosted the morale of the troops with her show *Peek a Boo* at the Whitehall Theatre during the war. Now, with her career on its last legs, she refused the offer of a showcase at the Revue Bar, deeming it pornographic and lacking in any integrity or artistic qualities, and went off to become a cook in Epsom until sadly and somewhat ironically she died of breast cancer. The part of her anatomy that had once made her famous eventually killed her.

I looked forward to these lunches with PR as well as the ride in the gold-plated Rolls-Royce, but most of all what I really valued was our friendship.

A few months after I left Madame Jo-Jo's he asked me if I'd consider taking over the running of both Madame Jo-Jo's and the Piano Bar, Jo-Jo herself having long since moved on. PR had big plans to gut the place, redecorate it and call it Savage's, with the emphasis on live comedy drag rather than singing. To clinch the deal he offered me both premises at a peppercorn rent of five pounds a week.

This was a seriously tempting offer as I'd always fancied myself as the proprietor of a nightclub, but Murphy put the kibosh on any such folly.

'Do you want to stand in a cellar in full drag night after night drinking yourself slowly to death and having to deal with drunken morons or would you rather be a successful comic?' he said, popping every bulb on the neon sign outside the newly refurbished Jo-Jo's that in my mind's eye now read 'SAVAGE'S', dragging me back to reality in a flash.

'Clubs are a fad, Savage, and the people who go to them fickle,' he lectured me. 'They don't last long when their popularity wanes, and the crowd soon moves on to the next place that's considered trendy, as well you know. Forget about it.'

PR was philosophical when I turned him down but we remained friends and he made a twenty-quid bet that I'd be a household name in a few years. I agreed, considering it a very safe bet, firmly believing there was no chance of that ever happening.

After I finished my stint at Jo-Jo's, Murphy suggested we take off for the Hebrides for a week of early nights, healthy food and lots and lots of walking.

'It'll do you good, you've been living like a bloody teenager running riot around Soho,' he said as we set off for Oban in the Citroën-cum-Lotus. 'It's time to calm yourself down, we're going to detoxify, eat good food, enjoy a bit of solitude and peace and quiet for a week.'

I could't wait.

I'd only fallen into bed at 4 a.m. and here I was five hours later crawling into the back of the car on my way to Scotland.

'Wake me up when we get there,' I moaned. 'I'm dying, in fact I doubt if I've got a pulse.'

'You ever heard of the word "hyperbole", Savage?' he asked me.

'No,' I grunted from the back.

'Well it describes you to a T,' he said, driving off.

It was dark when we got to Oban so we checked into the Oban Bay Hotel for the night. In the morning, before we got on the boat to Barra, we hit the supermarket to stock up on the week's groceries as we'd heard there was only one tiny shop on the island. Typically, instead of sharing a trolley like normal people, we went our separate ways, consequently purchasing a lot of the same things, except for one vital ingredient that would later cause an apocalyptic row.

'There's nothing between us and Canada,' Murphy said as we stared out of the window of the isolated croft we'd rented, watching the Atlantic Ocean crashing against the shoreline. 'Why don't we get the bikes out and go for a ride?'

'Are you crazy?' I said. 'It's pissing down, there's a gale force wind and it's freezing. I'm not going anywhere unless it's in the car.'

'Suit yourself. I'm going to make some soup then,' he said, going off to chop vegetables. 'Why don't you make a fire?'

I started to roll up the old newspapers conveniently left in a wicker basket by previous tenants, which was a slow process as I kept pausing to read some of them. The Edinburgh Festival, which had just ended, featured heavily in all the papers, stirring a pang of jealousy and regret as I read all about the insanity of those three weeks that every performer had seemingly enjoyed.

'Where's the onions, Savage?' Murphy asked, rooting through a cupboard.

'I don't know,' I said, engrossed in the write-up of a charity event at the Playhouse. 'Where did you put them?'

'I didn't buy any,' he snapped back, slamming cupboard doors. 'You did.'

'I didn't.'

'You did. I distinctly told you not to forget the onions.'

'You bloody well didn't.'

'Savage, where are the fecking ONIONS!'

The gloves were off. The blue touchpaper had been lit and the explosion was about to go off any second.

'If you hadn't gone running around the supermarket on your own,' he ranted, 'buying useless crap when there might, just might have been a bit of communication between us, I might be holding an onion right now, but oh no, you're not very good, are you, when it comes to anything practical? How am I supposed to make soup without any onions? Tell me that, you brain-dead moron!' He was fit to kill.

'Open a bleedin' tin,' I roared back at him. 'If you knew you were making soup why didn't you get your own onions, smartarse?'

'Because I thought you were getting them, Dumbo!' He was apoplectic and threw a King Edward potato at me, to which I retaliated by hurling a lump of coal at him.

Within minutes I was surrounded by a variety of root vegetables while he had a slag heap mounting up around him and the fury of the elements outside couldn't compete against the tempest raging inside our croft.

Two grown men fighting over an onion, or rather the lack of one, on the southernmost island in the Outer Hebrides, chucking vegetables and coal at each other, was not in any way unusual behaviour for Murphy and me. It was a fine start to a holiday of 'solitude and peace' but not in the least surprising for either of us, as we could argue over thin air, never mind an onion, and frequently did.

We were once watching a programme on the telly called *The Joy of Painting*, in which a middle-aged man with a frizzy Afro showed you how to paint landscapes. The guy with the Afro's technique involved the use of a variety of different brushes and lots of vertical lines, smudged to represent trees.

'That's not painting,' Murphy said. 'There's no art in that.' I disagreed, and by the time the programme had reached its conclusion and the frizzy-haired one was proudly displaying his finished masterpiece we were rolling on the front-room floor tearing lumps out of each other.

Car journeys to unexplored territory were always a nightmare as they involved map-reading, something that this former Cub Scout and Marine Cadet knows nothing about.

Irritating as the disembowelled voice of the satnav may be, it's probably saved a lot of relationships. In my hands an unfolded map could envelop the entire interior of the car and I never had the foggiest idea what I was supposed to be looking for. Murphy would then explode with frustration as he watched my desperate attempts to discover the route. Fisticuffs while driving on the motorway in a fast-moving car is not a good idea and I'm surprised we never had an accident. And after one of these rows I'd sit in the car with arms folded, silently fuming as I stared fixedly out of the window, hatred welling up inside me as I wondered for the hundredth time why the hell I bothered staying another minute with this snide, arrogant, bad-tempered arsehole.

The truth was we needed each other and, apart from the rows, the cruel cutting remarks we traded, the boxing matches and the moody silences, we were inseparable – a couple of mongrels scrapping in the gutter, vying for the position of Top Dog. Ours was a stormy relationship, and that's an under-statement, but deep down we were very much in love and always looked out for each other. Even though we rarely agreed, there was something that we never disagreed on: we both hated the same people.

Barra is a beautiful island blessed with deserted snow-white sandy beaches and magnificent views. On the rare less blowy days when it wasn't lashing down I'd take a walk among the rocks along the shoreline, listening to a tape of the haunting

*Derek Bell's Musical Ireland* or Capercaillie's *The Blood Is Strong* on my walkman, both of which I felt suited the mood and the location. We rode our bikes on the expansive empty beaches (Murphy brought his own, mine needless to say was hired), read Compton Mackenzie's *Whisky Galore* and walked for miles.

Our week was extended by another five days as the weather unexpectedly turned very nasty and all passenger ferries were cancelled, as were the flights from Glasgow that used the beach as a landing strip. We soon grew bored sitting in our croft of an evening with no TV or radio and attempting to read by the dim light provided by the Calor gas, so we did the sensible thing and adjourned to the bar of the Castlebay Inn and got drunk with some of the locals.

So much for detoxifying.

You go away for two weeks and the you-know-what hits the fan. I got back to find that for some unfathomable reason Chrissie had packed up and buggered off to live in Bangor, North Wales, and that Hush had lost a dramatic amount of weight in my absence and resembled a cadaver in a frock.

No amount of make-up could disguise how gaunt his face had become. When I gently tried to approach him about his weight loss in the dressing room of the Vauxhall as he was scraping off the slap, he was dismissive, claiming it was due to delayed shock following Roy's suicide. I didn't push him further as there was no need to. I'd seen it all before, too many times. The evidence was literally written all over his face. Hush had Aids.

# CHAPTER 2

I WENT BACK HOME TO MERSEYSIDE TO WORK AT JODY'S CLUB, luring Chrissie over from Bangor with the offer of a couple of nights at the Adelphi Hotel.

We loved this old Liverpool hotel. Once considered the most luxurious of its kind outside London, it was patronized by the rich and famous before they set sail for America. Roy Rogers and Trigger stayed here when they were appearing at the Empire, although Trigger, being a horse, slept in the stables round the corner. The Adelphi's glory days may have been behind her but Chrissie and I went down from our room to partake of afternoon tea in the Great Hall in the manner of two respectable Edwardian matrons.

'I wish I had a hat,' Chrissie remarked as he sipped his tea and nibbled daintily at the corner of an extremely unpretentious boiled ham sarnie. 'A big picture hat with a veil and a lace brolly to match. I could carry that look off, I could.'

'They could do with a few ferns and palms in here,' I said, relieved that he didn't have a hat and turning my attention to the Ionic columns and the glass panels in the ceiling. 'This room must have been something really special in its heyday.'

'I bet it was gorgeous,' Chrissie agreed. 'I could just see

meself in here back then. Big 'at and a ton of luggage waiting to get on a liner and fuck off to New York.'

'I hate to burst your bubble,' I told him, 'but if we had been around at that time the only hat you'd be wearing would be one of servitude as we'd have either been begging outside or below stairs, scrubbing floors and polishing boots.'

'Very true,' Chrissie sighed. 'Maybe I'll come back in the next life as a toff. Now is there any more tea going?'

I watched him as he set about looking for a member of staff. Apart from appearing slightly smaller than I remembered as well as, dare I say it, gentler, there was nothing I could put my finger on that would explain his sudden disappearance to Wales.

'D'ya want another sarnie, Lil?' he shouted from the other side of the room where he'd collared a waiter. I shook my head and sank into my chair. He hadn't changed yet there was definitely something different about him. Time would tell.

Chrissie went back to Bangor and before I went home to London I took the ferry over to Birkenhead to visit Aunty Anne. Like Chrissie, she too seemed to have shrunk, suffering badly from arthritis as well as a host of other illnesses. She was due to go into hospital in a few days' time for 'tests', a medical euphemism for 'we haven't got a clue what's wrong with you'.

For the first time in her life, since her sister, my aunty Chris, had died she was living alone in her little flat over the betting office, which, without her sister's presence and their constant banter, seemed empty and forlorn.

'D'you want a cup of tea, lad, and a little butty?' she asked. 'You look half starved.'

I could've waddled in the door weighing in at twenty-eight

stone and Aunty Anne would've still considered me to be wasting away. I sat on the sofa as she busied herself in the kitchen and stared at the empty armchair that Aunty Chris had held court in, swathed in her Brentford Nylon housecoat, pockmarked with fag burns and with her pharmacy of tablets and medication on the little table beside her.

Even though the amount of food Aunty Chris ate would hardly sustain a mouse, like her sister she was obsessed by it. I never left the flat without her slinging fifty pence at me across the carpet and ordering me to 'Get yourself something from Billy Lam's [the Chinese chippy across the road]. Although how you can eat that curry muck, stinking the bloody house out, is beyond me.'

'Here,' Aunty Anne said, stirring me from my memories as she bustled in from the kitchen with a mug of tea and a ham roll. 'Get that down your neck, it's a nice bit of ham off the bone from the market.

'So what brings you here then?' she asked, settling down to her crossword in last night's *Liverpool Echo*. 'I thought you were busy with work in London.'

I told her as I attacked the ham roll that I'd been working a club in Liverpool, answering her questions about how it had gone between mouthfuls.

It was good to be able to be truthful at last and come clean about what I was doing for a living and Aunty Anne had taken to the news that I was in showbiz, as she called it, with relish. In the last episode of *The Bill* I'd appeared in, my character had been badly beaten up and hospitalized and Aunty Anne had rung me up to see if I was all right, concerned that my assailants had taken all my money. Like a lot of people, Aunty Anne believed everything she read in the paper and watched on the telly as gospel.

44

The phone on the little table in the hall rang and she hurried to answer it. 'Fev, too, neen, siven,' I could hear her saying in the same clipped telephone voice my mother used to adopt, making me laugh.

'Our Paul's here, Tricia,' she was telling her daughter, dropping the telephone voice. 'He's just popped in, he had a club date in Liverpool last night . . . Yes, it went very well, earned a hundred and fifty quid,' she added, sounding like a seasoned pro discussing fees with another agent. 'He's sat here now, eating me out of house and bloody home.'

I spent a few hours with her and as I was leaving she wanted to know what was in the bin liner.

'Me wig,' I told her.

'Ooh, let's have a look,' she said as I dragged Lily's platinum barnet out to show her. I asked if she'd like to try it on as I could tell she was desperate to. Her tiny face vanished among the curls and it looked ridiculous on her as she admired herself in the mirror.

'Fancy carrying this in a bin liner,' she said with a quizzical expression as she bounced a few ringlets in the cup of her hand. 'It must've cost you a fortune. Our Chrissie would've loved this but I have to say I don't think blonde is my colour.'

Why didn't I have a camera with me? I'd pay good money for a picture of my aunty Anne, stalwart of the Union of Catholic Mothers, in a Lily Savage wig.

Taking it off, she stroked it gently as if it was a cat. 'It weighs a ton, it does. Is it human hair then?'

'Yes,' I lied. 'It's made from nuns' hair.'

'Really? I've never seen a peroxide nun,' she said knowingly, replacing it gently in the bin liner. 'Who'd have thought it.'

I promised to come back and visit her in hospital but she

was having none of it, telling me that I had more important things to worry about like my 'career'.

'You get out there, lad, and show them what you're made of. You're a star now, earning bloody good money and appearing in fancy nightclubs.'

I didn't want to shatter her illusions by admitting that I'd had to stand in my case to get changed in the cellar that passed as a dressing room at Jody's club in Liverpool, as the tide was high and the floor was soaking. I let her believe I was working among plush velvet seating, chicken in a basket and getting ready in a dressing room that had a mirror with light bulbs around it and a chaise longue to recline on like they did in the films.

Waiting at the bus stop for the 89 to take me to Hamilton Square and the train over to Liverpool, I realized that in all probability I would never see Aunty Anne again. 'You're like the fucking Grim Reaper,' I said aloud to myself. 'One visit from me and your number's up.'

'Well in that case I won't be inviting you round to our house for your tea then,' a fellah passing by remarked. 'And you're on the wrong side of the road for the bus to the cemetery.'

A few nights after Aunty Anne had gone into hospital I was working in a West End pub called the Phoenix, one of Tricky Dicky's venues. He was a popular DJ who held one-nighters in venues all over London. You worked on the dance floor there and changed in the boiler room, which was very dusty and whiffed of pee as the acts had a habit of pissing behind the boiler. Apart from the public loo, which was to be avoided unless you wanted to be confronted in full drag by punters, the boiler routine was the only alternative.

'You're quiet tonight,' Murphy commented as I wiped the

broken mirror clean with a pair of old tights. 'What's up?'

'Nothing, I'm just tired, that's all,' I said, unpacking the slap. The truth was I couldn't stop thinking about Aunty Anne. She'd gone into hospital and wasn't doing very well, whatever that was supposed to mean. Even after I'd done my spot and packed up the gear, making sure I hadn't included a stowaway mouse as I'd once done, I still couldn't shake off the uneasy feeling.

When I'd visited her we'd spoken about a programme she'd watched. It was a pilot for *Hetty Wainthropp Investigates*, much darker than the light-hearted series it spawned, and I'd taped it. As I settled down to watch it I could feel Aunty Anne's presence all around me and by the time my cousin Maureen rang in the morning I knew what the bad news was.

'Aunty Anne's dead, isn't she,' I told her before she could speak.

'How did you know?' a surprised Maureen asked me tearfully. 'I've only just found out Mum had died myself.'

'Because she paid me a visit last night,' I replied, and to this day I firmly believe that she had dropped by to let me know she was moving on. I'm not one of these people who claim to have seen a ghost; I'd like to say that I have but I haven't. I've smelt one but that's another story, and I will admit that there have been a few incidents in my house where I've been unable to come to a logical explanation, but that night I'm convinced I wasn't alone.

So that was it then. The last surviving member of the Savage Sisters had gone. There was nobody left to call Aunty any more and her passing affected me. Once again, without him knowing it Dave Lynn stepped in with the offer of a new project to take my mind off my grief.

\*

'Heaven want us to do a play,' he said. 'Can you think of anything?'

I certainly could. I'd always believed that the movie *What Ever Happened to Baby Jane?* starring Bette Davis and Joan Crawford would be a perfect vehicle for a couple of drag queens to spoof, and after watching the movie about fifty times I came up with a sixty-minute script that was faithful to the original but tailored to suit our audience.

Dave was to be the crippled Blanche and I was to play her psycho sister Jane. A very popular singing duo doing the rounds at the time called Katrina and the Boy, comprising a real-life girl called Katrina and her partner Ian who sang and played keyboards, became Blanche's confidante, the maid Elvira, and Edwin, Blanche's accompanist for her supposed comeback.

The management of Heaven went to town, building a set replicating the interior of the Hudson sisters' house. It was certainly no threat to Warner Brothers, nor, on reflection, would the staircase leading from the bedroom to the stage have passed today's demanding Health and Safety standards, but it was innovative, clever and just went to show what you could achieve with a limited budget and a lot of imagination.

The film opens with a pre-title montage of scenes showing the sisters' progression from Jane's early days as a monster child star to her decline into a washed-up alcoholic while her neglected sister Blanche's fortune ascends and she becomes a successful and glamorous movie star until a crippling car accident, supposedly caused by her jealous sister, confines her to a wheelchair for life. We made our own version of this, shot in black and white and shown on the big screen at Heaven before the curtain went up. I'd love a copy of it now but like a lot of things it's probably vanished in the mists of time.

My impersonation of Bette Davis wouldn't exactly have the late, great drag impressionist Charles Pierce worried but the mix of Birkenhead and Bette went down very well, as did Dave's homage to Joan Crawford. We were asked if we'd like to do it again at the Brighton Festival the following year, which of course we jumped at since all of us were desperately seeking a bit of diversity from the daily grind of the pubs.

Chrissie unexpectedly came back to live in London. He now had 'the look' and within days of moving back into his hovel of a flat in Victoria Mansions I got him admitted into the Westminster Hospital as he was clearly seriously unwell.

'I'm not going in there,' he wailed, throwing his arms out and upsetting the overflowing ashtray on the arm of his chair. 'I'm not sharing a commode with a gang of dying old queens.'

'You won't have to, Chrissie,' I tried to reason with him. 'You don't think they're going to risk putting a psycho like you in with sick people, do you? No, you'll have your own room, probably one with padded walls and bars on the window. It'll be just like your old cell.'

'Oh, very funny,' he said, glowering at me. 'Well, I'm not going in and that's that.'

'Chrissie,' I pleaded, 'you're not well, why suffer when you can get help? They can sort you out. Make you better.'

'Make me better?' he spat. 'I've got Aids, you stupid cow, there is no getting better so why don't you mind your own business. I'll decide when I have to go into hospital, not you, now fuck off.' He stood up and folded his arms in defiance, glaring out of the window into the yard below. 'Are you deaf? I said fuck off.'

It was the first time he'd actually admitted he had developed full-blown Aids and the news hit me in the chest like a blow.

I went home and rang Murphy to see if he could talk sense into Chrissie.

Apparently he could, and did, as within five minutes of him arriving Chrissie was all smiles and stepping into the car with a sponge bag, waving at one of the neighbours in the manner of a grand duchess about to set off on the Grand Tour.

'Don't forget to bring me some pyjamas,' he said, sliding the electric window down to give me my orders as I closed the car door. 'And slippers, I'm not walking barefoot in that place, you never know what you might catch. Oh, and ice cream – chocolate and vanilla – and some ciggies, sixty at least, and get me a jar of Oil of Olay while you're at it. I've run out and I don't want to end up with skin like yours.'

'Anything else?' I asked through clenched teeth.

'No. That'll do for now,' he replied, dismissing me with a wave of his hand and closing the window as they drove off.

Since neither of us possessed a pair of pyjamas I bought him some in the Army and Navy Stores, along with a pair of slippers. I had to fork out fifty quid for the slippers as they were leather and lined in sheepskin and, typically, the only pair in the shop in his size.

As the pyjamas were expensive as well I left the price tags on them so he couldn't call them 'cheap tat', as I knew he would.

'I thought you said I'd get me own room,' he bellowed as I walked on to the ward. 'It stinks of shite in here, and I'm going to murder that mouthy bitch over there. Did you get me ciggies?'

The mouthy bitch in the bed opposite Chrissie's shrugged, adjusting the sleeve of his pyjama jacket and picking a speck of imaginary lint off the cuff and dropping it contemptuously on to the floor.

He was a shaven-headed queen I recognized from the Market Tavern, a bit of a loner and obviously under the misapprehension that he was a match for Chrissie. Big mistake. The next morning they clashed in the corridor, the stands on wheels carrying their saline drips intertwining and setting off a slanging match that resulted in full-scale war.

'What happened?' I asked as I plonked my daily delivery of ice cream and cigarettes on the bed.

'He started it,' Chrissie said casually, inspecting the contents of the carrier bag. 'You didn't get that fancy ice cream again, did you? I only like Wall's.'

'Never mind that, what happened this morning? The nurse wasn't best pleased when she told me there'd been an incident.'

'Is that what she called it?' Chrissie said, lighting up another ciggie from the stump of the one he was smoking. 'Did she tell you how that queen deliberately blocked me way as I was going to the lav? And what he said to me?'

'No, what did he say?' It didn't take much to get Chrissie going.

'He said, "I'm surprised to see you on an Aids ward, how the hell did you find someone to have sex with you?"'

'Whatever happened to "we're all in this together"?' I sympathized.

'So I said, "Are you talking to me? Or is that jaw of yours slack because it's rotting away like the rest of you?"' He was prising the lid off the ice cream and scooping some out with his finger. 'Then I hit him.'

'What with?'

'Me drip stand. Picked it up and let him have it right over

the head. This ice cream is better than that crap you brought in last night.'

'Then what happened?"

'We ended up on the floor. The bitch pulled me drip out of me arm and tried to strangle me with it so I nutted her. There was blood everywhere and it certainly wasn't mine.'

'So this is why they moved you to a room of your own?' I said. 'To keep you away from vulnerable patients.'

'Not bad, eh? It's quite nice, isn't it? It's one of the private rooms.' Chrissie beamed, delighted with himself as he ate ice cream and smoked alternately. 'It gets me away from the riff-raff in there. Just because we've all got the same disease doesn't mean to say we all have to get on, you know? I wouldn't talk to the likes of that in the pub so why should I be expected to be its best mate just because we're dying alongside each other? Now gerrus a spoon, will yer, this ice cream is running down me arm.'

# CHAPTER 3

'*H*I-DE-HI, CAMPERS,' I SHOUTED IN A COD WELSH ACCENT from the stage of the ballroom, channelling the spirit of Gladys Pugh.

'*Ho-de-Ho*,' the happy campers replied, a tad lacklustre for my liking.

'Lily can't hear you,' I complained. 'I said *HI-DE-HI*!!!'

This time the timbre and tone of my voice owed more to Mussolini than Ms Pugh on her tannoy, but it had the desired effect.

'*HO-DE-HO*,' came the deafening response.

'That's better,' I said, reeling from the vocal blast and going into my spiel. 'Well, unless there's been an outbreak of acne rosacea overnight you're all looking very rosy-cheeked this morning. I hope you all partook of the luxurious slap-up buffet that our hard-working kitchen staff were up all night slaughtering. If not, then hurry along for a nice bit of pork served in the friendly ambience of the Spastic Colon Bar and Cafeteria.

'For my breakfast I had two sausages, a bit of bacon, half a bottle of vodka and an egg. Yum, yum.

'Ooh, what a fun-packed day we have in store for you today, you lucky campers. If you missed the aerobics on the beach at

7 a.m. this morning with the lovely Ebony, then don't worry as she'll be repeating that bracing experience again tomorrow.

'So what's on the agenda today? Well, for a start there's bingo in the Cabaret Bar this afternoon with me as your caller, for which I'm fully qualified having worked at the Mecca for eighteen months. Then there's the Who's Got the Best Bum competition around the olympic-sized swimming pool this afternoon, providing of course the weather holds out. Can all entrants please make sure that if you're going to expose your bum through a hole in a plank you give it a good wipe with a flannel first. We don't want to see anything unsightly like a stray clinker swinging in the breeze, now do we? *Hi-de-Hi!*'

'*Ho-de-Ho!*'

For an entire weekend, Butlins Skegness was invaded by hundreds of gay men and women of all ages from all over the country and transformed into Camp Camp, a homage to both the 'happy campers' spirit of post-war Butlins and the popular TV series *Hi-De-Hi!* set in the fictional Maplins Holiday Camp. The entire event was organized by Peter Searle (Adrella) together with a couple of entrepreneurs who, recognizing the power of the 'pink pound', persuaded Butlins, not slow at seizing a chance to make a fortune out of season, to go with the idea. Skegness in March was every bit as bracing as those old advertisements in which a fat bloke in wellies skipped along the beach proudly boasting that sentiment. It was more than bracing, it was bloody freezing.

The locals were not amused at the idea of Skeggy being overrun with screaming homos and dykes, and deliberately removed or changed road signs and directions to the camp, hoping that we'd get lost and end up in somewhere like Carlisle instead. Even the mayor expressed his vehement objection to such a carry-on in the press, but undeterred by the hostility of the welcoming committee everybody made it to Butlins on the Saturday morning for check-in.

Instead of Redcoats we became Pink Coats, a team who were surprisingly efficient and well organized. Each one of us was allocated a different role – sports Pink Coat, dancing instructor, lifeguard, entertainers, etc., with Lily acting very much in the manner of Maplin's Gladys Pugh in her capacity as Chief Pink Coat. Vera came along, taking on the mantle of Peggy, the chalet maid. Dressed appropriately for the occasion in a yellow gingham overall, mob cap and white pumps complete with ankle socks, she pushed her trolley around the camp screaming '*Hi-de-Hi*' like a mad thing to everyone she encountered.

Murphy and I drove up to Skegness in the car on the Friday afternoon while Vera, together with Chrissie, drew the short straw by travelling up in the Vauxhall Tavern Coach, a vehicle packed to the gills with pissed queens singing and dancing to the Hi Nrg that would've had the gals of St Trinian's shaking in their boots.

Chrissie, who was not very well, was fit to kill for the entire journey and had Vera's nerves 'hanging out' in case he kicked off and belted one of the poor hapless revellers.

I'd always wanted to go to a Butlins Holiday Camp since I was little, as I couldn't quite get over the fact that everything was all-inclusive. As many rides as I'd like at the fairground, all for free? A child's idea of heaven or at least it was for me, but my mother wouldn't ever have entertained the idea of going to a place as common as Butlins so we went to the Isle of Man instead, which she considered posh. Now, here at last was my chance to scratch that itch and get to sample the Butlins experience.

Our chalet was very nice – two bedrooms with a kitchen/living room and extremely clean and well equipped. I'm sorry to say that we didn't leave it in the same pristine condition as we found it. After a Saturday night party that went on until the very early hours of the morning it looked as if a couple of heavy metal bands and a herd of rhino had gone on the rampage.

Unfortunately, Chrissie and Vera were booked into one of the older original chalets that turned out to be damp, cold, with no electricity and decorated with dog shit. As maintenance were not available until the morning they temporarily moved in with us, which was fine until we all went for a walk and forgot to take the key, leaving us unable to get back in and forcing us to throw ourselves on the mercy of our neighbour, Regina Fong, who wasn't very amused at the intrusion.

Vera and Chrissie returned to the dog shit but even so it was a packed house with Reg sharing with Dave Rosen, the DJ from the Black Cap, and a couple of others. Needless to say, we hardly got any sleep and tempers were more than frayed around the edges the following morning. They were shredded.

'I'm knackered,' I moaned, as I sat at the breakfast bar back in our chalet once we'd eventually gained entrance, after a lot of hassle finding someone on the staff with a skeleton key. One of the many qualities this staff member lacked was urgency and Murphy, whose mood was fouler than swamp water and who had zero patience for bureaucracy at the best of times, called him a fuckwit and a jobsworth which nearly started a punch-up.

First a wild-goose chase around the camp in search of a key and now a boxing match, and it wasn't even 8 a.m. Great start to the day, I thought as I slumped over the laminated counter and rested my head on my arms, my eyes itchy and heavy from lack of sleep. 'Oh God,' I moaned again, 'I'll never get through the day. I'm ab-so-lutely knackered!'

'You're knackered?' Reg snarled, spinning round on his stool to face me. 'I'm fucking exhausted, dear, exhausted thanks to you.'

'Here, it wasn't my fault we got locked out,' I said, lifting my head up smartish and mentally squaring up for a slanging match.

'I never got a wink of sleep,' he announced, reeking of self-pity. 'It's not fair being invaded like that, we're not fucking Poland next door, you know, you could've all gone and stayed in Vera's chalet.'

'Don't talk daft, you know their chalet was unfit for human habitation. It had two single beds, where were me and Murphy going to kip? On the floor among the dog shit? God, you're a vinegar-faced owld bitch.'

'Oh, thank you for that appraisal, dear.'

'You're welcome, any time, just ask.'

'Oh, shut up, dear.'

'Shut it yourself.'

We sat on our stools festering with resentment like two rival tom cats with only the sound of sizzling bacon and a mad queen running past outside shouting, 'We've found it, Alice, we found it,' to break the silence.

'Somebody outside must've lost their key as well then,' I said in an attempt to disperse the cloud of animosity.

Reg sniffed as a signal that peace was restored.

'It's all right for you, Miss Saveloy,' Reg said eventually as he devoured yet another one of the many bacon butties that Murphy was churning out in our kitchenette. 'You see, you have a role as Head of the Pink Coats but what's my position in this affair, dahling?' he moaned, licking his teeth. 'And what's Adrella's role in all this?'

'She's supposed to be down from head office, a right bitch who's the boss's floozy,' I replied.

'Typecasting,' Reg sniped, taking a huge bite from his butty. 'But that's what I mean, you see, everyone has a character role except for me. I might as well pack up and go home as I feel surplus to requirements.'

'Don't talk with your mouth full,' I said. 'You look like Mr Ed. All you need to do is roll your lips over those teeth and the impersonation will be near perfect.'

'Thank you, dear, but impersonating a talking horse does not solve the dilemma of what I'm doing here.'

'Adrella said the reason you're here is because the camp was built on your family's land,' I explained. 'Supposedly you live in the hunting lodge, somewhere on the outskirts of the camp.'

'Why would the Romanovs have a hunting lodge in fucking Skegness, dear?' Reg asked imperiously, as Regina Fong was reputed to be the last surviving distant, very distant, family member. 'It just doesn't read, dahling.'

'Because the Romanovs once came here in the summer months to hunt,' I said, removing a long white wig hair from my bacon butty.

'There's a bloody big white hair in this, Murphy,' I shouted to Murphy's back as he fried up more bacon.

'Then take your wig off the counter then, dipstick,' he replied without turning round.

'But why would they come here?' Reg mused. 'And what would they hunt?'

'Locals,' I said, 'and the Lord Mayor. Now shurrup about it.'

'But what's all this about my eggs then?' Reg went on.

'I'm not doing eggs,' Murphy piped up. 'We haven't got any.'

'Not fucking fried eggs, dear,' Reg snapped. 'Fabergé eggs.'

'Somebody breaks into the lodge and nicks your priceless Fabergé egg,' I began to explain.

'But I don't live in a lodge, dear. There is no lodge. I live next door with Mother Rosen in number 4.'

'Following your burglary,' I ploughed on, ignoring him, 'there's a big egg hunt on Saturday all over the camp with cryptic clues and things to find it.'

'Why?' Reg drawled.

'For fun,' Murphy roared, finally turning round and waving a spatula. 'Now will you two maniacs shut up, eat your breakfast and get yourselves ready. Don't they want you in reception by ten?'

'Yes, the reception committee,' Reg ruminated. 'What am I supposed to be doing at that then?'

'Receiving,' Murphy said flatly. 'Now button it, you're getting on my nerves.'

'I'll tell you who gets on my nerves,' Chrissie said, marching into the room. 'Those two old queens, Mick Jagger and Bowie.'

'They're not here, are they, dahling?' Reg asked. 'Oh, and good morning to you by the way.'

'They're in reception.' Chrissie threw his overcoat off. 'Can I have one of these bacon butties, Murph? I'm starving.'

'Jagger and Bowie are in reception?' Reg was incredulous.

'On the big video screen, dancing in the street, Bowie flapping around in that mac with Jagger in his white shoes. They look a right pair of old marys,' Chrissie said, absently scowling as he opened his bacon sarnie and peered into it. 'Got any brown sauce, Murph?'

'Where's Vera?' I asked.

'Sorting out the chalet,' Chrissie said. 'I had a better cell in nick than that shithole we slept in last night. We both kicked off on that Adrella and we've been moved to a decent one with heating and hot water and no dog shit. Got any tomato sauce then, Murph? Or a bit of sandwich spread?'

'It's not a bloody café, Chrissie.'

'I'll nick some from that supermarket for you then.'

'Really, Chrissie,' Reg admonished. 'What happens if the store detective sees you?'

'They don't have store detectives in little mini-markets like that, Regina,' Chrissie scoffed. 'It's not 'Arrods.'

'They do in Kentish Town, dahling,' Reg said, yawning loudly. 'I don't know how I'm going to keep awake, really I don't.'

'Take a couple of these,' Chrissie said, casually rooting through the pockets of his overcoat and producing a pack of tablets.

'What are they, dahling?' Reg asked warily, suspicious but extremely interested nevertheless.

'Tenuate Dospan,' Chrissie said. 'Slimming pills. They keep you going all day and you lose weight at the same time. You could do with shedding a few stone, Regina, if you don't mind me saying, 'cos you're getting very hefty.'

Reg was momentarily speechless for a change.

'That's why they never gave you a pink coat,' Chrissie cackled, knowing exactly which buttons to push to get Reg going. 'Because you looked like a docker in it. A dirty great big pink docker. You should be carrying coal with a back like that, Regina.'

'Give me two of those tablets. Now, you filthy Liverpoolian trollop,' Reg demanded, holding out his hand, 'before I slap you.'

'Rock Ferry trollop if you don't mind.' Chrissie laughed, popping two of the pills into his hand.

'I'll have a couple of those as well, please,' I said.

'And me,' Murphy chimed in.

'You better save some for me,' Vera shouted with a hint of panic in his voice, coming into the chalet, 'whatever they are.'

'Eck, eck,' I said, swallowing the pills with a mouthful of tea. 'Here's Janis Joplin. Where've you been?'

We listened to the story of the confrontation with Adrella as Vera unpacked his chalet maid outfit. He'd already had a Dospan or two, judging by the way his tongue was furiously darting in and out as he stood shaking by the sink.

'I'm dry as a bone,' he tried to say but his tongue had turned to Velcro and was stuck to the roof of his mouth. Waving his hand in the direction of the tap, he said something that sounded like 'Gith a glath, Murth.'

'You're off your head,' I said, tingling all over, suddenly feeling highly elated and excited but with an uncontrollable urge to pee. 'As soon as I've been to the lav, I'll put your slap on and then I'll do me own. Come on, get a move on. You too, Regina.'

'I would, dear, but I'm having such a wonderful time on this fucking stool talking to my imaginary friend who is not only well versed in the workings of the Russian Orthodox Church and the dying art of polite conversation over the breakfast table but has a great-aunt who once sat next to my mother's wet nurse on a tram,' Reg drawled, waving a piece of toast as if it were a small fan.

'Then your friend is obviously not from the higher echelons of society, not if he or she was on a tram sat next to a lowly domestic servant,' I argued.

61

'The great-aunt was a suffragette, dahling, a very liberal-minded woman who didn't object to sitting in Third,' Reg replied grandly. 'Now if you don't mind I'm in the middle of a conversation about tropical fish.'

'I'm in a fucking madhouse,' Murphy said calmly, handing the shaking Vera a glass of water which he then proceeded to spill all over the kitchen floor. 'A madhouse.'

After the meet-and-greet with the campers, where our characters were established immediately as a deliberately very bossy Adrella introduced us all, I took the platform dressed in my pink blazer, pleated skirt and aviator sunglasses. Cracking a riding crop against my leg, I read out a list of rules I'd concocted that made a gulag seem like a very attractive holiday location in comparison. During this rant, Vera arrived on cue pushing a cleaner's trolley and screaming '*HI-DE-HI*' like a maniacal soothsayer. This gave me a chance to humiliate her in public by reminding her that she was a common chalet maid who would never make it to Pink Coat status as she was unfit to wear the hallowed pink jacket and should get back to work cleaning out toilets and chalets where she belonged.

Naturally Vera gained a lot of sympathy after one of my public beratings and did well out of it with consolatory drinks.

One of the security guards at the camp also worked on the door of the Two Brewers pub in Clapham and he had a ferocious-looking Rottweiler called Roxy who was in fact as sweet as a kitten. I'd patrol the camp with Roxy in the back of an open-top jeep, popping into the restaurant with her to enquire of a hapless camper who hadn't finished his lunch if there was anything wrong with his beans and if he was aware of world hunger.

\*

'How are you feeling?' I asked Regina in the cocktail bar as we attempted to take a break from the mayhem. He was wearing a fifties swimsuit, a swingback coat with a polka dot lining and an enormous straw hat and sunglasses.

'I can't see a thing, dear,' he confided. 'I was given these divine glasses by a queen in the Cap and they're perfect for this outfit (you don't think the coat's a bit short, do you?) but I think they may just have prescription lenses. Either that or everything's on a tilt.'

'The place is packed,' I said, looking through the window. 'Every gay pub and club in the country must be empty.'

Someone leaned over and plonked a bottle of cider in my hand, knocking Regina's cartwheel of a hat in the process.

'Mind the fuckin' chapeau, darlin',' Reg roared, more annoyed that he hadn't been given a drink than at having his hat nudged.

'This hat is going,' he hissed. 'It's gripped to the wig and I'm terrified that if it goes it'll drag the wig off with it. Imagine it, dear.'

I did and the image made me laugh.

'Very funny and I don't think, de-ar,' Reg sniffed.

'How's your tablet doing?' I asked, swiftly moving on.

'Wonderful, dahling,' Reg gushed. 'I'm full of energy. God bless Chrissie, although I'm peeing a lot, which is a bugger on the nails getting the old dickie-doo-dah out. I've got one lodged in my panty girdle and I stuck it on with superglue. Varda these two,' he added, nodding in the direction of two very smart young men wearing 1950s Hawaiian shirts and shorts coming towards us arm in arm.

'*Hi-de-Hi*,' they shouted, beaming from ear to ear and looking like a pair of all-American boys from a retro American

TV commercial for toothpaste, except for when they spoke. Then it was pure Salford.

It was amazing how so many entered into the spirit. Chalet windows were decked out with ruched net curtains and fairy lights, doormats appeared as did garden gnomes and pink plastic flamingos in the patches of grass in front of the chalets, their mundane interiors transformed by scatter cushions, throws and mood lighting, all brought from home. The camp was buzzing and so was I, and I was not in the least surprised, as I stalked the camp with renewed energy, that half the slimmers in the country were hooked on these Tenuate Dospan that Chrissie was, thankfully, handing out like Smarties.

After a long morning I escaped to the quiet of the dressing room I shared with Adrella at the back of the Showboat Lounge to repair the slap, but found that the toolbox I kept my jumble of greasepaints, powders and unmentionable things without lids in that I called my make-up case had been nicked. Security was called and there was a hoo-ha about it but it didn't turn up.

'What am I going to do without my slap?' I moaned to Adrella. 'Without my eyelashes? And false nail pads?' Suddenly these ridiculous-sounding items that the sensible would dismiss as unimportant and probably very easily replaceable became as vital as a wetsuit and oxygen tanks to a deep sea diver, the absence of which was guaranteed to tip the needle into the red area marked 'non-negotiable'.

Livid, I slammed out of the dressing room, incandescent with rage, and straight into the star of the show's young assistant, who was about to knock on his mistress's door.

'Whatever's the matter?' he asked in his soft accent.

'Some thieving bastard has stolen all my make-up, that's bloody what,' I spat.

'Oh no they haven't,' the soft-voiced one crooned.

'What do you mean?' the Philharmonic brass section enquired.

'Miss Kitt has it.'

*Eartha Kitt has got my make-up? My plastic toolbox from Mansfield Market with all me slap in it? Mother of God!*

A vision of the public health warning that lay inside that grubby box flashed across my mind but I swiftly banished this sudden lapse into weakness by remembering the words of Candy du Barry, 'A tidy make-up box means you're not working if you've got the time to tidy it,' and so I soldiered on in full high dudgeon mode.

'Did she now,' I hissed, through not quite slitted eyes as the slimming pills rendered the eye muscles incapable of anything other than a wide-eyed stare. I pushed him aside and grabbed the door knob. 'Did she now,' I said again only this time slightly louder, more for my own benefit, as running on a hot temper with right on my side or not, this was the legend that is Eartha Kitt that I was about to tackle.

*Steady the Buffs.*

I opened the door and marched in, ignoring the pretty little soft-voiced assistant's protestations, and bearded the dragon in her den.

I was unprepared for the delicate little woman in a brown sweater and slacks with her head bound up in a nylon scarf who was curled up on the sofa. She responded to this intrusion by making a nasal sound that resembled a cross between a yawn and a cat's yowl but which actually translated as 'Yes?' The sight of this little woman with her bare face and bare feet took the wind right out of my sails. Remembering that this was the predatory temptress I'd watched on the telly and heard on the radio for as long as I could remember, the woman who played Catwoman, albeit not a patch on her predecessor, Julie Newmar, but a Catwoman in the *Batman* series I was once devoted to nevertheless, I quickly remembered my manners.

'I'm very sorry,' I crawled, 'but I think my dresser might have put my make-up box in this room by mistake,' giving the old girl a get-out clause.

'Your what?' she asked irritably.

'Make-up,' I valiantly carried on in the face of that scowl. 'And there it is on the shelf over there, so I'll just take it and get out of your way, shall I?'

'Wait,' she said softly in that unmistakable growl. 'I borrowed it because I have none of my own. Not even a goddam lipstick or a little rouge, for Chrissakes. My luggage hasn't arrived yet, nor has my gown.'

Nor has your wig, I thought, looking at the makeshift turban but saying nothing.

'They said they'll send it on to my hotel in . . . what's it called?' She snapped her fingers at the boy. 'That place we're staying at?'

'Skegness,' he replied politely with a slight shudder.

'That's right,' Miss Kitt said. 'Skegness, where I'm freezing my ass off and want to go home. They told me if my luggage fails to arrive for the first show then they'll go into this Skegness and find me a selection of things to wear. And do you think they'd be able to find a stage gown in this Skegness? No. I didn't think so,' she went on without waiting for an answer. 'Can you imagine what they'd come up with? A little house dress from a department store.'

'It might be funny though, seeing the normally fabulously sexy Eartha Kitt slinking out in a nylon overall and carpet slippers,' I said, hoping to both flatter her and help ease the situation should the worst come to the worst.

This tickled her and she laughed, agreeing with me that indeed it might be fun but only for the first few moments, after which they'd expect her to ditch the overall and reveal the tight sheath dress underneath, slit to the hip and weighed down with sequins and crystal beads.

'I am after all supposed to be sexy,' she purred, stretching her leg out and stroking mine with her toe.

'Maybe they can go into Leeds or York for something suitable,' I offered lamely, stepping back a little in terror and safely out of reach of that toe.

'Maybe they can all go to hell in a handcart and take us with them,' she growled angrily, turning from coquettish kitten to spitting alley cat in a flash. She quickly finished off what was left in her glass and indicated that the audience had come to an end by standing up and handing me my make-up case.

'Thank you,' she said, 'although there was nothing suitable for me in there, nothing at all. On your way out would you mind asking the management where my bird is?'

'Your what?' I asked her, more than slightly puzzled.

'And my plants?' she said, ignoring my question. 'These guys need to get their act together or there'll be trouble. Big trouble. I'm a professional who performs all over the world, I was at the Café Carlisle last week and now here I am in . . . in . . .'

'Skegness,' the assistant prompted.

'Wherever,' she hissed, adding, 'You may go,' and dismissing me with a fearsome scowl and a flap of the hand.

'Well, what did you say to her?' Adrella asked when I escaped back to our dressing room.

'I gave her what for,' I lied. 'She's got the roaring arse because her slap and frock haven't arrived. What are you going to do if her luggage doesn't turn up?'

'Pray,' Adrella replied without irony.

'And she said she wants her bird.' I was rummaging through my make-up case to see if she'd nicked anything. 'And plants. What's she on about?'

'She likes live birds in her dressing room,' Adrella said, touching up his eye shadow.

'Flying about and shitting everywhere?' I asked incredulously.

'No, in cages. She also likes lots of plants but no cut flowers. There's a couple of budgies on the way and a canary, oh, and every cheese plant in Skegness. If she hadn't arrived so early we'd have had it all ready for her.'

'She's on the brandy already.' I sniffed as if I was unused to seeing an artiste in a dressing room drinking hard liquor.

'Oh dear,' Adrella groaned. 'It's going to be fun, fun, fun.'

It was actually. I called a marathon four-hour game of bingo in the disco (On Its Own – 62, Those Two Little Ducks – 17) and then staggered back to the chalet to change for the evening show that I was compèring in the ballroom.

As I weaved my way through the avenues of chalets in the fading light I caught sight of Vera still in his chalet-maid gear rattling around with his cleaner's trolley and knocking on doors asking if they wanted their beds turned down. Two Pink Coats passed me, greeting me with the ubiquitous 'Hi-de-Hi' and grinning like excited kids, still bright as buttons after an exhausting day. They made me marvel at just how much each and every one of us was putting into this event to make it a success. Billy Butlin would've been proud.

The show in the ballroom had an impressive line-up. We had the Mike Smith Orchestra, twenty-six musicians and three vocalists that brought the room alive and had the crowd jumping; Mike Terry, an international pianist, the 'Liberace of the North' decked out in a fake polar bear coat and sequins belting out Dorothy Squires numbers; George Logan, aka Dr Evadne Hinge in his first solo venture since he'd split from his partner Dame Hilda Bracket; and topping the bill the legendary Eartha Kitt.

The atmosphere in the ballroom gave off a bigger buzz than anything the slimming tablets could hope to achieve. People had really made the effort to get into the spirit. Two little middle-aged queens from Brum came dressed in full 1950s drag complete with little hats and gloves, and kept up the masquerade of being two genteel middle-aged single ladies all night. They even drank sherry, progressing to the more daring brandy and Babychams after a few dances.

There were soldiers, sailors, airmen and marines, elegant dykes in white tie and tails or teddy-boy drape jackets complete with quiffs and brothel creepers, and Vera had changed out of his overall into a dirndl skirt and cardigan as befitting his character's idea of high glamour. Even Chrissie had been affected by the mood. Smart in his suit, he was clapping and cheering and generally having the time of his life, in fact it had been quite a while since I'd seen him so relaxed and happy.

The show went down a storm with the crowd, who were virtually hanging off the rafters. The bars were packed with couples calling for more, as Cole Porter was wont to say, and by ten o'clock they'd virtually run out of booze, having to close briefly to restock. This caused mass panic among the happy but thirsty campers until I made an 'official announcement' from the stage to the effect that the bar would be opening again 'as soon as we've popped down to the off-licence to replenish'.

I stood in the wings with Eartha Kitt as I waited for Mike Terry to finish his final number. Eartha's kit had finally arrived (lousy pun, I know) and she looked beyond sensational in a clinging beaded black sequin gown and cock feathers, reeking of that unique and heady aroma that spelled Star.

'Are you ready, Miss Kitt?' I asked her, reverently.

She shook her head in reply and continued sipping whatever she was drinking, her eyes fixated on the stage.

'I'm going to be introducing you as soon as Mike Terry's finished,' I said in a voice loud enough to be heard in the front row. 'So are you ready?'

'Not yet,' she said, gripping my arm tightly. 'Give me ten to fifteen,' and I sensed that this great performer wasn't being arrogant, she was scared.

I managed to fill in, yacking about this and that and making various announcements while desperately turning to look into the wings now and then to see if Madame was ready – but there she was, standing as straight as a ramrod sipping her drink and shaking her head to indicate that she still wasn't ready quite yet. In the end I'd had enough of waffling and as time was marching on I thought perhaps the best thing for her was a little push, so I went ahead and introduced her. The band struck up her intro, she made an entrance like only a performer of her calibre can and the audience went wild. The nervous woman who'd stood in the wings had transformed into the international star and I fully understood as I watched her perform why she was known as 'the most exciting woman in the world'.

There was a cabaret after the show. Regina did a stint, as did the grande dame of drag, Maisie Trollette, whose drummer had gone AWOL.

'It's OK,' I heard myself saying, 'I'm a trained drummer, I'll stand in.'

I'd never played drums in my life but as soon as I sat down and got hold of those sticks I felt like Charlie Watts and found that, surprisingly, I seemed to have a natural flair for it. My dad had been a drummer with an Irish band in his youth so maybe it was in the genes. Whatever it was, Maisie gamely struggled on with 'Broadway Baby' as I battered the drums into something that sounded vaguely like a stripper's beat. I got a standing ovation for my efforts and it was one of the proudest moments of my life.

There was dancing to the band after the show and I jitter-bugged, waltzed, tangoed and lindy-hopped with the best of them. Vera and I executed a seriously energetic jive that nearly put us both in A&E, and at the end of the evening we all sang 'Goodnight, Campers' before returning to our chalets. I struck up a chorus of Gracie Fields's 'Sing As We Go' as we marched around the camp with a parade of pissed campers following behind me and joining in with gusto.

Nobody went to bed, we partied in our chalets into the early hours of the morning. Conga lines in the street below somehow always ended up weaving their way through our living room/kitchen until finally I collapsed on the bed at 7 a.m. still in full regalia.

Five hours later I was back on stage for the farewell show. My greeting of 'Hi-de-Hi' was no more than a hoarse whisper but the response was deafening, to which I merely groaned and staggered a little for added effect. At one point the show was stopped and Adrella walked onstage carrying a pink coat, announcing that she'd received a memo from the boss himself that stated Vera Cheeseman, chalet maid and all-round scrubber, was to be promoted. The crowd went berserk at this news. Vera rushed on to the stage, shed his overall and donned his pink coat with an expression of sheer joy written across his face.

'Wear it with pride, Cheeseman,' I said, kissing the exuberant Vera on both cheeks. 'And remember the honour of the camp.'

Eartha Kitt was announced but it was Adrella who strode onstage, sending up Eartha's 'Champagne Taste' song which he regularly performed in the pubs. The formidable Miss Kitt was a good sport about this. Making another grand entrance, she chased Adrella off the stage and took over.

Towards the finale the orchestra stuck up 'Lily The Pink', a song I loved as a child having bought the single in NEMS of Liverpool with Christmas money but was less keen on when I grew up. The entire audience started to sing as one and for the first time ever on a stage I wanted to cry. However, it wasn't until the final chorus of a suddenly poignant 'Goodnight, campers' that I let the tears flow and blubbed like a baby, as did most of us that afternoon.

The bar staff had told Murphy that they'd never made so much in tips before and how it had been a pleasure to serve such a happy, trouble-free crowd. The Butlins management were equally impressed by the way the weekend had gone and came to my dressing room after the show to say that Billy Butlin would be cheering in the heavens as this was the spirit in which he'd intended his beloved camps to be run. All in all the weekend was a massive success. The Pink Coats, with Spike Rhodes and Adrella at the helm (I was merely the figurehead), gave it 100 per cent and the cabaret was superlative.

My voice had been reduced to a feeble rasp, as had Regina's and Adrella's. Even though we were exhausted we had to play a benefit at the Hackney Empire the moment we got back, but it was worth it. My few days' playing a Birkenhead version of Gladys Pugh at a Butlins holiday camp out of season were three of the most extraordinary and indeed happiest days of my working life so far.

The tabloids had a field day as a few of their hacks, posing as campers, had spent the weekend undercover with us. The *Sun* devoted the entire front page to the event with a photo of 'Our man from the *Sun* and a member of the Vauxhall's bar staff known to friends and customers alike as Katharine Heartburn joining in the handbag-throwing competition. I believe the "man from the *Sun*" won it.' Says it all.

Due to the roaring success of Camp Pink, another weekend was planned for later in the year with Faith Brown and George Melly topping the bill. Tickets were going like hot cakes as everyone had heard about the first one and wanted to get in on the act.

For the next Camp Camp I was going big time. What I needed were pink patent-leather boots and as Hush and Doris (David Dale) were working at the Pulverfass club in Hamburg and had been banging on about this fabulous shop on the Reeperbahn that made shoes and boots for hookers, strippers and drag queens in every shape, size and shade I caught a cheap flight out there. They also made my trademark thigh-length boots. The Pulverfass club catered mainly to tourists who came to see the Travesties, the drag queens and trans-sexuals who performed there. It was what travel brochures would call intimate, small and dark with lots of dimly lit booths lined in red plush. There was also a curtained-off area near the kitchen where enterprising artistes could take a customer and earn a few bob for 'services rendered'.

The acts worked hard, four shows a night, and they all

shared one dressing room that only the management would describe as big enough for eight acts.

The compère was the renowned Ricky Renée. He had appeared as the drag queen in the movie *Cabaret* and being an enterprising act had traded on it ever since. He was American and despite not being in the first bloom of youth he looked sensational in drag. Hush worshipped him as the epitome of glamour and envied his skill at make-up as well as his magnificent blond wigs. It also helped that Ricky was a very nice person who'd had a long and successful career touring the world.

Predictably he opened the show with 'Willkommen', which he sang/spoke in his husky voice, slinking around the tiny stage like a world-weary fox draped in chic black velvet with a large diamanté question mark hanging from a chain around his neck. It was easy to understand why Hush was so captivated by him as he simply oozed that old Hollywood-style glamour. He was also a fabulous stripper and aficionados of the art of burlesque compared him to Lili St Cyr, one of the most sensational female burlesque queens of her day.

The majority of the acts on the bill left me cold. A couple of transsexuals, walking adverts for when to say no to plastic surgery, mimed through swollen lips amid a mass of feathers to a long and tedious ballad sung by some obscure Latino diva. An overweight queen from Denmark did a drunk act, miming away to a recording taped off the telly of Dorothy Loudon singing 'Vodka' at the Tony Awards. He lashed booze everywhere, mostly over himself as he mimed to the inaudible words of this lousy recording, sending the Germans into mass hysteria. I couldn't understand it until Doris explained later that the Germans loved slapstick and sloshing a bottle of water over yourself was a sure-fire winner, as was anything to do with pregnancy. Shove a balloon up your frock and mime to Ella Fitzgerald's 'I've Got You Under My Skin' and you'll get a telly contract.

I was seriously worried about Hush. He seemed tired and had now lost far too much weight, so much in fact that even though his costumes had been taken in many times they still hung off him. He and Doris were living in a flat that required a long climb up flights of stairs. It wasn't as bad as the two rooms we used to live in over Madame Arthur's club in Copenhagen but on the dump scale it certainly rated a high score. It also came complete with a lodger in the shape of a male stripper who worked at the club next door to the Pulverfass. He was a nice enough lad but he kept complaining of having a bent knob.

'Look,' he said, getting it out for inspection. Hush flapped his hands in mock disgust and turned away from the spectacle, while Doris and I studied it with a professional eye.

'It has got a slight curve, dear,' Doris said, squinting as he sized it up. 'Stand in the light so I can have a good look at it from a different angle.'

'Really, Doris,' Hush said disapprovingly, 'I've just washed my hair,' which made us all laugh as it had nothing to do with the problem of the bent knob.

'Does it hurt, dear?' Doris asked, sounding like a school nurse.

'Has it always been bent – not bent,' I quickly corrected myself, 'but with that bit of a curve?'

It was bent, in fact you could've hung your coat and hat on it, but I didn't say that of course.

'It's benter now than it used to be,' the stripper said, all wide-eyed in his charming German accent. He really was quite lovely, the archetypal strapping Teutonic youth fresh from the country, blond and wholesome and working in the fleshpots of the city with a bent knob.

'But does it hurt, dear?' Doris persisted.

'Only if I've been fucking for a very long time,' he replied earnestly, 'then it gets a liddle bit painful.'

'Oh, honestly,' I heard Hush say, 'put it away. You'll be wanting him to try it out next.'

I liked Hamburg. My hotel was in a little square that despite being littered with hypodermic syringes and dog shit had character, as did the hotel. The bar to the left of reception was what the tabloids would describe as 'a haunt of rent boys'. Hush and I went in for a drink without realizing that they were all on the bash until a couple of them approached us offering to make us 'happy'. Hush explained we weren't punters but 'artistes' from the Pulverfass, at which they immediately stopped their hustling and treated us instead as kindred spirits.

The infamous shoe shop where I managed to obtain a pair of metallic pink thigh-length boots was sandwiched between a sex shop and an 'Erotic Theatre' that I was desperate to have a look at, but as the other two wouldn't come in with me I had to pass it by.

'Filth, Savage, filth,' Hush said, pursing his lips and giving me a shove as I studied the picture of a naked man and woman outside. Apparently the woman was blessed with a deep throat, which was probably just as well as the same poster plastered across their pictures also claimed that her gentleman friend was in possession of ten inches.

'Now you just get in this shop and get yourself a sensible pair of shoes for work,' he ordered in his affected Hyacinth Bucket voice. 'Never mind filth like that, it'd put your mother in hospital if she were alive.'

\*

Murphy picked me up at Gatwick.

'I've spent a bloody fortune on boots and shoes,' I told him as I got in the car laden down with bags. 'It's just as well I'm earning good money at Camp Pink.'

'No you're not,' he muttered in reply.

'What do you mean?' I nervously asked.

'It's been cancelled,' he said.

Butlins had lost their nerve. They worried about mass cancellation because of the negative press following the first event. There'd also been quite a lot of in-house fighting between the organizing companies and in the end Butlins withdrew quicker than a panicking teenager indulging in a spot of coitus interruptus.

The Aids scare was still widespread and prejudice was rife. The campers who frequented Butlins claimed that they didn't want to risk catching Aids after occupying the chalets that a bunch of contagious gays had used, and the homophobic gutter press who feigned outrage at the idea of a bunch of 'poofs' taking over one of the country's national treasures for another weekend of debauchery helped hammer the nails into the coffin. Consequently, what could've been a great money-spinner for Butlins out of season and a wonderful, not to mention lucrative, weekend for the acts and staff died a death. A lot of people were understandably bitterly disappointed and the fallout over cancelled tickets was nasty, with Adrella undeservingly bearing the brunt of it.

Butlins later asked me if I'd like to compère at one of their proposed 'Adult Weekends'. This outraged the tabloids, who threw up their arms in horror that the home of good clean family entertainment was being reduced to a latter-day Sodom and Gomorrah. I don't know if those weekends ever happened but I never fancied it and turned them down flat. Nothing to do with the press, but I didn't want to chance sullying the memory of a fabulous weekend by having a bad time under the banner of 'Adult Entertainment'.

# CHAPTER 4

'Y̲o̲u̲ ̲c̲a̲n̲'̲t̲ ̲s̲i̲t̲ ̲t̲h̲e̲r̲e̲,' C̲h̲r̲i̲s̲s̲i̲e̲ ̲s̲a̲i̲d̲ ̲f̲r̲o̲m̲ ̲h̲i̲s̲ hospital bed, digging into the tub of ice cream I'd brought him. 'That seat's already taken.'

'Who by?' I asked, giving the empty chair the once-over just in case a teeny-weeny little visitor might have escaped my notice.

'Jesus is sitting there,' Chrissie replied calmly, licking his spoon. 'And you can't sit in the other chair either.'

'Why, who's sitting there then?'

'The Virgin Mary.'

'Where can I sit?' I said, bored now with this game. 'I'd hate to unwittingly end up on Our Lady's knee.'

Chrissie looked outraged. 'Shut your filthy mouth,' he snapped, his mood suddenly switching. 'That's his mother you're talking about, if you don't mind. Show some respect, you common slag. Jesus was only saying to me before you barged in that I shouldn't have anything to do with you.'

'Why?'

'Because you're a bad influence on me, that's why,' he shouted, his face now scarlet with rage. 'If it wasn't for the likes of you I wouldn't be in here,' and with that he fired a spoonful of ice cream straight at me, hitting me in the face.

Not for the first time since Chrissie had fallen ill I wondered if a judge and jury would show leniency if I cracked and retaliated with some force, but as usual instead of committing murder I took myself off to the kitchen to clean myself up. Chrissie's health was deteriorating alarmingly fast. I wasn't sure if it was the cocktail of medication that Chrissie was on or the early onset of dementia that was causing him to act like this but whatever the reason, it was worrying. Yesterday was slowly setting in and I was getting used to days like this. Yesterday it had been the Pope who popped in and then there was the time an envoy from Buckingham Palace had dropped by to discuss the stained glass window he'd promised to repair in the Queen's downstairs lav. It was painful to watch, and also very confusing as most of the time Chrissie was his old self, moaning and carping and wanting all the gossip. Then slowly his eyes would glaze over and you had to make room for Edith Piaf.

In the kitchen a patient I recognized from one of the pubs was mixing up a sachet of Build Up with some milk. He was usually to be found in Heaven nightclub, stripped to the waist on the dance floor waving a pair of large paper fans around his body with considerable dexterity. There was a craze for dancing alone with fans in the clubs and some of these fan-dancing queens were exceptionally good at it, spinning these paper fans around at great speed. They could also be a damn nuisance if you were attempting to get across a crowded dance floor with a couple of drinks in your hands. The inevitable collision broke their concentration, turning them angrier and fouler of mouth than one of those serial London cyclists with a camera on their head.

'Lo, Lil,' he greeted me cheerily, leaning on the lid of the blender while mixing his protein shake. 'May I be so bold as to enquire if that substance dripping off your chin is what I think it is?'

'It's ice cream,' I replied. 'Vanilla, to be precise.'

'What a disappointment you are,' he sighed. 'I thought for a moment there you'd been at that Kiwi doctor. So come on, what's happened then?' he continued, switching the blender off and picking up a dishcloth, dabbing my shoulder with it. 'How did you manage to get vanilla ice cream all over yourself?'

'Chrissie lobbed it at me,' I told him as I wiped my face with a paper towel that was harder than concrete and equally rough and non-absorbent.

'Oh dear,' he remarked, rinsing the cloth out in the sink. 'He's been on one all day, refusing to take his medication, saying that he wanted to come off it and then changing his mind a moment later. He's been as good as gold for the ward sister though.'

'It must be me then,' I said, thanking him for the wipe-down. 'I obviously set him off.'

'Don't take it personally.' He folded the cloth neatly over the sink. 'They always look for a scapegoat to have a go at, usually someone they're very close to. Turn the other cheek. I know he's got a right mouth on him, I've heard it, but just try and remember that it's the medication and the illness talking, not him.'

'Listen,' I explained. 'Chrissie's always had a temper on him as well as a mouth like a bee's arse, regardless of his state of health. I'm used to that. This is different, it looks as if he's losing his mind as well as his eyesight and it's all happening overnight. I don't blame him chucking ice cream around . . .'

I shut up quickly when I realized spouting off to a man with the same terminal illness as Chrissie and possibly reminding him of what horrors could be in store at any moment showed a disgusting lack of tact.

'Well, just keep telling yourself that it won't be for much

longer,' he pointed out. 'I doubt if either your pal or yours truly here will be around for Christmas,' he said without a jot of self-pity. He gave his protein shake another whizz and poured the pale yellow liquid into a glass.

'Banana-flavoured,' he said grimly, pulling a face. 'When I think of the times that I've tried to lose weight in the past. All those diets I put myself through and now, thanks to the miracle of Aids, here I am with the twenty-six-inch waist I always wanted and shedding pounds by the day with no effort at all.'

'I'm sorry,' I said, and to change the subject asked, 'Where's your fans then?'

'Oh, those?' He laughed. 'They fell to bits, dumped on the dance floor and swept away with the rubbish. The story of my life really. Anyway fans are passé now, you know how it is on the gay scene, nothing lasts for ever. We all get bored and move quickly on to the latest craze.'

'What is the latest craze then?' I asked.

'Dying,' he answered with a wry smile.

Chrissie was perfectly lucid when I returned to his room. He acted as if nothing had happened and allowed me to sit down without objection, Jesus and his mother having apparently left.

'I hope you haven't forgot the promise you made to me,' he said, flicking ash on the counterpane as he juggled with a spoon of melting ice cream and I wondered if I should get ready to duck. 'Remember what you agreed to in the Adelphi.'

During our weekend at the Adelphi he'd opened up and spoken about the death of his mother, telling me how when he went to pay his respects to her, laid out in her coffin in the Chapel of Repose, he'd been horrified by her appearance.

'They'd made her up so that she looked like an old tart,'

he'd said grimly. 'She looked ridiculous, not peaceful at all, not even like her in fact. They'd plastered her in make-up until she was unrecognizable and I don't want the same happening to me.'

'I'm sure they'll do a good job when the time comes,' I'd replied, not really wanting to get on to such a premature, if not macabre topic.

'Well, I'm not taking that chance and that's why I want you to lay me out,' he announced as casually as if he'd asked me to pop down to the shops for him. 'You'll do a good job with my make-up.'

'You're joking.'

'I'm deadly serious.' He was looking me straight in the eye. 'Will you promise to do my slap when my time comes?'

'I promise,' I said reluctantly.

'Seriously? You swear on your mother's grave to do my make-up?' he persisted.

'I swear on my ma's grave to do your make-up.'

'And not make me look like a tart?'

'I promise. Honestly, I will when the time comes, which hopefully won't be for ages yet. I promise and swear on a stack of Bibles to make you look fabulous.'

'I'll get that Bible out of the drawer and you can swear on it. It doesn't matter if it's one of them Gideons, does it?'

'Is there something you should be telling me,' I'd asked him, hoping for an honest reply, 'something about your health maybe?'

'There's nothing wrong with me,' he'd said. 'I'm just planning ahead, I'll be around for years yet.'

But it hadn't been years and now here I was with him in hospital listening to the same request again.

'You really promise to do my slap like you said you would?' he pressed anxiously.

'I promise,' I replied.

'That's settled then,' Chrissie sighed happily. 'And you can't change your mind because I've got a witness who'll back me up.'

'What witness?' I dared to ask.

'She's behind you,' Chrissie said gleefully, sounding like a kid at a panto. 'She's listening to every word we're saying, so mind your language.'

'Who is?'

'Joan of Arc, of course,' Chrissie replied, deadly serious. 'St Joan to you.'

'Bonjour, madame,' I said to a commode. 'Comment allez-vous?'

Chrissie sniffed disapprovingly. 'She's not stood there, she's over here now.'

'Shouldn't she be on the burns unit?' I asked flippantly, unable to resist. I was rewarded with a death-ray glare from Chrissie.

'Take no notice, Joan,' Chrissie was saying in the direction of the wall behind me. 'Just back me up, will ya, if this one welshes on the deal.'

A short conversation followed between Chrissie and St Joan that was so realistic that I began to question what sanity I had left. Was the Maid of Orleans, even if I couldn't hear or see that good woman, really present in the room?

'Joan's leaving now,' Chrissie said eventually. 'Show her out, will you, and bring us a cup of tea – black, no sugar.'

'Yes, ma'am,' I said, ushering St Joan out of the room and pointing her in the direction of the exit. 'Thank you for coming,' I said, 'and don't worry, I have every intention of keeping my promise.'

'Who are you talking to?' I heard a voice from behind me and turning round I saw to my shame it was Chrissie's consultant.

'Joan of Arc,' I answered him honestly, as who's to say she wasn't clanking down the corridor in a full suit of shiny armour, dragging her sword behind her?

'Keep it up,' he said without stopping, shouting, 'Sorry, can't talk, I'm late,' as he hurried on past me. With his white doctor's coat flapping behind him he put me in mind of the White Rabbit from *Alice in Wonderland*, only this was no fantasy. It was all hideously real despite the Mad Hatter moments and the gallows humour born out of appalling tragedy.

Being able to laugh in the face of misery sometimes provided momentary resilience when faced with a desperate situation. It was a hideous day-to-day routine that had become a way of life. Watching your friends slowly dying around you was now all too commonplace, part of the daily routine like cleaning your teeth or making tea, and with each death I understood what people meant when they claimed to feel as if a light somewhere inside them had been switched off.

Quite a few of my inner bulbs were dud now but as I said before, just like that wartime saying we see plastered everywhere, I kept calm and carried on.

Professionally life was good but privately it stank higher than a rotten fish. We'd given the Brighton Festival our *Baby Jane* to capacity business and excellent reviews, as they say in *The Stage* newspaper, and I had more work around the pubs and clubs than I could handle, but friends were dropping like flies.

Chrissie got out of hospital and went back and forth to Bangor for a while, returning to London when he got ill. These bouts of sickness were becoming increasingly frequent, each one more severe than the last, and I begged Chrissie to ring his family and tell them he was sick.

'I don't want that lot down, worrying,' he grumbled. 'I'll hang on a bit yet.'

Eventually he did ring his sisters and within days the three of them arrived from Birkenhead.

'Thank God you're here,' he told them in a voice that was barely audible. 'I've had no one to look after me, they do nothing for me, you know, absolutely nothing.'

I could've killed him there and then.

Chrissie and I had a stormy relationship. Blazing rows that could clear a pub in seconds, usually followed by a lengthy bout of ignoring each other's existence, coexisted with periods of amnesty and a close friendship. We both possessed hot tempers and could easily lay claim to having tongues like vipers when crossed, but despite everything our friendship had endured down the years and I stubbornly refused to accept that this disease would claim another victim in Chrissie.

One of Chrissie's sisters just happened to be very religious and I wondered how Chrissie would react to her brand of fire-and-brimstone Christianity. He did after all have Aids and a lot of so-called devout and loving God-botherers were going around preaching that Aids was divine retribution on gay men. Thankfully she was not judgemental, or if she was she kept a lid on it when Chrissie was around, and despite his initial protestations Chrissie enjoyed the ministrations of his sisters and having his family fussing around him.

During one of his spells in hospital I paid a visit to Lambeth Housing to see if I could get him transferred to a decent flat. His current lodgings in Victoria Mansions were verging on the uninhabitable. I'd already spoken to social services at the hospital and they in turn had written to the council explaining his circumstances, as had Chrissie's doctor. Nevertheless I took copies of the letters with me, as my experience of dealing with the council had taught me to do.

Three different people interviewed me at length, all of them sympathetic but all unable to help. Despite his condition they claimed that they couldn't find him anywhere suitable to live at the moment, but as one housing officer explained, strictly off the record of course, if I kept at them then his chances of getting a very nice flat were good as they didn't mind housing Aids tenants. They inevitably didn't live long and the council got their flat back quickly.

The 'very nice flat' Chrissie was offered was over a wet fish shop in the Elephant and Castle. It made his place back at Vicky Mansions look like a suite at the Mandarin Oriental. I stupidly took him round to see it before investigating the place myself, just after he was discharged from hospital.

'I'm not living in this doss hole' was all he said, and without another word he marched smartly back to Victoria Mansions.

He stayed with me for a few days but soon moved back to his old flat, declaring he needed his own space but would I mind if he returned each day for a bath, his meals and to watch the telly. On good days, when he felt more or less like his old self, we'd go down to the Vauxhall Tavern, returning to the flat much later with Vera in tow.

Chrissie had hardly any appetite for anything other than ice cream and those jars of sandwich spread and so, courtesy of our friendly neighbourhood dealer upstairs, I'd buy some dope and we would proceed to get heavily stoned as we sat watching videos and having a few drinks. Round about the fourth joint we'd all get the munchies and I'd vanish into the kitchen to churn out tinned salmon sandwiches, prawn cocktails and chips. Once, at 2 a.m. when we were particularly ravenous, I made a full roast dinner.

Murphy would occasionally drop in on his way back from the West End to find us sitting on the floor around the coffee table devouring a week's shopping and talking nonsense.

'Like the Mad Hatter's tea party,' he'd remark, but regardless of what it took it was good to see Chrissie eating properly for a change, and if that meant breaking the law then it was about time the law changed.

Chrissie was eventually moved to a hospice run by nursing nuns. I worried about this as apart from the occasional visit from Jesus and Mary, Chrissie was not one for religion and viewed nuns and priests and all things holy as a load of old papist mumbo-jumbo. Nor was he a fan of the royal family. He claimed they were total anathema to him, so it was of some concern when it was discreetly announced that Princess Diana was to make a visit to the hospice.

'Are you looking forward to Diana's visit, Chrissie?' I asked, tentatively broaching the subject of royalty.

'Not bothered,' he grunted.

'You're going to be nice, aren't you?' I pressed on bravely, listening to the multitude of eggshells I was standing on crunching beneath my feet. 'I mean you know it's amazing what she's doing really, and she's had to put up with a lot of stick from some of the press for it.'

'Fuck 'em,' Chrissie snapped.

I couldn't have put it more succinctly myself. I just hoped that Chrissie wasn't going to be quite so brutally frank when dealing with the princess.

*

It was a remarkably compassionate action for Diana to take, choosing to ignore her detractors and continue to quietly go about her business visiting the Aids wards and hospices unannounced. Not only did she lift the spirits of patients and staff alike, her actions did so much to help remove the fear, prejudice and stigma surrounding HIV/Aids at a time when being associated with anything Aids-related was not only distinctly uncool but potentially damaging.

It turned out Chrissie was putty in Diana's hands. She declined the offer of a chair and sat on the bed instead, holding Chrissie's hand throughout their chat.

'She told me that she'd become an expert at identifying which shops everyone's pyjamas had come from,' a glowing and animated Chrissie relayed to me later. 'She said mine came from Marks.'

'And was she right?' I asked.

'Well, you should know, you bought them.'

'She was right, I got them in Marks.'

'Oh, she was lovely,' Chrissie gushed. 'Really . . . normal.'

Her visit had certainly had a profound effect on him. It had also done his sisters, who had been present at the time, a world of good and he seemed to rally after his royal visit. However, a few days later he quietly slipped into a coma.

'It won't be long now,' a kindly nun told me in the corridor after I'd lost control and broken down one night. 'You go home, we'll let you know if anything happens.' Chrissie was right, the nuns were lovely. They were also practical, sympathetic, caring and non-judgemental.

I was in the process of preparing for a Christmas show that Murphy had engineered with our friend Mig Kimpton, only this time it wasn't round the pubs but at the Bloomsbury Theatre.

Usually I got together with Adrella at this time of the year and we worked up a couple of seasonal numbers and called it a Christmas show, but this was different. I was to have a troupe of dancers, new costumes and it was to happen in a bona fide theatre. My excitement at getting the show together was dampened as Chrissie declined and after each trip to the hospice I invariably ended up in Westminster Cathedral lighting candles like a pyromaniac on a bender to St Jude, the patron saint of lost causes. Even though I was no longer supposed to believe in such things, I would hold my breath and concentrate intensely on the candle, as if to infuse it with my desperate sense of urgency as I silently pleaded for a spot of divine intervention.

Predictably, it never came. St Jude wasn't taking any calls and within two months Chrissie was dead, passing away on the same day as Freddie Mercury.

I was sitting round a table at the Bloomsbury with all the people involved with the production side of the show when Murphy walked in and broke the news.

'Chrissie's dead,' he said. Simple as that, no warning, no 'Can I have a word with you quietly outside', no 'Brace yourself, Savage, I've got some bad news for you', just 'Chrissie's dead.' Two little words delivered stone cold that completely floored me.

Those gathered around the table sat in disbelief, I suspected more at the callous way the news was delivered than at the news itself.

I didn't know what to do. Cry, rush out of the room and hail a cab to the hospice, or just sit there and carry on with the meeting? I chose the latter, although I didn't take in a lot nor did I manage to contribute much. Even though

I'd prepared myself for this day it still came as a shock.

As soon as the meeting was over I rang Vera at the hospice.

'You'd better get up here,' he said. 'All the family are in the waiting room and if you're going to lay Chrissie out and do his slap you'd better get a move on as they want to see him.'

Oh Lordy, why did I ever agree to this? I thought as I sat in the car with the make-up box on my knee. I had no experience whatsoever in the laying out of corpses and nor did I want any when it came to corpses that I knew. However, there was no backing out now. Joan of Arc had witnessed my pact with Chrissie and it wouldn't do to piss off the likes of her.

After I'd said hello and offered my condolences to Chrissie's nervous and subdued family, an Irish nun showed me into Chrissie's room.

'Just give me a shout when you're done,' she said in a manner that suggested she believed I was used to embalming dead people every day of the week. 'Would you like a cup of tea?' she asked. 'I bet you'd kill for one.'

Not the best choice of words given the circumstances, but I said that I would and she left me to it.

Death had not been kind to Chrissie. One side of his face had turned a deep purple where the blood vessels had haemorrhaged and I wondered how the hell I was going to cover it up.

'Now,' the nun said cheerfully, returning with the promised cup of tea, 'I've brought you a biscuit as well, just in case you were peckish.'

I smiled weakly and thanked her but the idea of dunking a Jaffa Cake in my tea as I laid my friend out seemed wholly inappropriate.

Alone again with Chrissie I removed my coat, unpacked the slap and sat down to think as I drank my tea and smoked a fag.

Being alone with Chrissie's earthly remains didn't bother me in the slightest for that's all his body was. What was within had called a cab at the moment Chrissie had taken his final breath and there was nothing left behind except this empty shell. Getting down to the job in hand proved to be not as daunting a task as I'd first imagined. Dressing him was possibly the most difficult bit and at one stage in the proceedings, as I was attempting to get his arm in the sleeve of his jacket, I ended up lying on the bed with Chrissie on top of me. The situation was verging on farce but it was the kind of black humour that in life Chrissie would've relished, and as I lay there laughing it occurred to me that even in death Chrissie could be stubborn.

I was glad to have been able to perform this service for my old sparring partner. He'd undoubtedly enhanced my life, even though at times he'd driven me to distraction and I could've cheerfully wrung his neck. I was going to miss him.

When the job was finished I lit a scented candle, turned the lights down and stood back to admire my handiwork. He looked fabulous, even if I say so myself, better than he'd looked for months. Satisfied with a job well done, I went in to tell his family that he was now available for viewing, although I didn't quite put it like that.

'Bloody hell, Lily, you've done a marvellous job,' Vera said admiringly. 'It's a shame to bury her, she looks so well.'

'Thank you,' one of his sisters said, 'for making him look like our brother again.'

'Come on, let's get you home.' Murphy put his arm around me. 'Don't forget you're working tonight.'

So I was. Hoop-de-doo. Life goes on, as must the show, and whoever said that was talking through his arse. Thank God for Lily, a nice tough shell to hide behind and forget for a while.

Chrissie went back to Birkenhead as he'd wanted and was cremated at Landican Cemetery on a cold November morning. The fool in a dog collar, a supposed man of God, more or less implied in the rant he mistakenly called a sermon that Chrissie's death from Aids was divine retribution that he'd brought upon himself. The congregation flinched as one, apart from Chrissie's religious sister that is who'd organized this joke and remained tight-lipped as the rest of the mourners considered walking out in protest.

Murphy was livid and I knew in my bones that he was about to get up and take this fire-and-brimstone fanatic to task. I pleaded with him to reserve the well-deserved lecture he was about to deliver until the service was over, which thankfully he did.

'And now I believe a friend of the deceased is going to play a selection of music that was close to the late departed's heart,' the preacher said, glaring down from the pulpit at me as if I were shit and he was Ajax.

With great pleasure I stepped up to the altar with the enormous ghetto blaster I'd bought specially for the occasion and switched on the tape of music that Chrissie had selected. It started gently with Mahler and the music used in the film *Death in Venice* before moving swiftly on to David Rose's version of 'Night Train', and concluding with a blast of the old school song 'You Gotta Have A Gimmick'.

I thought the preacher was going to have a stroke. The expression of horror on his unlovely face as his ears were assaulted by what he probably considered to be the devil's own tunes was a joy to behold.

After the service, this preacher was ignored by everyone except the religious sister, who fawned all over him, and Murphy. As expected, Murphy confronted this miserable bigot and in no uncertain terms 'marked his cards', as they say in the trade. Chrissie would've approved.

Back in London, there was a show to create. Simon Green, a professional dancer and choreographer who found fame and fortune as Betty Legs Diamond, came on board. He and Murphy auditioned a group of boy dancers – Simon to assess their talent and Murphy, who as producer insisted on sitting in at the auditions, to weigh up the totty.

It wasn't a complicated show. I wrote a load of Christmas-related patter padded out with some of the old tried and true, and closed the first half with a potted history of Lily's arrival in London. This told of what happened to her after she fell into the hands of a procurer at Euston station and was sold into slavery as a hostess at the most notorious bar on south London's Barbary Coast, the Royal Vauxhall Tavern.

We'd rehearsed at the Drill Hall, Simon choreographing an elaborate fight/dance routine for the boys and an energetic Apache dance for me in which my 'pimp' flung me about the bar room, dragging me across the floor by the hair (the wig was virtually nailed to my head) before throwing me over the bar. For the bit where he swung me around his head, a life-size doll was substituted. As Chrissie was no longer with us and Hush, though very ill, was working away in a club in Hamburg, the job of making this dummy fell to me.

I had no idea how to use a sewing machine so I had to hand-sew the two crude life-sized body shapes together that I'd cut out of strong lining material, and stuff the result with those awful multicoloured foam pieces that my two cats just loved getting stuck into, scattering them all over the flat. Once Lily's stunt double was well and truly stuffed I made a crude copy of the outfit I was wearing, sewed a wig on its misshapen head and finally painted a face on it. The result looked like the Elephant Man in drag – that's if he had one leg shorter than the other by over nine inches – but it did the job and got big laughs as it was so obviously made by a rank amateur.

When I eventually left Victoria Mansions, that doll stayed curled up in the corner of the kitchen like a murder victim and I often wonder what the poor sod who moved in after me must've thought. I just hope he didn't think it was some kind of sex toy, albeit one without any orifices.

Simon certainly got his money's worth out of the dancers, for as well as chucking me around in the Apache dance they did a parody of 'Diamonds Are A Girl's Best Friend', only in this instance Marilyn's best pal was a shop called Argos:

> A wok on the stove may be quite oriental,
> But Argos is a girl's best friend.
> And you won't find the price in the least detrimental
> For in their catalogue
> Is just the job for thirty bob . . .
>
> I don't run to Smith and Son when on a pen
> I know a fortune I will spend
> But you won't blow those giros
> If you rob those little blue biros
> At Argos, Argos,
> I don't mean Ratners,
> Yes, Argos is a girl's best friend.

Hardly Rodgers and Hammerstein, I know. Even though the

show sold out, after all the bills had been paid I didn't earn very much – a little detail that would normally dampen my mood, in fact would positively drown it after all that hard work, but it gave me the opportunity to do things that previously I didn't think I was capable of. Having made a success of it I now wanted more, promising myself that no matter how long it took I was going to stick at this game until that one big break came my way.

'Next year I think we should give the Edinburgh Festival a go, Savage,' Murphy said. 'Are you up for it?'

'Open the cage, Murph,' I replied, 'and let me out.'

'Are you any good at sign language?' Mr Lawrence Gordon Clark, director of the miniseries I was auditioning for, asked. 'It's just that we'd heard that once upon a time you did something useful in social services and we wondered if one of those things might be signing?'

'Oh yes, I can sign,' I replied, looking him straight in the eye as I lied through every tooth in my head without the slightest hesitation. 'I'm fluent.'

'Excellent,' he said, obviously delighted. 'If only it was always this easy.'

I silently prayed that he didn't want me to demonstrate my signing skills, or rather my total lack of any.

'Well, I'm a little rusty,' I heard myself say, shamelessly coming out with the understatement of the year. 'But I'm sure I can get back up to scratch with a bit of homework.'

'Excellent,' he said again. 'In that case, welcome aboard. I think we've found our Donaldson the social worker.'

'You mean I've got the job?' I almost shouted. 'Seriously?'

'Yes,' he laughed, 'the character is northern and so are you and, more importantly, you can sign. We'll be in touch with your agent. I look forward to working with you.'

It was that easy, I told myself as I left the building. I didn't even have to audition, I just walked in, chatted for a bit and left with a part in a telly series. No sweat, not scary, a piece of piss.

*Hang on, what about the little matter of signing?* the voice of sanity said in my ear. *You lied to get the job and now the piper must be paid.*

'Oh, it can't be that hard to learn,' I told it. 'I'll get a book on it.'

*We'll see*, the sceptical little voice replied ominously.

The first thing I did on my way home, apart from buying a Birds Eye boil-in-the-bag cod in parsley sauce from the Mace shop for my tea, was to pay a visit to the library on South Lambeth Road to see if they had a book on signing. They did, which didn't surprise me as they seemed to have a book on every subject under the sun, no matter how obscure.

While the cod was boiling away, being transformed from fish to mush as my timing was always lousy, I studied the book. There were lots of diagrams explaining the different signs for all sorts of useful words and slowly through the night I transcribed my script into sign language. There were a couple of words that the book didn't have a diagram for so I made those up, hoping that if I waved my hands around fast enough no one would notice.

I practised every day until I more or less had it off pat, driving everyone round the bend in the process, Murphy in particular.

'D'you know what this one means?' he asked, sticking two fingers up at me. 'Give it a rest, will you.'

*

I was in the front room giving it my daily Annie Sullivan with the cats watching me, mesmerized, from the sofa and the top of the telly respectively, when the phone rang. It was a call to tell me that I had an appointment with someone called Peter Elliott who was going to show me how to sign.

'Oh, I already can,' I said airily. 'I've gone over the script and worked it out—'

'Very nice,' the clipped female voice at the other end said, cutting me off in mid-self-congratulatory flow. 'However, Mr Elliott really would like to see you on Friday afternoon at 2 p.m. Here's his address, do you have a pen?'

Peter Elliott is the performer inside those ape costumes in films such as *Gorillas in the Mist* and *Greystoke*. He's more primate than King Kong and his ape performance, whether in or out of costume, is startlingly realistic. No wonder he's regarded worldwide as the best in his field.

As well as swinging from the pelmet and peeling bananas with his toes, the man is also a proficient signer. He'd made out a script for me complete with diagrams explaining the sign for the words, similar to my library book although these signs were different from the ones I'd been learning for the past ten days.

'It's Amslang,' Peter explained. 'It's American and different from BSL. Do you know it at all?'

I didn't. Of course I bloody didn't. I didn't even know that BSL meant British Sign Language and since my call time was for Monday that gave me two days to unlearn it all and then teach myself this bloody Amslang. I'll never do it. I'm working tonight and Saturday . . . This stream of undiluted blind panic ran through my head like a ticker tape machine announcing the Wall Street Crash and if there'd been a window handy with

a decent enough drop then at that moment I might have considered jumping.

Peter's script became my Bible. I studied it incessantly, trying
to drive out the BSL and replace it with this Amslang.

'Why would a Bradford social worker be using Amslang?' I
asked the cats, who ignored me. 'And who is this Lucy that
I'm signing to? What if she's an expert and shows me up when
she has to sign back? They've only given me two pages of
script with my lines on it, why didn't they give me the full
script? It would help if I knew what I was supposed to be
doing. Acting? No wonder they're all half soft.' Dolly yawned
and remained aloof but Lucy got up and stalked out of the
room, tail erect, in high dudgeon as if I'd said something to
offend.

Maybe she's been an actress in a past life, I wondered. Mae
West perhaps, she's certainly got that rolling gait and look
how she uses her tail, waving it languidly like a feather boa . . .
I was allowing the most ridiculous thoughts to distract me
from the job of learning the sodding, boring, driving-me-up-
the-friggin'-wall Amslang!

By the time the car came to pick me up on Monday morning
at the ungodly hour of 5 a.m. I might have been gibbering but
at least I was more or less proficient in Amslang. I sat in the
back of the car, unable to stop running the lines through my
head and twitching my fingers.

'Is that a nervous complaint?' the actor who was travelling
with me asked, obviously irritated by my Riverdancing fingers. 'It's extremely distracting.'

'Sorry,' I replied, 'I'm doing imaginary knitting, I can't help it.'

He gave me a pitying look and for the rest of the long journey
to the location we never spoke.

'You're playing a northern social worker, aren't you?' the make-up woman asked, speaking to me in the mirror as I sat in the chair. 'You won't want any make-up then. You're perfect as you are.'

I was quite flattered to hear that my face could withstand the scrutiny of the lens without the assistance of make-up, even though I thought that after the stressful weekend of learning and lack of sleep I was looking a little rough – dog rough to be exact – and privately believed that major renovation work was required. But no, according to the expert, I didn't need any.

'Yes,' the make-up woman went on, inspecting me closely, 'he'd be drawn and pale like you, wouldn't he? Tired around the eyes and a bit worn out. That shaving rash you've got is brilliant as well. Yes, I believe you'll do exactly as you are.'

I sat and waited in a tiny little cell on wheels for the best part of the day, dressed in the dowdy tweed, brown and beige combo complete with a grey cardigan that the wardrobe department considered was what northern social workers wore, going over and over the now brain-rotting Amslang. Eventually I was called on to the set to do my bit at 4 p.m.

*Chimera* was a science fiction/horror three-part series about the result of a bit of genetic engineering between ape and man. The product of this experiment, the chimera in question, half man and half beast, had escaped and a social worker who could sign had been brought in to get information about how this had occurred from someone who was obviously deaf.

That someone turned out to be a chimp. A chimp called Lucy to be precise, and as cute as hell. She was very young and after a spot of bribery with a couple of Polo mints she was putty in my hands, and me in hers.

'Do you think I could have her on my knee when I question her?' I asked someone on the studio floor who looked important. I was desperate to get her out of the cage. 'It might look better.'

'The shot's been set,' he said dismissively. 'The chimp stays in the cage and you'll stay on your mark . . . if you don't mind.'

Kenneth Cranham played the sinister government official who'd summoned me to talk to this chimp, which was presumably a highly intelligent creature if it understood sign language. I just hoped it would be able to come to grips with my particular brand of Amslang. If it didn't and the scene took ages because the chimp couldn't interpret my signing, then I'd blame it on my accent. That's what I told myself anyway.

Before I shot the scene, KC asked me to come into his dressing room for a line run, which has nothing to do with chasing cocaine on a mirror by the way.

'How are you going to play it?' he asked.

'Intimidated,' I replied, which wouldn't be hard as I was.

The chimp behaved beautifully. She sat mesmerized with wide eyes staring at me lovingly through the bars of her cage as we went through the scene, and as I managed to remember my Amslang it was all over in two takes.

'But she didn't sign back at me,' I said to the disembodied voice of the director who was lurking and watching from somewhere in the ether.

'You didn't honestly expect the chimp to actually sign, did you?' The director's voice boomed all over the studio. 'Well, that's made my day,' he said, barely able to suppress the laughter in his voice.

The entire crew laughed as one and I wanted to turn into liquid and slide under the door.

'They get an actor in wearing chimp gloves to do the signing and cut it in later,' KC explained.

How could I be so bloody naive? Simple, in those early days I still believed in the magic of film and television and if I'd been told they had a monkey who could sing, let alone sign, then I wouldn't have been surprised.

'She likes you, that chimp,' Kenneth C said as we left the set. 'Listen, she's screaming the place down now you've walked away, yet she never moved during the scene.'

'She might do,' I told him, 'but then again she might prefer the Polos she knows I've got in my top pocket.'

'Crafty bugger,' he said. 'I know what to do now if I'm ever cornered by a gorilla.'

'What?' I asked.

'Offer him a Trebor mint.'

Privately I didn't think much of *Chimera*. It wasn't the least bit scary and could've quite easily passed as an early *Dr Who* episode, but it developed cult status among schoolkids and students. For a while afterwards, deaf gays in nightclubs would always approach me and hold lengthy conversations in sign. I was too ashamed to admit that I didn't have a bloody clue what they were saying, so I just did a lot of nodding and smiling and pretended I was drunk.

'Why can't we do *Baby Jane* at the Edinburgh Festival?' I argued as I pounded the slap on in the upstairs bathroom of the Vauxhall that had been designated as my dressing room. 'I don't want to do it on my own.'

'Here we go again,' Murphy sighed, clearing costumes from the corner of the bath so he could sit down. 'Why do you always do this, Savage? Convince yourself that you can't do it on your own when you've been doing exactly just that for years? This is a golden opportunity for you to show them what you can do and you're not going to blow it with *Baby* soddin' *Jane*.'

'Yes but it's just that I reckon *Baby Jane* would go down better than just me on my own,' I wheedled. 'I mean, what am I going to do? The stuff I do round the pubs? I can't do that at the Edinburgh Festival, it's all lads in T-shirts talking about the contents of their fridge and which teacher they hated at school.'

'Of course you can,' Murphy exploded. 'What do you think made you successful in the first place? God, you're a fuckwit, Savage. Listen to me, the mind is a strange place. You start filling it with thoughts of self-doubt and it'll start believing them, then you'll have convinced yourself you're incapable of doing anything outside the confines of a pub.'

'I know. But—'

'Look how confident you were about the Christmas show,' he rattled on. 'Well, adopt that attitude again and start thinking positively for a change, have a bit of faith in yourself. We'll go up to Scotland and have a gas for three weeks, end of story.'

I couldn't argue with that really – there was no point – but I did manage to convince him to allow Katrina and the Boy to come with me to do a spot in the show.

I didn't know a great deal about the Edinburgh Festival at the time. I just knew there were hundreds of acts performing throughout the day and night and I reckoned that I'd go unnoticed outside of the gay crowd.

For some inexplicable reason I'd decided to advertise myself as a Radical Marxist Sex Kitten. These were PC times and a drag act was not what you'd expect to see on the comedy circuit, never mind at the Edinburgh Festival, and I reckoned I'd need a handle to catch the punters' attention. What I knew about Marxism wouldn't fill the back of a postcard but I knew enough to recognize Lily as one of the lumpenproletariat class, and the city was bombarded with posters declaring that you could witness this spectacle first hand every evening at the Assembly Rooms. 'The most prestigious venue of the festival,' Murphy said as we set off in the Citroën, filling me with self-doubt. If that was the case, what was I doing there? Lily Savage with her singing fox fur and lousy fire-eating? What the hell was I letting myself in for?

We arrived in Edinburgh fairly late. Murphy had been given directions over the phone as to the exact location of our rented flat, which saved me the horrors of map-reading and the inevitable argument that followed. Consequently and unusually for us, our entry into this beautiful city was strangely amicable.

When we stopped at the traffic lights I noticed a hoarding absolutely smothered with bills advertising a variety of acts: Jack Dee, Jo Brand, Eddie Izzard and the Marxist Sex Kitten herself, Lily Savage, the sight of which released an entire kaleidoscope of butterflies into my stomach and stirred up a mixture of excitement and terror.

Our flat was conveniently placed just off Broughton Street with all the amenities that a turn at the festival needs to survive close at hand – a couple of pubs, a sandwich shop, a grocer's, an off-licence and a chip shop. Perfect. It was also handy enough for the Assembly Rooms for me to walk in each night, thereby saving on taxi fares.

Katrina and Ian shared this flat with us. Katrina's bedroom unfortunately had a hole in the wall above her bed that led

**Right:** Twenty to two in the morning. Thursday night at the Vauxhall.

**Above:** The early days. With Hush and Doris, LSD.

**Left:** Pat McConnon, landlord at the Vauxhall.

**Above:** The two moods of Chrissie.

**Below:** Reg and Murphy, 1987.

**Right:** Murphy and Angela Walsh, Vauxhall Tavern.

**Left:** Bloomsbury Theatre.

**Below:** 'You want to start something?'

**Left:** Opening a pub in the West End. Peter (Adrella) in background.

**Above:** Another B&B. Touring the clubs with Murphy.

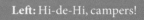

**Above:** Madame of the house.

**Left:** Hi-de-Hi, campers!

**Below:** Vera at Camp Pink.

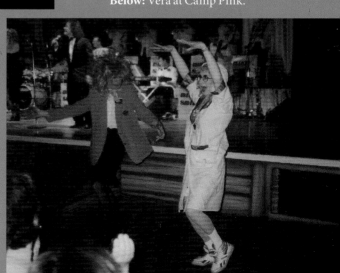

**Above:** The leeches!

**Right:** 'I am big, it's the bush that got small.' Paying homage to Skippy the Bush Kangaroo.

**Left:** Australia – the Daintree.

**Below:** 'Go for a paddle in the river,' Murphy said.

**Below:** With Lady Bunny and Regina at the PETA do at Heaven. I think Lily has had a few . . .

**Above:** With Tiny Tim and Bob Downe.

**Above:** As dressing rooms go, this one ain't bad. Melbourne.

**Right:** Touring eventually gets to you. Melbourne.

**Below:** Sweating like a couple of whores at confession. In the jacuzzi with Bob Downe, Australia.

**Above:** Murphy, me and Stomp and the crew, swimming with dolphins.

**Above:** My mate the cassowary.

**Above and right:** The Blue Mountains, Australia.

into the cupboard in the hall and on nights when I'd had a few I'd stand in this cupboard and shine a torch through the hole on to her bedroom ceiling, proclaiming in an Irish accent that I was the Virgin Mary – although why a resident of Galilee would sound like a character out of *Darby O'Gill and the Little People* escapes me.

At the sound of this heavenly voice Katrina would obligingly get out of bed and kneel devoutly in front of the hole-in-the-wall like the good daughter of the Legion of Mary that she used to be, and wait for the apparition to appear. In due course it did, only not in the saintly form of Linda Darnell in the movie *The Song of Bernadette*. Instead Skippy the fox fur popped its head out and drunkenly sang the few choruses of 'Faith of Our Fathers' that he could remember.

The atmosphere at the Edinburgh Festival is as intoxicating as it is infectious, although for those three weeks it becomes an insular environment and anything happening in the outside world is of little concern to the acts performing there. The stand-up comics scoured the papers for reviews in the artists' bar of the Assembly Rooms, all of them eager for a good crit. They'd play it cool in front of their peers while slyly enjoying the Schadenfreude of a lousy write-up for a rival. A front-page headline proclaiming 'Bomb drops on Houses of Parliament' would be given scant attention compared to the reviews, unless you happened to be a topical comedian, then you'd go away and try to think up a few smart and satirical gags for that night's show.

The guide to the festival was as thick as the Yellow Pages and it was unbelievable just how much was on. In 1991, comedy was being hailed as the new rock and roll and suddenly the expression 'Comedy God' was in common usage, with the successful stand-ups revered in the broadsheets by the comedy 'experts', particularly the American stand-ups who I gathered were considered the best. I can recall quite a few female journalists who allowed their hormones to get out of control as they shamelessly lusted after the handsome Rob Newman with the same gusto as groupies at a Kiss concert.

By all accounts there was quite a lot of shagging going on in Edinburgh during those three weeks. It didn't matter if you had all the appeal of a whelk with dysentery, if you were a male stand-up then it seemed that those two little words 'Stand' and 'Up' were the ultimate leg-opener and a more potent aphrodisiac than a brandy and Babycham – that's if you believed the gossip and the bragging that went on in the Gilded Balloon and Assembly Rooms bar.

A friend of mine happened to encounter a well-known comedian and actor getting out of his rather flash sports car one afternoon.

'Nice car,' she said, for want of something to say, 'that must have cost you a few bob.'

'Yes, but it's paid for itself in pussy,' he bragged, to her disgust. 'A real fanny magnet, this beauty is.'

While the heterosexual contingent appeared to be bed-hopping all over the city, the gay performers and their retinue, myself included, lived a fairly celibate life. In fact there was probably more action in a monastery.

'And they call us permissive,' a friend said wryly as we witnessed a woman down on her knees, giving a blow job to one of the comics round the back of the Playhouse Theatre.

The Assembly Rooms were very impressive, although I wasn't keen on the Wildman Room that I was working in.

'The Brit's bigger than this,' I moaned, referring to a tiny

East End pub I frequently worked at with an act called Dockyard Doris. 'There's no stage and look how low the ceiling is, it's like a bleedin' cupboard.'

'Well spotted, Savage,' Murphy said, patting me on the head. 'That's possibly the very reason why there is no stage as the ceiling's too low to accommodate one. Ten out of ten for that.'

He walked around the floor of this black box that was probably the porter's lodge or the cleaners' cupboard when not substituting as a venue during festival time.

'It's not so small,' he declared after giving it his full inspection. 'You can probably get a hundred in here at least.'

'A hundred!' I almost choked. 'We're going to get rich quick working to a hundred a night, aren't we?'

'That's if we're lucky enough to sell out each night,' Rick, one of the producers, chipped in, unwittingly adding fuel to my fire. 'There's a lot of shows on in this town, particularly comedy, and if we're going to sell tickets then we've got to work at it.'

'How d'you mean?' I asked.

'Well, that all depends on you, doesn't it?' he said.

I didn't enjoy the humiliation of the many publicity stunts I had to go through to drum up business. I was photographed in full drag at nine in the morning in the entrance of the Assembly Rooms standing next to a life-sized cardboard cut-out of Lily we'd brought with us in the back of the car from the Bloomsbury Theatre. It got nicked, turning up days later on an island in the middle of a busy junction. Murphy made sure it was chained up to the radiator after that, buying a bike lock for the job and giving Security down the banks for being so negligent, claiming the cardboard Lily was worth more than the real thing and a lot less trouble to deal with.

I went shopping in Jenners on Princes Street for the telly cameras but was thrown out. Oh, the shame of being frog-marched out of Edinburgh's poshest shop wearing thigh-length boots and a zebra-skin coat by two security guards, to find an enormous crowd of curious onlookers outside wondering what the hell this apparition was doing on Princes Street on a Saturday afternoon.

I don't know whose bright idea it was for me to dress as an usherette and flog ice creams for publicity as people came into the Assembly Rooms, but that's what I ended up doing each night. I was given a tray full of ice creams and five pounds' worth of change just like the regular ice cream sellers dotted around the building, and flogged choc ices and lollies to the punters. If I'm honest, I ended up enjoying it.

I might've sold out of ice creams but selling out the Wildman Room was another matter. We hadn't opened yet and so far advance ticket sales weren't as good as we'd hoped. If we wanted those 'house full' signs outside every night, the only way to do this was by creating a three-ring circus of publicity, not easy when, as Rick had pointed out, the competition was so fierce. Everywhere you turned, someone was handing out flyers and plugging a show. Acts were performing in every available space in Edinburgh, you couldn't walk down the street without tripping over a juggler and each time I visited the launderette I half expected to find a comic in the tumble dryer trying out a bit of improv.

On the first floor of the Assembly Rooms, they'd portioned off a part of the ballroom as a dressing room for the acts and filled it with rows of long tables that we shared to get made up on. I shared mine with an actor called Bob Kingdom who was performing his critically acclaimed one-man show about Dylan Thomas. I expected Bob to be a serious thespian, which indeed he was at work, but offstage he had a great sense of humour. Among his many other talents he had once been a voiceover artist and would often greet me with his uncannily accurate impersonation of Neil Kinnock.

I told him about a conversation I'd overheard between two young Americans who were studying his show poster outside the Assembly Rooms.

Boy: 'You wanna go see a show about Dylan Thomas?'

Girl: 'No, but my mom and dad love him, they've got all his albums.'

Boy: 'That's Bob Dylan.'

Girl: 'Oh, who's this guy then?'

Boy: 'He used to date that Oscar Wilde, you can tell by his scarf.'

In return Bob told me about two old men he'd overheard discussing my poster.

Man 1: 'It'll be a load of lesbian leftie claptrap.'

Man 2: 'She doesn't look like a lesbian.'

Man 1: 'Don't let the make-up fool you, Tom, she's as hard as nails. I bet she's got a pair of balls underneath all that.'

The majority of acts appearing at the Assembly Rooms used the same big dressing room. Actors, comics and performance artists from around the world, including the percussion group Stomp, who made extraordinary music out of everyday objects, and an all-male troupe called La Gran Scena, who dragged up and spoofed opera. Before you can send a subject up you have to be expert at it yourself. Les Dawson was an accomplished pianist and that's the reason he was able to play so brilliantly out of tune, and Les Ballets Trockadero de Monte Carlo, an all-male ballet troupe, are classically trained ballet dancers who have the talent to burlesque the classics to perfection.

The same was true of La Gran Scena. They had unbelievably extraordinary voices, worthy of La Scala or Covent Garden, and their assassination of grand opera was priceless. Their show was on in the afternoons so our paths rarely crossed and on the odd occasion we did meet they were polite but reserved, as you'd expect any self-respecting opera diva to be when encountering a single mother of two who swore like a trooper and entertained gentlemen in exchange for cold, hard cash.

There was great camaraderie in the dressing room, where the closest thing to a circus atmosphere prevailed and where everyone was supportive, enthusiastic and friendly. As one of the Stomp group pointed out, we all had the same goal in mind and that was to be a success at the Edinburgh Festival.

On my opening night the Wildman Room was only half full. The Liverpool writer Frank Clarke had turned up with a load of his mates, thank God, as they were very vocal and laughed in all the right places. Even though the crowd was small it seemed to be going well. Katrina and the Boy did their bit in the second half, allowing me to charge up the stairs past bemused punters and get changed for the fire-eating.

'I can't wait to work to half a dozen people each night,' I said angrily as Murphy helped me out of my leopardskin coat. 'It's a waste of time. I don't know what else I can do to drum up business. I've been made a show of in the street, I'm flogging ice cream, I'm getting up at all hours to put all this crap on and I'm made to do stunts. I'm spending more time in drag than I am as myself and I'm sick of it. All this just to flog a couple of fuckin' tickets? I want to go home.'

'Don't worry,' he said, aware that the end of my rope was in sight. 'Things will pick up. We'll think of something to get them in and get them talking.'

Madame Fate must have been listening, for the moment I lit up my fire rods the fire alarms went off. That damn low ceiling with a myriad of super-sensitive smoke detectors dotted around it went into overdrive when faced with two blazing rods, and the entire Assembly Rooms were evacuated. Every show was stopped mid-flow and the crowds spilled out on to the pavement as half a dozen fire engines turned up with sirens blaring.

I crawled into the back of the Citroën to hide my utter mortification and shame but Murphy was having none of it.

'Get out here,' he said, 'and get yourself with them firemen. It'll make a great picture.'

In the end he talked me into showing myself and I was photographed sat on the fire engine surrounded by firemen as the crowd, far from appearing angry at this disturbance, cheered good-naturedly.

'Thank God you set those alarms off,' one comic told me later. 'I was dying on my arse in there until you tried to burn the place down. When we went back in, the mood had changed and I played a blinder.'

My attempt at arson made all the papers and the picture of me and the Fire Brigade was on the front page of a lot of them. It even made the local evening news and I sat on the sofa groaning with embarrassment.

'Well done, Sav,' Murphy said, beaming with pride. 'You can't buy this kind of publicity, you're the talk of the Festival.'

*

As the Wildman Room was so intimate I thought it a good idea to serve drinks in plastic cups to the audience from a little hostess trolley. It was a very limited bar, serving only Thunderbird, a cheap fortified wine favoured by the winos of the city that turned the lips and tongue blue-black if you drank enough, and Buckfast, a sickly syrupy wine that had earned itself the slogan among those who necked it in bus stops of 'Buckfast, the drink that gets you fucked fast'.

The audience were a real mixed bag including the odd committed festivalgoer, the type who trawled Edinburgh armed with a bottle of water and a *Guide to the Fringe*. This character went in search of more artistic endeavours that usually involved a semi-naked performer delivering a lengthy and excruciatingly worthy monologue by the light of a forty-watt bulb but would sometimes wander into my show, thanks to the radical Marxist blurb on the poster, believing that they were in for an evening's discussion on the polarization of capitalist society.

Naturally, they weren't disappointed. Not.

Despite being on the go all day and partying all night I had masses of energy, fuelled by adrenalin, phials of royal jelly and fish suppers from the chippy over the road. Business was suddenly booming and I was invited on lots of television and radio shows. The celebrated Streatham madam, Cynthia Payne, was also in town promoting her one-woman show and it suited both of us to occasionally team up together at TV and press events.

I spun a tale, one I think a few people believed, that Cynthia and I were sharing a flat on Leith Walk and were operating a part-time brothel in our spare moments. On a live programme called *Edinburgh Nights*, Cynthia announced to the presenter

Tony Wilson that 'Lily is one of my best girls. She doesn't mind doing anything required of her.'

'Although not for luncheon vouchers, Cyn,' I added.

You were only asked to do a three-minute spot on these TV shows promoting the festival and I found this harder to do than an hour. It took me fifteen minutes to get around to saying hello on stage and although three minutes might not sound much it's a lifetime on television, particularly if you're dying on your backside. After giving it a lot of thought, I put together a spot suitable for the telly that was full of local references along with some of my best funnies. Prepared for anything, I was then able to relax and have a blast.

I quickly cottoned on to the fact that if you could make the crew laugh then you were on to a winner and I was always full of myself if I managed to achieve that. On one of these *What's Happening at the Fest* shows, usually pre-recorded in the morning, a young woman from Manchester dressed up as an Irish nun did a very funny spot.

'How many Protestants does it take to change a light bulb?' she asked. 'None, for they all live in eternal darkness.'

She was hilarious and her real name was not Sister Mary Immaculate but Caroline Aherne and I liked her immediately. She was very 'northern' and I mean that as a compliment, and also as smart as a whip. She had given up the day job as a typist for BBC North TV and branched out into comedy. Murphy really liked her as well and we became mates, later touring together.

The phone rang at the crack of dawn one morning and I staggered out of bed and into the hall to deal with the offender.

'Hello,' I croaked, sleepily answering the front door to no

one, still slightly drunk from the late night before and a bit confused.

'It's the phone, not the door, you dozy sod,' Murphy shouted from the bedroom.

'Then why don't you shift your fat arse and answer it yourself?' I snarled, making for the phone. Who the hell could be ringing at this hour? Someone must've died.

No one had died. It was Nica Burns, a director and producer of the Perrier Awards, the golden chalice that was the ultimate prize for all the stand-ups appearing at Edinburgh.

'You've been nominated!' she was screaming down the phone. 'Nominated for the Perrier Award. Congratulations!'

'Oh' was all I could muster before thanking her and going back to bed.

'Who was it?' Murphy asked.

'Nica Burns going on about fizzy water.'

It was around midday when Katrina burst into the bedroom with the newspaper in her hand.

'Have you heard?' she was asking. 'You've been shortlisted for the Perrier Award. It's between you, Jack Dee, Eddie Izzard, Frank Skinner and Avner the Eccentric. How fab is that?'

The fog in my brain quickly evaporated as I started to recall a phone call in the middle of the night from Nica that suddenly made sense.

'The phone hasn't stopped all morning,' Katrina said. 'There's a whole list of people who want to talk to you.'

'And you didn't want to come to Edinburgh,' Murphy said, laughing as he read the paper. 'Well done you. Now come on, get up, there's work to do.'

For the next week until the winner was finally announced

my feet didn't touch the floor. Extra shows were added thanks to the sudden demand for tickets, I made endless radio and television appearances and was interviewed and photographed by just about every newspaper. The press were wonderful, the Scottish papers in particular rooting for me unashamedly. In one paper there was a little cartoon of Lily sitting on an upturned bucket with the caption 'OOR LULLIE' written underneath as a homage to the *Sunday Post*'s Oor Wullie.

None of this attention turned my head, I'm happy to say. I simply kept it down and got on with the job, feeling as if I were on a runaway train. It was all very gratifying though. It did wonders for the confidence and gave me the energy I needed to get through the workload. There were afternoon shows and early evening ones, fifteen-minute spots with the other Perrier nominees in circus tents and the Playhouse Theatre, and endless interviews.

One day I got up at 6.30 to be on camera for eight to do some stunt for breakfast telly and didn't stop until 1 a.m. the following morning. Seventeen hours in drag, no wonder I felt rough.

I sat in the now empty dressing room following my last show, too shell-shocked to even reach across the table for my pot of Crowes Cremine to take the slap off with. I hadn't been able to feel my feet since around teatime and my left leg had come out in sympathy and was now completely numb, thanks to the pressure from the corset.

'Oh, my good God,' I groaned to my reflection in the mirror, which bore a startling resemblance to Alice Cooper's grandmother. 'Stop the train, I want to get off.'

'Give over, you've never been on better form, you're cooking with gas,' Murphy said, coming into the dressing room. 'I'm proud of you, Savage, the way you're just getting on with it.'

A rare compliment coming from Murphy was enough to shake me back into life.

'There's a woman downstairs who wants to say hello,' he went on, all smiles. 'She said her name's Xaviera Hollander.'

'The Happy Hooker?' The pitch of my voice had hit a double octave high A sharp with delighted surprise. 'I thought I recognized that woman in the front row.'

'Not another prozzie?' Murphy said. 'How in God's name do you know her?'

Xaviera Hollander had once been New York's premier madam, presiding over a brothel that went by the interesting name of the Vertical Whorehouse, a title that implies they certainly didn't take it lying down. It was a very respectable establishment, depending on your idea of respectability, of course, but unfortunately the grandees of that city didn't take too kindly to that sort of operation. They closed her down and slung her out of the country.

In the seventies she wrote a series of autobiographical books that became an international success. We'd all read these books and were mad about them as they were very frank and out-spoken for the time. I even had a promotional T-shirt with 'The Happy Hooker' emblazoned across the front and once got propositioned in Woolies in Crouch End by a seedy old man holding a bag of cat litter who took it literally.

Ms Hollander in person was a quiet, highly charismatic, dignified lady and I was over the moon to meet her. She was full of compliments and we sat and chatted for a while like old friends, with me promising to get in touch the next time I was in Amsterdam – which of course I never did as it was over a decade before I next visited the city and by then I thought she'd have forgotten who I was.

'First Cynthia Payne and now this Xaviera Hollander,'

Murphy said after she'd left. 'What is it with you and brothel madams? Is there something you're not telling me, Savage?'

'Give me the likes of Xaviera any day,' I replied. 'Now do us a favour, will you? Pull this bloody boot off, me leg's gone dead, and let's go home.'

Frank Skinner won the Perrier in the end and the train didn't so much stop as come to a grinding halt. From being everyone's darling I suddenly became Mr Cellophane overnight. It happened to all the nominees, but I still went back to London having had one of the most exhilarating times of my life. I had a carrier bag full of great reviews, lots of offers of work and, surprisingly for a first-time act on the Fringe, some money in my pocket from all the extra shows. My liver followed some days later by train, having been discovered early one morning lying in the gutter outside a public house in Rose Street.

I'd also met and made friends with a wide variety of people. Katrina knew Julian Clary quite well and she brought him round to our rented flat one evening. Julian was already an established star. Wondering if he would be as cutting as he was on stage, I mentally sharpened the tongue as well as a couple of claws just in case. I needn't have bothered as my first impression of Julian was of a shy and somewhat reserved person, though of course I know differently now. As I write, the old slapper is in the house down the hill, no doubt attempting to get into that rubber catsuit that's got more punctures than a busted lilo.

'You've got a lot of furniture,' he said, looking around the front room.

He was right. We had two sofas, four armchairs, two dining tables, a dozen hard-backed chairs, a variety of occasional tables in all shapes, sizes and condition, a sideboard, a bookcase and a hostess trolley with a telly on it. It looked like an auction saleroom.

'We do a lot of entertaining,' I told him, offering him a glass of wine. 'And on Wednesday night we hold seances and I give private sessions in the back bedroom. There's usually quite a queue, hence all the chairs.'

I think he thought I was mad.

Katrina also introduced me to Mark Trevorrow, the man behind the Australian Prince of Polyester, Mr Bob Downe.

I'd not seen any shows at the festival. I didn't have time, for a start, and nor did I have the inclination as I don't particularly enjoy sitting through an evening of stand-up. It's a precarious evening out for me. If the comic goes down a storm and I think he's crap then I get the hump, and if the poor sod is struggling and dying on his proverbial backside, I suffer along with him and spend the evening resisting the urge to self-harm.

Mark was different. His brilliant comic creation who sings, dances and takes very good care of his hair was a hoot, a brilliantly observed parody of all those cheesy safari-suited, over-made-up celebrities popular on TV at one time. This Australian crooner of 1970s classics lives with his mother, Ida Downe, in a caravan on the Now or Never Caravan Park and was once the darling of regional TV as the host of *Good Morning Murwillumbah* until he was usurped and replaced. These days, when he's not touring, he can be seen flogging men's jewellery on the Home Shopping Channel throughout the night.

Bob leapt out on stage like a firecracker and whipped the audience into a frenzy with a rendition of Georgie Fame's 'Yeh, Yeh'. His boundless energy never flagged and it was of such force that had the lights gone out in Edinburgh the Electricity Board could've shoved a lead in his mouth and used him as a generator.

After we got to know each other we appeared together on the bill at a charity show at the Playhouse Theatre singing a version of 'Something Stupid' ('I'll be frank, very Frank, and you're Nancy'). Bob, a mummy's boy with his dubious sexuality and unnatural obsession with his hair, wasn't exactly Lily's type but the relationship worked and we made plans to tour Australia.

The Edinburgh Festival changed my life. The experience opened doors for me that would otherwise have been firmly closed, exposing me to a much wider audience than I'd previously been used to. After it was all over and I was swept out of the city along with the empties and back to London, I was booked for three nights at the Purcell Room on the South Bank, a venue more familiar with classical recitals than a drag queen. I also turned up at the Royal Festival Hall and compèred a comedy show every Saturday night for six weeks at the Hackney Empire, that beautiful Frank Matcham-designed theatre where I'd made my first video the previous year. I didn't really think much of the video but I felt totally at home at the Empire.

The venues might be changing but the act was more or less the same. Regardless of whatever flash gaff I found myself in, every Thursday night I was back at the Vauxhall Tavern as per usual.

# CHAPTER 5

In 1992 I invaded Australia, touring the comedy festivals in Sydney, Melbourne and Adelaide for three months with Bob Downe. I was nervous but looking forward to this big trip down under and nearly everyone I knew had some information to impart concerning that continent.

'Oh, I loved it when I was there. It's just like England was in the fifties,' an elderly queen reminisced. 'They still have trams, so quaint.'

'There's no ozone layer left over Australia,' someone else informed me. 'You can't lie on the beach without an official coming up to you and covering you in factor one hundred.'

'Watch out for the funnel web spider,' another friend warned. 'They hang around toilet seats and one bite will kill you in minutes.'

'All the men have mullet haircuts and the women are as rough as arseholes. Well, you've seen *Prisoner Cell Block H*, haven't you?' It seemed everyone had their own opinion on Australia.

Even a fortune teller in Covent Garden who read my tarot cards had something to say about my forthcoming trip.

'Don't go near Australia,' she said ominously. 'Travel just yet, especially to Australia, wouldn't be a wise move.'

Great. Just what I wanted to hear when I was leaving in three days. That woman's words rang in my ears for the entire time I was in Oz and in the back of my mind I was always waiting for some misfortune to happen. Consequently I've never had my cards read since.

The night before I left for down under I worked the Vauxhall, to say goodbye to everyone. As I was putting the slap on in the dressing cupboard the feeling of trepidation that I'd been trying to suppress all week finally took hold. What the hell was I going all the way to bloody Australia for? They might not like me . . . I'll probably die on my arse . . . What about what that fortune teller said? . . . Why am I leaving the security of all that I know for territories unknown? . . . Oh bloody hell, why did I say I'd go?

It was a raucous evening and it only reinforced my reservations about leaving. After consuming our fair share of booze at the lock-in Pat, the landlord, and I got slightly maudlin.

'Listen to yourselves,' Murphy laughed. 'You'd think you were being transported to a penal colony in Hobart for life. You'll be back before you bloody know it and at each other's throats again.'

Fortified by pints of Guinness Murphy got up and sang the Irish ballad 'Slievenamon', all two thousand verses of it, during which Vera had a punch-up with a highly opinionated and aggressive regular who overstepped the mark. All in all, it was quite an eventful send-off.

We ended up virtually going from the pub to the airport, stopping off at the flat on the way to collect the luggage, which, thankfully, I'd had the sense to pack earlier. It was a dishevelled mob, stinking like a brewery, who staggered into Heathrow and up to the Qantas check-in that morning: Murphy, Joan, our friend Lewis and Vera, who had bloodstains all down his

T-shirt from the fight earlier on. I'd left the cats and the flat in Vera's charge and as we said our final goodbyes I felt as if I really was emigrating and could've cried like a baby.

Qantas Economy should be administered as a deterrent for young offenders, as they'd certainly never offend again. My seat was in the middle of the centre aisle, wedged in between a very large Chinese gentleman who kept clearing his throat and an even larger Aussie on the other side who spilled out of his seat and over into mine, forcing me to sit bolt upright and spend the journey staring at that infernal map that shows the flight's progress. From where I was sitting, it seemed to be interminable.

We stopped in Thailand to refuel and to allow those lucky enough to have reached their destination to get off, Murphy among them. He'd planned to break the journey and have a few days in Bangkok. I got off with him to take a look at the airport again. It had been a long time since I was last here and had to sleep on the floor when I was stranded getting back from the Philippines. As we walked towards immigration, Murphy suddenly stopped dead in his tracks.

'Jesus, Savage,' he hissed, the hand that had been furiously rooting in his inside pocket suddenly motionless, indicating that he'd either forgotten or discovered something he'd rather he hadn't. 'I've got a lump of dope in my pocket.'

The bloody fortune teller was right.

'Please tell me you haven't,' I groaned, the film *Midnight Express* instantly springing to mind, complete with a vision of Murphy and me sharing a rat-infested cell with John Hurt for the rest of our miserable lives.

'I haven't worn this jacket for ages,' he said. 'I had no idea it was there.'

'You bloody fool,' I said sotto voce as I saw to my horror two armed guards walking towards us. 'We could've been arrested at Heathrow and if you're caught with it here we've all had it.'

'I'd better get rid of it quick,' he said. 'Can you see a bin?'

There was no sign of a bin anywhere and the guards were getting closer. There was only one thing for it.

'Give it here,' I said in the voice my mother used when she spoke about cancer or lesbians, and taking it off him I popped it in my mouth and washed it down with the can of Coke I was holding.

The rest of the journey was euphoric. The passengers had thinned out and I moved to a double window seat, stretched out and spent the rest of the flight blissfully out of my mind. Twenty-eight hours after leaving Heathrow I arrived in Sydney, the flight having taken longer than usual due to high winds that had been against us. There'd also been a delay at Bangkok and by the time I finally fell out of the airport and into the back of a cab I felt like I'd been turned inside out and nailed to a door by my tongue.

I gave the driver the address of the hotel we were staying at in a place called King's Cross.

As he dropped me off the cab driver warned me to 'watch myself' around King's Cross. I told him that back in the UK our King's Cross was an area of mean streets, prostitutes, pimps and pushers.

'That's about right,' he replied. 'You'll find no change here then.'

For the month we were staying in Sydney the producers had booked us into a room that was more like a small apartment. The first thing I did after unpacking the all-important wig, which thanks to its time imprisoned in a case now resembled roadkill, was to inspect the toilet and beds for any of those funnel web spiders that just about everyone back home had insisted on warning me about.

I'm not in the least bit scared of spiders, I like them, but I didn't fancy getting bitten on the arse as I sat on the lav, particularly if that bite meant I'd die in agony within minutes as the Delphic sibyls back home had prophesied. I poked and prodded around the back of the toilet bowl with a wire coat hanger and gingerly peered under the seat in search of anything with eight legs and a mark on its back. Finally satisfied that there were no killer spiders lurking I dutifully used it and then collapsed on the bed.

When I woke up, which was quite some time later, I had absolutely no idea where I was. I lay on the bed as if coming out of an anaesthetic and wondered why there was a ceiling fan above me as I slowly struggled through the fog that enveloped my brain, attempting to recall the last twenty-four hours.

Australia, you're in Australia.

The fog lifted and everything became crystal clear. The fight in the Vauxhall, the torturous flight, the dope, the cab ride, yes, I was in Australia and more importantly I was here to work. This realization suddenly made me nervous but the urge to eat overcame pre-show jitters and after a shower, a cup of tea and a root through the case to find something clean to wear that didn't look like a dish rag, the nerves had turned into excitement. It's hard to be dispirited when the sun's out and even though the Cross was undoubtedly sleazy there was a sort of party mood and I set out in search of food.

'Wanna see a show?' a guy with a mullet (so they were right) slouched in the doorway of a dubious-looking club asked me.

I resisted the temptation to say, 'Yes please, I'd like two in the stalls for *South Pacific* and tell me who cuts your hair so I can avoid them,' and declined the offer instead with a polite 'No thanks.'

'Where you from, mate?' he asked.

'England,' I said cheerily.

'Oh, right,' he said, yawning, clearly not very impressed.

Welcome to Australia, I thought as I moved on and looked for a shop that might sell something other than dildos and fetish gear.

On the corner of the street stood a group of Native Australians, busy haranguing another group on the other side of the road. A woman was angrily waving a bottle and screaming abuse, while the small child in the filthy vest standing beside her seemed nonplussed by the commotion and continued to suck contentedly on whatever he had in his hand.

'Bloody drunken Abbos,' a rat of a man with spite written all over his mean little face said as I stood waiting to cross the road. He had more tattoos on display than twenty rock bands put together. 'A fucking mess, the lot of 'em.' He spat, taking a swig from the can in his hand. 'Look at 'em, drunken bastards.' He dragged the word out so it sounded like 'Baaaaaaaasteds'. Pot calling the kettle and all that, I thought as I quickly crossed the road to get away from him.

Next door to a budget hotel was a mini supermarket and as I hunted around inside for basic essentials such as tea, sugar and milk, a woman who could've been the half-sister of Stig of the Dump accosted me by the deep freeze.

'Give me twenty bucks,' she demanded.

'No,' I told her, quickly turning my attention to the frozen pizza I was holding and becoming fascinated by it.

'Go on, it's only twenty lousy bucks,' she whined as if she were a teenage girl asking her father for money. 'Help me out, will ya.'

'Why do you want twenty bucks?' I foolishly asked her.

She explained that she had to get to somewhere that sounded like Mooohollhoolaborrowbrow as an old friend had told her that there was lots of lucrative work there. Her only problem was getting the fare together.

During this conversation I'd made my way to the till in an effort to shake her off, but with no success. She clung to me like a limpet to a rock.

'Ask him,' she said, pointing to the guy behind the counter. 'Tell him what I was telling you yesterday arvo about me job.'

'Out,' the guy behind the counter said firmly. 'I've warned you about hassling the customers, now out or do I call the police?'

'I was only asking for—' she tried to protest.

'Out!' he yelled, interrupting her mid-flight and coming out from behind the counter. 'Or do I throw you out?'

'Fuck you!' she shouted resentfully as she slipped out on to the street, ranting to no one in particular.

'These junkies,' the man behind the counter muttered as he rang up my goods. 'The police should do something about them.'

Reaching into my back pocket to pay, I found that my money had gone. I ran out into the street to see if Miss King's Cross 1962 was anywhere to be seen as she was the number one suspect. She'd vanished.

Cursing my stupidity and feeling like a right mug, I told the shopkeeper to hold my shopping as I'd be back once I'd got some more money from the hotel.

Mugged in a grocer's by a junkie! It wouldn't happen in our local Mace on the South Lambeth Road.

As I made my way angrily back to the hotel, I felt something dragging on my flip flop. Looking down, I found it was a syringe that had imbedded itself in the side. Another couple of centimetres and it would've stuck in my foot.

My first impressions of King's Cross and indeed the entire country were most definitely far from good and I returned to my room empty-handed, hungry and feeling very stupid like the hick tourist I was for allowing myself to be rolled.

The phone was ringing when I got in and I just hoped it was Murphy. I'd give him down the banks for dumping me in this hellhole and buggering off to Bangkok.

'Hiya, doll, welcome to Sydney.' It wasn't Murphy, it was Mark. 'I thought you were going to ring me when you got here.'

I explained I'd been asleep, which sent Mark off on a lecture about what I should be doing to combat jet lag and that going to sleep was a massive mistake. In turn I told him about my experiences in King's Cross and that for two pins I'd go home.

'Oh, that's King's Cross,' Mark said airily. 'Don't judge Sydney by the Cross. Jump in a cab and get down here to my place. I'll take you over to Kinsella's and we'll have a late lunch.'

Kinsella's was the venue we'd be working in. It was a nice big room with a great stage that in a past life had once been a funeral director's. We changed downstairs in a room we shared with a family of cockroaches who had a predilection for wigs. There were always a couple nesting among the curls, sticky with hairspray.

We'd decided in a reckless moment to recreate the Apache number from the Christmas show, so we rehearsed what moves

I could remember in the hotel room, flinging ourselves about until by the end of the afternoon I was covered in carpet burns again. We also went over the songs that we were doing together, 'Baby, It's Cold Outside' and 'Something Stupid', with Mark singing out at full throttle. God knows what the neighbours thought.

Murphy arrived from Thailand full of the joys of spring and waxing enthusiastic about the place. He'd loved the cuisine, in particular the food sold on the roadside by street vendors. 'They cook it there and then for you,' he enthused. 'Right there in the road, they even deep-fry cockroaches and crickets. Right up your alley, Savage.'

In that case the Thais would have considered our changing room at Kinsella's a valuable source of income as a fast food outlet, but it all sounded pretty disgusting to me. The more I heard about Bangkok the more I wanted to avoid the place, unlike Murphy, who thought it one of the most exciting locations in the world. It was Bangkok this and Bangkok that, and even the gay bars of Patpong were a revelation.

'I bet they were,' I sneered. 'And how many Bangkok scrubbers did you go through?'

Ding-ding, round one. We were at it again, arguing, and he'd only been back half an hour. Still, we were glad to see each other really.

Before we opened both Mark and I did as much press as we could to generate business. Apart from press interviews we appeared on *Tonight Live with Steve Vizard*, which was obviously modelled on one of those formulaic American chat shows that had mine host sat at a desk with a scenic view of the city at night behind him and the obligatory house band who laughed and cheered on cue, giving him a rim shot on the cymbals at the tag line of his lame jokes.

I disliked this autocue merchant, unable to fart unless it was written down for him, and felt uncomfortable on the show.

However, after our appearance on *Tonight Live* I received a letter from a young man in Perth called Martin Taylor, who told me that he was returning to live in London and if I ever needed anything made then I was to get in touch. He enclosed a couple of photographs of some costumes that he'd created and they were magnificent. Martin was going to prove a godsend.

The show went down very well and the *Sydney Morning Herald* gave us a glowing review, which we hoped would have a positive impact on ticket sales. Relaxing a little at the prospect of possibly earning some money, I began to settle into Sydney life.

Sydney certainly didn't remind me of England in the fifties, not that I had first-hand knowledge of that period as I was only a baby at the time. Even so, it didn't remind me of anything except . . . Australia.

The Apache dance was scrapped after the first few shows, much to my relief. Lots of fake bottles are broken over each other's heads in that number and although they look real enough, in the UK the glass is made out of sugar and breaks easily without harm. However, Australian sugar bottles are made of much sterner stuff, in fact I'd say that they're pretty damn close to the real thing, and as a result we were torn to pieces, me in particular as I was the one dragged across a stage littered in the razor-sharp shards.

We did all the sights, but one of my favourites was a trip to Waratah Park, the home of Skippy the Bush Kangaroo. Murphy didn't share the same enthusiasm as I did for this marsupial from my childhood. Neither did Mark, but one of the sound guys from Kinsella's did so we set off on our pilgrimage to see Skippy together.

I loved Skippy when I was a kid, loved everything about the programme from the catchy theme tune to the way that remarkable beast was able to communicate, by means of a series of tutting noises, that Sonny was trapped down a disused well. I didn't realize at the time that when Skippy attacked the villain the effect was achieved by chucking a kangaroo across the room at a stuntman. Apparently they went through quite a few Skippys during the making of the series. Now here she was, a miserable, moth-eaten old kangaroo at the back of a cage, staring morosely into space underneath a sign proclaiming that this derelict was indeed the very same world-famous Skippy the Bush Kangaroo that had appeared on the show, making this raddled geriatric the oldest living kangaroo in history.

'Yep, that's the original Skip all right,' one of the staff humoured me when I asked him. 'Kangaroos can live into their twenties, that's if a truck don't get them first.'

'Is that really you, Skip?' I asked the poor animal through the bars. 'Look at you now. To think you used to be big . . .'

The kangaroo shot me a defiant look à la Norma Desmond and responded with a series of grunts which I interpreted as 'I am big, it's the bush that got small.'

We ate out every day in one of the excellent and, more importantly, inexpensive restaurants that were on offer all over the city. Mark has an insatiable appetite and was always dragging me into cafés between meals for coffee and cake. I accused him of having a tapeworm as he never stopped eating, yet somehow he never put on any weight.

'I burn it off on stage, doll,' he explained as he munched his way through a chocolate gateau.

The food was good and I developed a love of Thai cuisine, much to my chagrin and Murphy's amusement.

'The moral of this tale, Savage,' he lectured as I devoured my second bowl of Tom Yon Gun in our local Thai restaurant, 'is not to knock it until you try it.'

'Does that go for necrophilia as well?' I asked, between slurps. 'Or just soup?'

'You know what I mean. Don't be so dismissive, be more receptive to the world around you. Experience all that life has to offer.'

'Blah, blah,' I responded and peeled a prawn that up to then I wouldn't touch as in their pink shells they reminded me of one of the undersea band from *The Little Mermaid*.

We went out every night as usual, mostly to the pubs and clubs of Oxford Street and in particular to a pub called the Albery, where a group of highly inventive drag queens performed their own version of the movie *Cry-Baby* behind the bar. Give a clever drag queen like Hush and this lot twenty quid and a couple of yards of fabric and they'll put on a show for you that looks like it's had a bit of money spent on it.

Sadly, the Albery has gone now, demolished to make way for a block of luxury apartments, but every time I hear Tammy Wynette's 'Justified And Ancient' I think of that pub.

Sydney was buzzing with the forthcoming Mardi Gras and the most frequent question asked around the bars was 'Have you got your drugs yet?' Apparently it was de rigueur to go to the Mardi Gras party bombed out of your head, and unthinkable to turn up stone cold sober. I didn't fancy the party at all and would've been happy to just watch the parade down Oxford Street and then go to the pub, but Mark and Murphy were having none of it and insisted that I go.

On the night I dutifully dropped an 'E' to get me in the party mood. Instead of me hitting the dance floor like a maniac, it had the opposite effect and all I wanted to do was sit quietly and pretend I was somewhere else, preferably somewhere quiet, and read. So much for ecstasy, I was the least ecstatic person at the Mardi Gras.

The venue in the park was vast and the noise deafening, and I wandered from tent to tent until Barry, a friend of Mark's, found me and put me in a taxi. Then I had a sudden burst of life and instead of going back to the hotel I got the cab to drop me off at the Taxi Club, a twenty-four-hour drinking dive that was wall-to-wall pokey machines (one-armed bandits) and had a clientele reminiscent of the Cantina bar in *Star Wars*.

Barry was great fun, cool, calm and collected, and I liked him from the minute we met. He reminded me of an illustration of Spiller, the wild Borrower from Mary Norton's book *The Borrowers*. He had a sly smile and a permanent twinkle in his eye and nothing on the planet seemed capable of stressing him out.

With our season at Kinsella's over and before we left for our next port of call, which was Adelaide, Murphy, Barry and I spent a weekend in the Blue Mountains, staying at the slightly faded grandeur of the Hydro Majestic Hotel, which boasted magnificent views. We walked the Giant Stairway, a lengthy track that leads down into the Jamison Valley, roaming the rainforest for hours and turning back only when we realized that it was getting dark.

'How do we get back up?' I asked naively. 'Is there a lift?'

'No, Savage, we walk,' Murphy said evilly.

Halfway up the seemingly never-ending track a violent electrical storm broke, the forked lightning above so close that it literally made the hairs on our heads and arms stand up. It was strangely energizing as we stood in the shadow of the Three Sisters, an enormous rock formation, and marvelled at the violence in the heavens, watching the lighting display with our hair on end like the twins in the Broons.

We were sharing a room at the hotel to save money (three beds, no orgy) and getting undressed for a shower I discovered a trail of blood running down my arm.

'I must've cut myself,' I said as I examined myself for a wound.

'No you haven't, Savage,' Murphy cried, pointing to my back in horror. 'You're covered in leeches.'

On further inspection, we were all covered in these disgusting expanding black blobs, although I seemed to have the lion's share, counting ten on my back and over twenty on my right leg. Ugh.

Dinner was late that night as we spent quite a bit of time burning them off each other with a lighter and dropping them down the toilet. They were enormous by now, having spent a few happy hours gorging themselves undisturbed on our life blood, and by the time we'd dropped the last one in, the toilet bowl resembled an abattoir and the towels were like Sweeney Todd's laundry basket.

I was going to miss Sydney and so was Murphy. We'd settled in nicely, finding it a beautiful, unpretentious city with a rough-and-tumble attitude that suited us. Our next port of call was Adelaide and as we'd nearly emigrated there in the 1960s when my dad considered becoming a 'Ten Pound Pom', I was interested to see the place I almost grew up in.

'There's no dressing room, how the hell do they expect us to change?' I moaned to Mark as we had a look around the venue that was playing host to the Adelaide International Comedy Festival. It looked very much like a temporary building and it frustrated and annoyed me that when they were erecting this corrugated edifice whoever slung it up didn't think to provide any facilities for the acts, such as a toilet, somewhere to make up and get changed and maybe even, and I'm really pushing the boat out here, a sink with a tap that actually worked for a wash. I won't mention hot water as that would be a step too far. I was obsessed with dressing rooms. Both Mark and I were, although after years of getting ready in appalling conditions we didn't ask for or expect much, just somewhere private to get ready and if possible within reasonable proximity of the stage.

If my mother had been on holiday or on a day out to a stately home or perhaps for a coffee and a sandwich in a reputable department store and you asked her how she'd enjoyed herself, the first thing she always commented on was the condition of the toilets. They were either immaculate, the floor entirely suitable for eating your dinner off should you choose to do so, or they were 'bloody disgusting' and the equivalent of a sailors' latrine on a Friday night in Port Said. A toilet that wasn't up to her high standards could make or break a place.

'The hotel was nice, but the state of the toilets . . . Mother of God, I said to Jessie Quigley, the last time they saw a bit of bleach was when the Virgin Mary appeared.'

That was said of a hotel in Lourdes. My ma could've written a Michelin Guide to public conveniences and I was the same about dressing rooms. In the pubs and clubs this invariably meant the lavs, the cellar, the manager's office or, in the case of Adelaide, no bloody dressing room at all.

'Well, it ain't the Palladium, that's for sure,' Mark observed wryly, sitting down on one of the long, low benches and tipping the bag of backing tapes out on to the table. 'Let's get the sound check out of the way and then see if we can sort something out, otherwise we'll be changing in the street. I've done that before and I ain't doing it again.'

We collared the producers of the tour and let them have it, and they in turn nervously assured us that a dressing room would be found for us by tomorrow.

'They better bloody had as well,' I grumbled. 'And it better hadn't be the toilet either, otherwise I'll set Murphy on them.'

Our hotel was on Hindley Street, which had a reputation for being seedy and dangerous although I didn't think it deserved it. Apart from a few undesirables and drunks it seemed fairly tame. The hotel was extremely handy as it was across the street from the venue. A fairly new, formidable red-brick building that we quickly christened 'Wentworth', inside it was very pleasant as the rooms were more like studio apartments.

My bête noire was the little Asian chap who checked and stocked the minibars in our rooms. Each and every day as regular as clockwork he would wheel his squeaky trolley packed full of nuts, miniatures of spirits and cans of Coke around the open walkways and corridors, announcing his coming like a Victorian street vendor by shouting at the top of his lungs as he rapped on your door: 'Mee-bar, mee-bar!'

I wanted to kill him, particularly first thing in the morning when he started his rounds and I was trying to sleep in. Had he never heard of show-business hours?

Before we opened we had the usual round of press and promotion to get through. One critic, notorious for his scathing and vitriolic reviews and justifiably feared by every performer in southern Australia, was very keen to meet me.

135

'Why me?' I moaned. 'He'll probably tear me to pieces.'

'Don't talk daft,' Murphy said, pushing me in a taxi to go and meet this ogre in his den. 'Switch the charm on and you'll have him eating out of your hand.'

As it happened, we got on like a house on fire and found we shared a lot of the same interests. He had a genuine passion for theatre and after a couple of bottles of wine we were like old friends.

'Thank you for a very pleasant afternoon,' he drawled as he saw me out of the house. 'But just because we've had a jolly time doesn't mean to say I won't give you an honest review if your show fails to impress me.' No pressure then, as a damning write-up from this guy could ruin business. In the end he gave both Mark and me an absolute love letter of a review, half a page of glorification that brought a few more punters in.

Every town in Australia had its own regional programming with the obligatory morning show and Adelaide was no exception. Theirs was called, not surprisingly, *A.M. Adelaide*, presented each day by an Australian television legend, Anne Wills, or Willsy as she was better known to her legion of fans. Willsy was smart, slick, warm, funny and, above all, genuinely interested in her guests. She had the rare knack of being able to put you at your ease immediately, and watching her at work it wasn't hard to see why she had won more Logie Awards (the Aussie equivalent of a Bafta) than any other television entertainer in their history.

When her marriage broke up because her husband was having an affair with a younger woman, Willsy let rip on live television and, not sparing any of the details, proceeded to tell her errant spouse as well as the good townspeople of Adelaide just what she thought of him.

We need women like Willsy on British TV. We really do, as

it's becoming extremely anodyne. Within seconds of meeting this remarkable lady both Mark and I fell in love with her and became firm friends. To this day, every time Mark is working in Adelaide he always does a spot in his show with Willsy.

Our brand new dressing room turned out to be a wooden shed that had been assembled using a particularly noxious solvent and erected in a corner of the room, nowhere near the stage. Mark had asked for shelves and some hooks and the management had obligingly supplied us with a hook each and a shelf that was eight foot high.

When the room outside filled up with punters this Black Hole of Calcutta grew hotter than a furnace, intensifying the vapours from this poisonous glue which sent us reeling. It was a running battle to keep the make-up on and for some reason my left false eyelash would droop as it grew more sodden, making me look as if I'd had a slight stroke. Hair lacquer was out of the question as it refused to dry in the wet heat, my Lily wig had shrunk in size to virtual respectability and what were once fascinating curls now hung like wet rats' tails clinging to my face and perspiring shoulders. Mark's Bob Downe wig was no better, hanging on his head like a damp flannel.

If we thought the dressing room was hot then it was nothing compared to the heat on the stage, especially if I was fire-eating dressed in fake fur, three pairs of tights and a corset, not to mention the boots and the wig. Both Mark and I sweated like a pair of whores in confession every night and would come offstage wringing wet and gasping for air.

There was a bottle shop (off-licence) next to the venue and most nights I'd drop in and buy myself a pint bottle of cider. They didn't sell it behind the bar and a pint of cider with a ciggie as I put my slap on had become a ritual, the legacy of working the pubs and clubs.

There was nowhere to wash or shower after the show and the only toilet was outside. As I wasn't prepared to hike through the crowd in full drag when I wanted a pee, I took advantage of the collection of empty cider bottles I'd accumulated on the top shelf. Once filled, I'd put the bottle back safely out of the way on the unreachable shelf until I could dispose of it.

It was unfortunate that Mark, parched with thirst during a quick change, looked around the dressing room for something to drink and spied what he thought was a full bottle of cider on the top shelf. He took a hefty swig. I should imagine the expression on his face when he realized what was in the bottle was not dissimilar to one of those Warner Bros cartoon characters who suddenly discover that they've run off the end of a cliff and are furiously pedalling thin air.

When he joined me on stage I noticed he kept giving me funny looks and making pointed remarks about having a nice glass of cider after the show. The penny eventually dropped as to what had happened in the middle of our closing number and I couldn't speak for laughing, in fact I sniggered for the rest of the night as Mark sat purse-lipped, feigning wounded indignation.

We shared a bill with Dillie Keane of Fascinating Aïda fame and Stomp, who I knew from the Edinburgh Festival, so there was usually quite a gathering of us in the outdoor bar area after the show. That's one of the good things about touring on a bill with other acts, there's always a great social life.

When I wasn't chewing the cud over a bottle of something with the boys and girls of Stomp, I could be found in Adelaide's solitary gay bar. It wasn't a particularly busy place, in fact on most nights there was just me and the barman knocking back shots in an empty bar with a *Looney Tunes*-style decor that resembled a set from *Beetlejuice*.

Most days when the weather was good we'd take the historic old tram to the beach at Glenelg. There I'd fling myself on a borrowed hotel towel and roast in the afternoon sun, half expecting an official to approach and slather me in a high-factor sun cream as I'd been warned back home would happen. None did, but even so I was heavily policed by Murphy and Mark, who were constantly at me to cover up. Murphy would examine my sun cream with the intensity of Poirot scrutinizing a piece of evidence to make sure it offered adequate protection, and when he discovered that it didn't the same old argument would invariably break out.

'This is no good, Savage, it's only factor ten. Put this on.'

'No, that's factor thirty and I'll never get a tan through that. I might as well lie under a shagpile rug.'

'Don't talk stupid, get this on you. Do you want skin cancer?'

'No, I want a tan, now bugger off with your factor thirty.'

'Well, don't come crying to me when you're burned to a crisp. Your back is already bright red, you look like a typical gobshite Brit abroad. Get a hat on . . . and get this cream on.'

'He's right, Sav,' Mark would chip in. 'Get the cream on.'

'All right, all right, give me the bloody cream and shurrup!'

On the way back we always stopped off at a little old-fashioned ice cream shop at the top of Hindley Street for a coffee and one of their homemade granitas, just the thing when you've been sweating like a hog roast on the beach all day and you can feel your back and legs burning hotter than a griddle. I'll never learn . . .

*

The regal old queen who'd said Australia reminded him of England must've been speaking about Melbourne. The evening we arrived it was cold and raining and my first impressions weren't very good, as I thought we could've been in any dreary provincial British town. We'd missed our plane because Murphy was late getting to the airport and our tickets were not transferable, so we'd had to pay for another set. Needless to say, we had a huge row and hadn't spoken a word to each other since we'd left Adelaide and the mood in the taxi to our digs complemented the weather outside: grim and stormy.

However, we perked up and became almost sociable when we pulled up outside a peculiar little house in Yarra that was almost Arts and Crafts in design, painted a worn-out salmon pink with an overgrown semi-tropical garden. It had an air of faded grandeur about it that suggested that this house had once known a glamorous past. It turned out the house had belonged to an old-time television star who no doubt had hosted fabulous cocktail parties here, sipping a Manhattan around the cut stone fireplace with Bert Newton and listening to Toni Lamond sing at the piano.

There were still traces of her Hollywood lifestyle around the house. In the bedroom stood a 1950s kidney-shaped dressing table where I imagined Madame had once sat studying herself critically in the rose-pink tinted mirrors. The dressing table had no handles left on it and a long, dark fag burn had eaten its way into the top where a past tenant had rested their cigarette and forgotten about it. Long gone were the swans-down powder puffs from Caron in Paris and the expensive perfume, to be replaced by the debris one accumulates from living out of bags and suitcases for months. The rose-tinted mirrors, which could've benefited from a wipe-over, were reflecting a very different vision of loveliness this morning.

I stared at my sorry reflection in these mirrors from the bed, examining the wreck looking back at me who sat supping a mug of tea and smoking a fag in the early morning light. Murphy shouted from the kitchen that he was making breakfast and if I wanted any then I'd better get my arse out of bed and get a move on as it was half past eight and the film crew would be here at ten.

I sighed and took a slurp of tea, imagining that the great star of Australian television was more than likely woken by a maid, who would gently rouse this Belle au Bois Dormant from her slumber not with love's first kiss but with orange juice and black coffee served on a white wicker breakfast tray.

'Savage! Will you shift your sorry arse!'

I yawned so violently I nearly dislocated my jaw. Not for the first time I wished I'd chosen an occupation that didn't involve so much effort and preparation.

'Did you hear me, Savage?' Murphy demanded, coming into the bedroom holding a fish slice and a tea towel. 'Do you want some bacon or not?'

'Please, Murph,' Mark shouted from his bedroom before I even had a chance to answer. If, God forbid, Mark was ever in a coma all I'd have to do is wave a cream cake under his nose and he'd be out of that hospital bed and up and running in a flash.

There was a room just off the patio that contained a giant sunken jacuzzi, another remnant from the glory days that could no doubt tell many a tale. We had a crew coming from the local television station to interview us, along with a press photographer. We had hit upon the bright idea that it would be a wonderful photo opportunity without having to go to a lot of fuss if both of us got in the jacuzzi with full slap and wig ('We won't have to frock up, we can just wear shorts, paint the

141

face and shove a wig on. It'll be over in a tick . . .'). We'd cover our modesty with lots of bubbles. In the end we were in the tub for over three hours – things always take longer than anticipated – and when we were eventually released from the bubbling cauldron our muscles had weakened in the hot water and we were barely able to walk. What once was flesh had been transformed into the consistency of warm tripe that hung as withered and flabby as the neck of a geriatric tortoise, while our genitals had vanished without trace.

We were inexplicably tired. It was a real effort to pull a towelling dressing gown on as it suddenly felt as heavy as a sack of coal. Our life force had been sucked down the plughole, leaving behind two empty, comatose husks. People on Zimmer frames in care homes moved faster than us as we headed towards the bathroom to take our slap off.

'What the hell did you put in there to make those bubbles?' Mark asked wearily, barely able to form words as he wiped his face with a flannel.

'Two big bottles of Radox and some bath oil Murphy had for muscle strain,' I managed to slur back.

'Oh Jeez, Sav,' Mark moaned. 'No wonder we can't move, our muscles have atrophied with all that bloody Radox.'

Thankfully we soon recovered and normal service was resumed, although we did stink of pine for a few days.

If Sydney and Adelaide were like spending time with a particularly raucous family of young cousins, then Melbourne was the equivalent of a month in the company of a very proper maiden aunt who was a bit pretentious and a terrible snob. It's a beautiful city with huge sprawling suburbs that look exactly like the houses in *Neighbours*. We appeared on *The Bert Newton Show* in the studios where they filmed *Prisoner* and I instantly recognized the red-brick corridors that were used as a location for the prison. This had the effect of releasing my inner crazed fan and getting me very excited, insisting that Mark take my photo before we went any further.

We'd been asked to appear at the Palais Theatre in St Kilda in aid of a charity and even though it clashed with our opening night we were both keen to do it. There was such an eclectic line-up on the bill of Australian television and theatre stars, including some of the cast of *Prisoner* and two very interesting cherries on the cake, Bea Arthur and Tiny Tim.

I knew Bea Arthur from the Edinburgh Festival as we'd appeared at a few Sunday charities together. As it happened, these were usually held in circus tents. We once shared a corner of the Chinese State Circus tent and Bea had some interesting tales to tell of working on the film *Mame* with Lucille Ball.

'Bette Davis wanted the role, you know,' she growled, referring to her part as Vera Charles. 'She harangued Miss Ball for the part. *Harangued* her, for weeks on end but Miss Ball was not about to share the limelight with a woman of Davis's reputation and chose to ignore her.'

Bea was a formidable lady and made it clear that she was no fan of Tiny Tim, announcing that she loathed every hair on the man's greasy head.

'I refuse to be photographed with that freak,' she snarled in her basso voice, putting the fear of God into the young PR woman. 'I won't even be in the same room as him.'

I, on the other hand, was fascinated by the man and had been ever since I'd first seen him on *Top of the Pops* when I was a kid, warbling 'Tiptoe Through The Tulips' in his falsetto voice. He was a genuine curio, a peculiar-looking man, ugly even with his hooked nose and long, straggly hair and although he was repellent to most adults, including my mother and father, his eccentricity made him compulsive viewing and listening for children.

I had an LP of his called *For All My Little Friends*, which I've still got somewhere. One of my favourite songs was 'I'm A Lonesome Little Raindrop' and I was very keen to meet him.

I dragged Mark down to his dressing room with me, both of us in costume, to see if we could have a five-minute audience with this marvellous creature and get a photo with him at the same time.

His assistant told us to come back in ten minutes, which we duly did, and though Tiny Tim was still a giant of a man, with the same greasy locks, I was taken aback by how old he looked. He seemed frail, dabbing at his face with a hand towel to mop up the perspiration that was causing havoc with his clown's white make-up. It slid from his face like a slow-moving landslide and left behind a residue trapped among his many deeply etched wrinkles and lines.

If my parents thought he was scary back then, they'd probably run for the hills if they saw him now, but Mark and I were both polite and courteous and I told him I was a great fan and what a privilege it was to meet him.

'Oooooh' was his only comment.

'I have a record of yours with one of my favourite songs on it,' I carried on enthusiastically.

'Oooooh' he said again, the vibrato working at full throttle.

'Yes, it's called "I'm A Lonesome Little Raindrop",' I pressed on undaunted. 'Do you remember it?'

'Noooooo,' he replied after giving it a moment of thought.

As I appeared to have dug a hole for myself that was going to be hard to climb out of, I sang a few lines of it for him.

'Ooooh,' he said, sounding more confused than ever, but he

picked up his ukulele from the side of his chair and plucked out a few notes as I sang the bloody song in its entirety, much to Mark's amusement and my mortification. 'Ooooh, yes . . .' he said vaguely and proceeded to play a tune that bore no relation to 'I'm A Little sodding Raindrop' whatsoever as I bravely battled on.

It was an excruciating five minutes, but it was fascinating to meet one of show business's greatest oddities. Even though he didn't say much he was very affable.

Apparently after we'd left he turned to his assistant and said, 'Isn't that Bea Arthur a charming woman.' I didn't dare tell Bea that she'd been mistaken by Tiny Tim for Lily Savage. I doubt if she'd have been best pleased at that, but what would really have upset her was the thought that Mr Tim believed she'd bothered to pay him a call in his dressing room and been so complimentary about him.

The show overran, as these things usually do, and after getting caught in the Melbourne rush hour we were late arriving at the Universal Theatre for our own show. We literally had to go straight on stage, to a hostile audience and a very sniffy critic who didn't think much of me at all.

Nevertheless I really enjoyed working that little theatre. The audiences were good and we spent a lot of time there after the show, drinking at the bar with the gang from Stomp and getting together with other acts who were working the festival, who seemed to head for the Universal after they'd finished their own stint.

Julian Clary turned up one night. He was very popular in Oz and was playing one of the big theatres. 'You've ballooned,' he said cheerfully when he saw me, and he was right. As Murphy had pointed out a few days earlier, I was getting to be the size of a house.

There were a lot of good cheap restaurants close to the theatre and when we weren't there we could usually be found in our favourite, eating, eating and eating. I needed a couple of the lads from Stomp to hold the corset together so Mark could get the zip up, I'd put on so much weight. It was so unbearably tight that my back and stomach were covered in scarlet welts, making me look as if I'd just come from a particularly energetic S and M party. Better the corset than going on stage with love handles and a belly hanging out any day of the week though. To help work off the result of this unusual intake of food, I started to walk to the theatre each afternoon along the Yarra River and cut down on the cakes.

Sitting in the cinema one evening watching the film *Hook*, I was hit with the force of a punch in the stomach by an unexpected bout of homesickness as I watched a scene shot on a snow-covered Tower Bridge. Suddenly I missed everything about the UK. My flat, the cats, friends, family, the lesbian bus driver who used to beep her horn underneath my flat window and shout up each time she pulled up at the bus stop, the Vauxhall Tavern, *Coronation Street*, just about everything in fact, and I had to fight to hold the tears back.

I couldn't shake off this feeling of melancholia. I'd been away for nearly three months now and the longing to go home intensified daily.

'You'll be going home soon enough, although when the time comes I bet you'll want to stay,' Murphy said when I admitted how I was feeling. 'Enjoy yourself while you're here. Stomp have asked us if we'd like to go swimming with dolphins tomorrow. It sounds great, they take a boat out to where the dolphins play and you can get in with them.'

'There's one small snag, Murphy,' I pointed out.

'What's that?' he asked.

'I can't bloody swim.'
I learned three things on that trip.

1. Dolphins are remarkable and really are as intelligent as they're made out to be. In fact I'd say they were psychic.
2. Fear can be conquered.
3. I look like a skid mark in a wetsuit.

I stood on the deck of the boat with a member of Stomp, who like me couldn't swim, pretending to be not the least bit bothered that Murphy and the other Stompies were having a wild old time being tossed in the air and dragged through the water by the dolphins.

One of the crew, a strapping German blond in a clinging wetsuit, asked us if we would 'like to go with him', an offer that ordinarily I wouldn't have hesitated to take up even though it would've taken me a good hour to get out of the wetsuit that was meant for someone a lot shorter than me. Unfortunately, in these circumstances 'go with him' meant jumping in the ocean and without giving us a chance to hesitate he wrapped his arms around our waists and leapt in.

Jumping off a boat and into the sea was one of my worst nightmares and had been ever since I'd seen *A Night to Remember*. When we hit the water he had a job stopping me from crawling up his back and on to his shoulders, the way a drowning cat would.

'Just relax,' he said in his hypnotic voice. 'You're quite safe, keep calm and we might see the dolphins.' I clung to him like Andromeda to the rock as I knew for damn sure that if he let go I'd sink like a stone straight down to Davy Jones's Locker.

The two guys who ran this trip were conservationists and

they'd been observing this pod of dolphins for some time, in particular a pair who had just sired a pup. Contrary to popular belief, dolphins aren't a monogamous species and they don't mate for life, quite the opposite in fact. They're extremely randy little buggers who mate not only for reproductive purposes but because they enjoy it, and will have numerous partners of both sexes. There's a veritable aquatic bacchanalian orgy going on under those waves that I don't recall seeing any of on *Flipper*, do you? They're also very sociable mammals and when they're not shagging everything with a fin they enjoy a spot of hunting, playing and just plain lazing around in the water with each other.

We bobbed around in the water like a trio of shipwreck survivors. I was silently praying that any dolphins in the vicinity would keep their distance and prefer to join the rest of their kin, who were busy hurling Murphy and the Stompies into the air.

'Look,' the big, blond German said. 'Dolphins, and it's the breeding pair.'

I didn't like the sound of 'breeding' and tried to dismiss any thoughts of a dolphin mistaking a human in a wetsuit for a skinny member of their species who might be up for a good time.

'Keep very still and quiet and we might get to see their pup if we are lucky.'

'Shit' was the first word that came to mind as I watched a couple of the buggers coming towards us. One of them appeared to be more daring than the other as it swam slowly around and then underneath me. I wasn't very happy about this. Any minute I expected to feel a snout rammed forcibly up my hoop and find myself ejected out of the water and into the heavens with the speed of *Thunderbird 1* on take-off. Convinced that death by drowning was imminent, I offered up a silent prayer. Thankfully this dolphin, although obviously very curious, was extremely gentle and eager to prove he wasn't a roughhouse type like his mates. He hovered close, allowing me to stroke him.

'He knows you can't swim, that's why he's so gentle with you,' the German told me as we watched him swim away to join his partner.

It was as if he were explaining to her. I could just hear him: 'It's only a couple who can't swim with that nice human we already know. Why don't you come and have a closer look at them?'

The pair slowly approached us.

'Put your face in the water, we might see the pup,' my human life jacket urged us. Put my face in water and open my eyes? Was he out of his mind? I was a borderline hydrophobic who'd sooner put his face in a cowpat than immerse it in water.

'Quickly,' he insisted.

Taking a deep breath, I plunged in and was glad that I did, for the dolphins briefly parted to reveal their tiny offspring behind them. We had the rare privilege of seeing a dolphin pup in the wild. That's a bit of magic I'll always remember.

Murphy had been right about the homesickness phase. On the last night of the show there was a party in the theatre and I suddenly didn't want to leave all these people that I'd spent the best part of three months with. In fact I didn't want to leave Australia at all as I had become well and truly Aussified. I hadn't liked Melbourne at first, I'd thought the people stuck up but they weren't, just slightly more reserved than Sydney folk. Now I felt less alien. Having got to know my way around the city and made friends with some of its inhabitants, I'd gone from aching to go home to couldn't give a monkey's if I never went back.

The drag was packed up and sent on ahead. Mark went off to San Francisco and Murphy and I flew to Cairns, hired a jeep and drove up to Port Douglas and the Daintree Forest.

The first place we stayed in was a sort of a camp with tents on stilts in the rainforest. Inside our tent were a number of bunk beds even though Murphy and I were the only inhabitants, or at least I foolishly believed we were until I discovered a rat-like creature munching its way through a Body Shop moisturizer right next to me in bed. I let out an almighty yell that woke up half of Queensland. I don't like rats very much, you see. I don't mind tame ones but I don't like the idea of a big, wild, unpredictable one running across my face, dribbling pee and droppings into my open mouth during the night.

We moved in the morning to another place that was still in the rainforest but was more 'secure', with nice, rat-free bungalows on stilts to keep everything out and wooden walkways that led through the forest to the main building.

There was something about this rainforest that made me want to get up early and go for a walk through it, which is surprising in itself as I love my kip. Each morning I spent there I'd get up around 6 a.m. and leave the wooden walkways to walk into the forest, taking a banana or an apple with me to snack on as it seemed the right thing to do in the circumstances, being at one with nature and all that.

As I ambled along I had no idea that I was being watched, and that hidden among the fronds and ferns a heart was beating with lust and desire.

He was tall, with long skinny legs and a face that only the most charitable of beings would call pretty, but he had beautiful

150

eyes and was certainly striking even if he did nearly give me a heart attack, appearing like that out of nowhere and blocking my path.

'Hello,' I said lamely, but he wasn't keen on small talk. He seemed far more interested in my banana.

I broke a bit off and held it out to him, and without any hesitation he strolled towards me and snatched it out of my hand. 'You're a charmer, aren't you?' I said. 'Do you want some more?' I gave him the rest of the banana and considering the size of his beak he was extremely gentle.

'What are you?' I asked him. 'You look like an ostrich yet you've got a blue neck and a red wattle, and I've never seen an ostrich with a Mohican hairdo like that.' The bird stared at me with his big red eyes as I prattled on and I wondered if he was tame and had possibly escaped from an enclosure as he didn't seem the least bit bothered by my presence.

I'd certainly never seen anything like him. 'You're not a mutant turkey, are you?' I said conversationally. The bird threw his head back indignantly and gave me a look which I read as meaning 'Who are you calling a fuckin' turkey?'

'Sorry,' I apologized, not wanting to rile him as he was quite a size. Luckily he overlooked my faux pas and was more than happy to walk with me back to the hotel, where he lurked, half hidden by the foliage, to watch me go in for breakfast.

I told Murphy about my encounter and brought him out to see if my new mate was still there but he'd gone, vanished back into the bush.

'Are you sure about this?' Murphy asked doubtfully. 'A multicoloured ostrich?'

'Just his face,' I said huffily and went back in to finish my cornflakes.

Every morning for three consecutive days the bird was

waiting for me. I'd give him his banana and we'd walk together, and he'd even let me stroke his neck and the back of his head. He loved it, closing his eyes and lowering his head to enable me to give it a good scratch.

Eventually I asked the man who owned the place what sort of bird this was that had latched on to me. When I described it to him he went off to get a book. 'Is that it?' he asked, pointing to a large colour plate of my bird, and was visibly shocked when I told him it was indeed the same critter I went for a walk with each morning.

'But it can't be,' he said. 'What you're describing is a cassowary. They're an endangered species and I've never heard of one in these parts before. Are you sure the bird in the book is the same one?'

'Yes,' I snapped, fed up at being doubted. 'That's the one, I've taken pictures of him.'

'And you say you've been walking with it and stroking it?'

'Every morning. He's very friendly.'

'The cassowary is one of the most dangerous birds on the planet,' he said, totally bewildered. 'They've been known to decapitate people, rip their guts out with those razor-sharp claws.'

'Oh,' I said, as if he'd just told me he was thinking of getting double glazing, possibly because I was a bit taken aback on hearing that what I'd thought was a type of ostrich, one that I'd been treating like a friendly budgie, was the Jack the Ripper of the rainforest.

'They're notoriously shy and getting scarcer by the minute,' he went on, 'and I can only assume that he travelled this far in search of a mate.'

'And what does he find when he gets here?' Murphy chipped in cheerfully. 'Savage. Oh well, any port in a storm, I suppose.'

'It's incredible,' the owner said, too stunned to pay any attention to Murphy's rapier wit. 'Absolutely astonishing.'

The same could be said of Australia and if I'm ever asked to compile one of those ubiquitous bucket lists of the ten things you must do or see before you die then Australia would be right up there, in particular the rainforests and the endangered Great Barrier Reef, threatened by shale oil operations.

Those ten days we spent in Queensland were one of the best holidays of my life. Good food, sunshine, horse riding on a wide expanse of beach, snorkelling on the reef (wearing a life jacket), nature walks with a bushman and his parrot as a guide and making friends with a cassowary. What's not to like?

The bushman made tea in a billy can and served it in chipped enamel mugs. 'If you want some lemon, then pick an ant off that tree and lick its arse,' he told us. 'They're called green ants or the weaver and you'll find they taste of lemon. Go on, give it a lick.'

'No way am I licking an ant's arse,' Murphy laughed.

'Why not?' I said, plucking an ant off a tree. 'You've licked worse.'

Before I could change my mind, I gave the ant's posterior a quick lick. Surprisingly, it tasted delicious – sharp, citrusy with buttery undertones and even perhaps, if I may be so bold as to say, a tad oaky due to its being aged in wood. And delicious served with jet-black builder's tea. No ant was harmed in the process. After I'd given it quite a few licks, prompting Murphy to accuse me of formicaphilia, the ant was put back on the tree where it scuttled off to ring the ant equivalent of Operation Yewtree.

Yes, Australia was indeed incredible and astonishing.

# CHAPTER 6

'SAVAGE, WILL YOU GIVE IT UP,' MURPHY COMPLAINED AS we drove through the Hollywood Hills in a beautiful Mustang convertible with cream leather interior that we'd rented. 'You've been whistling that same tune since we got here.'

'Sorry, Murph,' I apologized, 'I wasn't aware that I was doing it. Shall I sing it for you instead?'

'You can shut up, that's what you can do,' he replied, 'or we're not going to Disneyland.'

Murphy was right to complain. The song 'Hooray For Hollywood' had been going through my head on a loop tape from the moment we'd arrived in LA and the urge to keep whistling the damn thing was irresistible.

We'd broken our journey home from Australia for a week in Los Angeles, arriving late afternoon and after checking into our hotel on Santa Monica Boulevard I'd plagued Murphy with childlike impatience not to unpack or shower but to come with me immediately to a place I was desperate to see. As we were yet to rent the beautiful Mustang we took a cab to my destination. When the driver dropped us off at the corner of the fabled Hollywood and Vine, the place I'd wanted to see so badly, he warned us to be careful.

'So this is Hollywood Boulevard?' Murphy sounded

disappointed. That odour, so familiar from the lifts of run-down council blocks and doorways where drunks congregated, assailed our nostrils. 'Bit of a dump, isn't it.'

I had to agree, but there was still more than a whiff of the glory days of Hollywood hovering underneath the stench of decay and it was glorious . . . I knew all about Hollywood Boulevard thanks to various books I'd read over the years and a long-suffering Murphy was treated to a guided tour whether he liked it or not.

'Take a photo, Murph,' became a mantra as we came across landmarks that had once been at the heart and soul of the old Hollywood. The Knickerbocker Hotel was one, where Mae West had lived in a gold and white apartment with a mirror over her bed so she could 'see how she was doing' and where the likes of Valentino and Pola Negri had danced the tango in the Lido Bar.

Sadly, the Knickerbocker was a retirement home now. I stood on the pavement outside looking into the lobby where William Frawley, who played the Ricardos' irascible neighbour Fred Mertz on *I Love Lucy*, had died from a heart attack. I wondered which window the celebrated costume designer Irene had jumped from when the poor woman found she couldn't cope with the news that her great love, Gary Cooper, had died. All of them ghosts now, long gone and, in the main, long forgotten, haunting the stairways and corridors, wondering what happened to the bar and why the music had stopped playing.

'Frances Farmer was arrested here.'

'How do you know all this stuff, Savage?'

'I just do. Take a picture, Murph.'

Sandwiched between the cheap liquor stores, fast food shops, tattooists and fortune tellers, there were a number of shops on Hollywood Boulevard that could only have been designed with drag queens in mind. It was a drag queen's paradise.

Wig shops proudly displayed magnificent creations in their windows, the work of the Filipino women who sat in the back of the store chattering away above the noise of the hairdryers as they worked their magic. There were fancy dress shops, specialist stores dealing in shoes of every size and stores where all the paraphernalia required of every self-respecting stripper could be found. At the end of the row sat the jewel in the crown, Frederick's of Hollywood.

This store had once sold Hollywood glamour at affordable prices. For a few bucks a suburban housewife could dream she was Lana Turner as she mopped the floor in a leopard-print chiffon housecoat with matching turban, Capri pants and kitten-heel mules, although I don't recall any of our neighbours in Birkenhead dressed like that as they donkey-stoned their front doorsteps. Shame really.

I never normally bought anything off the peg for Lily but there were some choice items on offer at Frederick's that begged to come home with me. I had a browse around the tiny museum displaying apparel worn by famous film stars. Then, after a root around the shop, I bought Regina Fong a waist clincher and for myself an assortment of evening gloves that went right up to the armpits, impossible to find in the UK, as well as a padded girdle, complete with a bum and hips that looked faintly obscene.

The motherly little Jewish lady who served me was straight out of Central Casting. According to the badge on her little black dress she was called Rose and she was elegant, dry-witted and the ultimate professional. Wild horses wouldn't have been able to drag me into a shop in London to buy such an intimate piece of feminine apparel that had slightly kinky overtones about its padded contours, but here in Frederick's nobody batted an eyelid at who you were or what you bought.

Lily's padded backside had finally called it a day in Melbourne. The elastic around the thighs had long since withered and the sponge padding had a tendency to escape its moorings and slowly slide down my legs, giving me an arse like the Elephant Man.

'Oh, we get all sorts in here, honey,' Rose said after I explained the purpose of the false bum. 'You're a professional and you're in a famous store that caters to people in your business, so there's no need to explain anything to me. Now, how ya gonna pay?'

'American Express.'

'You got any ID to go with that? A passport, driving licence?'

'No, I'm afraid I haven't. I've left my passport back at the hotel.'

'Then since I can't make a transaction without ID, would it be inconvenient if you called back with your passport? I'll leave your goods safely behind the counter for you.'

That same day a jury acquitted a number of police officers who were on trial for unnecessary brutality inflicted upon a man called Rodney King during his arrest. Localized riots started to break out all over the city as a consequence, starting small and then igniting into an orgy of violence, looting and murder.

'It'll all die down soon,' we told ourselves optimistically as we watched the news on telly, convinced that it wouldn't spread to our part of town.

I returned to Frederick's with my passport the next day to collect Lily's arse, only to find hardly anything left of the store and Rose standing among the ruins.

'Oh, honey,' she wailed tearfully, 'look at what they've done. It's as if a bomb's hit the place.' It wasn't just Frederick's that had been visited by the looters, the rest of the boulevard looked like it had been hit overnight by the Luftwaffe. The charred remains of buildings were still smoking and there was broken glass and rubble everywhere.

'I suppose you've come for the goods, have you, honey?' Rose enquired mournfully. 'Well, I'm afraid I have some bad news for you. They've taken everything, they even looted the museum.'

She pulled a handkerchief from under the cuff of her cardigan and delicately blew her nose. 'They not only took Ava Gardner's lingerie and Madonna's corset but they took your padded girdle as well.'

At least I was in good company, I told myself as I made the journey back to the hotel, aware that total anarchy was breaking out as I watched the mood on the streets from the back of a cab.

'The riots are getting worse,' Murphy told me when I eventually got back. 'The manager's told me that he's bringing down the metal shutters and nobody is allowed to leave.'

'I'm not sitting banged up in here,' I wailed. 'What are we going to eat? They don't do food in this place.'

'Well, he suggested we go to that Häagen-Dazs next door and stock up.'

'On what, ice cream and milkshakes? We've got to get out of here, Murph,' I said.

'Exactly, I vote we go and see Mark in San Francisco,' Murphy said. 'Otherwise God knows how long we might be holed up in here with nothing but a gallon of ice cream to eat. Are you willing to risk it?'

I most certainly was. From what I could see from our window, the number of fires breaking out all over the city was increasing alarmingly and the street outside was growing busier, with gangs that didn't look as if they were out doing a spot of leisurely shopping.

We packed quickly and checked out, leaving by the back door as the shutters were already down.

'I wouldn't go out there just yet if I were you,' the security guard warned us as we headed for the car park.

'We'll take our chances,' Murphy replied grimly. Despite the very real danger, I felt as if we were characters in a movie about to face a shoot-out.

Predictably, Murphy took no prisoners and he drove down Santa Monica Boulevard at breakneck speed, jumping red lights and swerving to avoid rubble on the road with admirable dexterity. From seemingly out of nowhere a man appeared standing stock still in the middle of the road, holding a shotgun menacingly and looking as if he was about to take aim.

'Put your foot down, Murph,' I shouted. 'Run him over if you have to.'

'Don't worry, I will,' he replied calmly as the car roared towards this nutter who stood rooted to the spot pointing his gun straight at us.

I closed my eyes as I didn't particularly want to see his entrails slathered all over the windscreen but thankfully he jumped out of the way in the nick of time. Just in case he still fired at us, Murphy drove the car in a zigzag fashion, like in the movies, making us less of an easy target. It was all very exhilarating and both of us discovered what we already knew:

that we weren't averse to danger, quite the opposite in fact. We both found it thrilling.

Apart from our being pulled over for speeding by a traffic cop who wouldn't have looked out of place in a porn film, the journey to San Francisco was uneventful. On arrival, we got lost – not surprising since neither of us had ever been to the city before. Pulling up at a phone booth, I rang Mark for directions to his friend's house where he was staying.

'Whereabouts are you, doll?' he asked anxiously.

Of course, I didn't have a clue but I described the area and read out a few road signs for him.

'Get out of there, quick,' he ordered. 'Riots have broken out here as well and you're in one of the worst areas. Get back in the car and get the hell out of there – now!'

A case of out of the frying pan and into the fire. We found Mark's friend's house eventually without being killed or, indeed, running over any gun-toting looters.

The gay community of San Francisco, like London, had been ravaged by Aids. Despite this, the Castro was putting on a brave face and continuing to keep the flag flying even if it was war-torn and tattered. The San Franciscans were a lot more approachable and affable than the folk in LA. A guy in a bar asked me what I was treating my psoriasis with, referring to the bites on my arms from the sand flies in Queensland. Not the ideal chat-up line but I told him that I had them on my back as well and that if Helen Keller was to run her hand over me she'd have thought she was reading a Chinese menu in Braille.

He told me he liked Chinese food and could he see the menu please? So I took up his offer of a ride up to Twin Peaks, where we sat in the car and smoked a joint watching the lights of the city below. I spent a few nights with him, much to Murphy's disgust. Despite us having ceased all intimate relations apart from the odd kiss and hug, and Murphy being on intimate relations with half of the West End, he went into a jealous sulk which pleased me no end.

I was a right old tart in Frisco and had quite a few flings while I was there, but all good things must end and after nearly four months away it was time to go home.

Murphy was driving the car back to LA but as I had work commitments I couldn't go with him. I was to fly home alone, slightly apprehensive at what felt like returning to civilian life.

At the check-in I was recognized by a member of the cabin crew, who turned out to be a regular patron of the Vauxhall Tavern. God bless Lily Savage, I thought, as I miraculously found myself upgraded to the luxury of business class. Turning right on a plane is fatal as once you've flown in first or business there's no turning back to cattle class. The seats in business were roomy and comfortable and reclined until they were almost flat. Food came served on a tray with a choice of wines and a continuous supply of bread rolls. No more the torture of Qantas economy for me, I vowed, as I slipped down into my seat and covered myself with the blanket thoughtfully provided.

The blinds had been drawn and apart from the odd reading light the cabin lay in silent darkness as my fellow passengers slept. How lucky they were to travel like this all the time, I thought, and wondered what luxuries awaited those who could afford the price of a first-class ticket. You probably got a four-poster bed and your own private bathroom, I ruminated, as I tried to settle down but found it impossible. I was too excited for sleep.

I watched as one of the crew members that I'd been chatting to crept quietly down the aisle. He was carrying a glass of brandy and kneeling down next to my seat he spoke quietly.

'I'm afraid I've got some bad news for you,' he said solemnly.

Bollocks, I thought, I knew it was too good to last. He's going to tell me the plane's about to crash or, even worse, I'm getting moved back to economy.

'Here, you might need this stiff drink,' he said, handing me the glass.

'What?' I whispered, really worried by now.

'Marlene Dietrich has died. I thought you should know.'

I played the game and pretended to have the vapours at this news, gripping the seat and knocking the brandy back while muttering, '*Gute Nacht, Marlene, meine Liebe. Ruhe in Frieden.*' At this, the crew member, suitably rewarded for his news by my display of grief, respectfully retired to the galley.

I was genuinely sad at the news, not weeping and wailing and tearing at my hair, you understand, but I'd liked her as she'd reminded me of my aunty Chris. My aunty did indeed bear a resemblance to her, only she worked on the buses and the closest she ever got to Hollywood was her Max Factor face powder.

I imitated Marlene a lot on stage. She wasn't hard to do, you just lowered your eyelids, remained motionless and spoke through barely moving lips in a deep, rhotacistic voice. Now the eternal glamour girl was gone, along with Hollywood Boulevard and the great soundstages of the film studios that had long been abandoned and converted to indoor tennis and squash courts.

The first thing Vera said to me at the airport was 'Marlene's dead.' In fact a lot of people were keen to tell me over the next few days, as if she were a close friend or relative. Vera and Joan had come to pick me up. They hadn't recognized me at

first what with the tan, the extra weight and my new wardrobe courtesy of R. M. Williams, a shop that specialized in
traditional Australian outdoor clothing. I was a walking advert
for them, attired as I was in moleskin trousers, leather boots,
a khaki shirt and an Akubra Cattleman hat which made me
look more outback than Crocodile Dundee. Even the cats
didn't recognize me when we got home to Vicky Mansions.
Lucy spat at me and ran to Vera for protection from this
stranger. Maybe it was the hat, I told myself, having been put
out by this blatant display of disloyalty. It made me empathize
with a soldier who came home from war to a child who didn't
have a clue who he was.

The flat seemed smaller than I remembered it, plus it was a
lot cleaner and tidier than when I'd left it all those months
ago. I felt like I was intruding.

'Anything gone off while I was away?' I asked Vera as I sat
down to a mug of tea.

'No, nothing really,' he replied airily and by the expression
on Joan's face I knew that he was lying.

'What's happened then?' I grilled Joan. 'Come on, I can read
you like a tuppenny novel.'

'Nothing,' Vera protested, giving Joan a look to silence her.

'Well . . .' Joan started to say, before Vera interrupted her.

'What happened was this.' Vera was about to launch into
what was obviously a carefully prepared speech. 'You see, it
was getting a bit nippy so I thought I'd light a fire.'

I'd opened up the old 1930s fireplace in the front room, had
it swept and then started using it again. It was very welcome
when the weather turned cold as there was no central heating
in the flat, although I hadn't lit a real fire in it for ages, relying
instead on the convenience of a two-bar electric fire.

'Go on,' I said to Vera.

'Well, I'd just had me tea and settled down to watch *Corrie* when I heard all this commotion outside, so I had a look out of the window.'

'And what did you see?' I asked tentatively, aware that Joan was trying to suppress a smirk.

'Six fire engines,' Vera replied matter-of-factly. 'Well, I wondered, as you would, where the fire was when all of a sudden there was all this banging on the front door and someone shouting through the letter box.'

'What's the odds it wasn't Cilla Black doing a *Surprise Surprise*?' I said, already knowing what to expect next.

'It was a gang of firemen.' Vera's voice rose in pitch as he recalled the incident. 'Well, my nerves went, didn't they.' Holding out his hand, he shook it slightly by way of a demonstration.

'The two flats upstairs had phoned them because they were filling up with smoke that came seeping out from behind their gas fires,' he explained. 'The council had blocked the chimney up or something.'

'Then what happened?' I was probably going to be booted out for this.

'The Fire Brigade put the fire out.'

'With a hose?'

'No, with a fire extinguisher,' Vera explained dramatically. 'There was smoke everywhere and the flat was full of firemen, with me screaming at them to shut the door in case the cats got out. Oh, I was mortified.'

So that was that then, no more coal fires for me.

Murphy got back a couple of days after me, having decided not to stay as long as he'd thought. He was just in time for my first night back at work in the pubs.

I'd been furiously writing up a wealth of material that I'd gleaned since I'd been away. The gags just kept coming, which made a pleasant change from sitting there sucking on a pen and staring at the only two words I'd managed to come up with so far: 'Good evening', a greeting I rarely if ever used.

I was doing a double, starting at the Two Brewers in Clapham then a return to my alma mater, the Vauxhall Tavern. I had a ball at both places and it was more than good to be back. After the show, familiar faces and old friends piled into the tiny dressing room, each of them bringing me a drink of either cider or whisky or both.

Murphy appeared and as he couldn't make himself heard above the din he ordered everybody out.

'Hop it,' he told them. 'I want to speak to Savage in private.'

'You were something special tonight, Savage,' he said proudly, slightly pissed and uncharacteristically emotional. 'All that stuff about Australia was just brilliant.' Rare praise indeed. Embarrassed by this unexpected outburst as I'm not good at taking compliments, I busied myself packing up my gear.

'It does you good to have a break from the routine,' he said. 'You come up with all sorts of new stuff. It stops you getting stale.'

'I'm not a large sliced loaf, Murphy,' I replied, shoving the wig in the bin liner. 'It's hard, you know, working the same circuits week in week out and constantly having to come up with stuff.' 'Coming up with stuff' meant writing new material but as that sounded pretentious nobody said it.

'You need to be seen by a much wider audience,' he announced importantly. 'We need to get you on prime-time telly.'

'Well, you sort it out and I'll be there but if you want my opinion you've got two hopes – no hope and Bob Hope,' I said, quoting my mother. 'I'd like to think differently but I bet you that I'll still be out there on that stage in thirty years' time, tottering around stinking of cider and stale piss, in front of an audience of bemused teenagers who'll look upon me in the same pitying way that we did with Shufflewick in her declining years.'

'You see,' Murphy suddenly exploded, 'there you go, negative as always.'

'I'm not being negative,' I tried to explain, 'I'm only being practical. So I've done the Edinburgh Festival and been on Channel 4 a few times and won awards. But I always end up back in a pub, don't I? It's my natural home.'

'I agree, but tell me, where does it say that a pub performer can't go on to better and bigger things?' he asked.

'Well, the only ones I can think of who got off the gay scene were Hinge and Bracket, and I can't see me on the BBC at seven o'clock, can you?' I said. 'So tell me, what's the master plan?'

'You leave it with me, sugar.' He winked and tapped the side of his nose as he went to leave. 'I'll do my bit and you do yours. Oh, and by the way,' he said, spying the mountain of drinks on the side of the sink. 'You wanna lay off the sauce, Ruthie, you're beginning to look an old bag.'

It was a line spoken by Jimmy Cagney from the film *Love Me or Leave Me*. Cagney plays Marty 'the Gimp' Snyder, the short-arsed, short-tempered gangster manager/lover of the singer Ruth Etting, played by Doris Day.

When I'd first met Murphy he knew nothing of and cared even less about this genre of film, but after years with me he could now recite entire passages word for word. I used to do the same with Hush and David Dale, only then it was dialogue from *Gypsy* and *Female Trouble* that we quoted ad nauseam. It passed the time in the dressing room and put us in a good mood, although outsiders used to wonder if we were the full shilling.

Murphy booked the Bloomsbury Theatre again for a few nights. There were no dancers or sets this time, just me doing what they call stand-up although in drag queen circles it's known as patter. I had the excellent Caroline Aherne as support, giving them her Irish nun as well as an embryonic Mrs Merton.

After Dietrich died her daughter had published a book about her that amounted to nothing more than a character assassination, so to defend the old girl's honour I parodied the Cole Porter classic 'Laziest Gal In Town' and hit upon the bright idea of standing underneath a lamp post. Attached to the back of my mac, the lamp post would follow me around as I walked. It was real and had been mounted on a board with castors for easy mobility. Nevertheless it was hard work dragging it around and if I was on a stage with a steep rake I had my work cut out to keep the damn thing from pushing me into the orchestra pit.

'My daughter, she's a cretin,
Wrote a book that's most upsettin'
Claiming that me and Claudette Colbert indulged in heavy
  pettin'
How could I you see, for I've a lamp post attached to my
  mac . . .

The lamp post became my bête noire as I was to include it in quite a few shows.

The rain was coming down quite heavily as I walked over Vauxhall Bridge on my way to see Hush in the hospital and, as is the case in lousy weather, there wasn't a taxi to be found. I really should've sheltered somewhere until the rain at least died down, but I was in a hurry. I was always in a hurry, so instead I ran through the streets towards Westminster Hospital and arrived like a drowned cat.

'You're soaked through, wench,' Hush exclaimed when I sploshed into his room. 'What did you do, swim here?'

I was shocked at Hush's appearance. I hadn't seen him for a while as I'd been away and he'd been working in Germany with David Dale. He'd lost a whole lot more weight. Hush had always been big. I used to tease him and David about their weight all the time, calling them the Hoop Sisters on account of their ample derrières. Now he was half the size of me and as emaciated as a famine victim.

'I'm not dead yet, wench,' he said, reading the expression on my face as I pulled up a chair and sat dripping beside his bed. 'I've just been on a light diet, that's all.'

He looked dreadful and despite the banter didn't have the strength to sit up in bed without assistance.

'I had a dream,' he said resignedly after I'd pulled him up in the bed and sorted his pillows out. 'The cow came into my room, only she wasn't dancing and smiling this time, she was wheezing and kind of sad like. She came over to my bed, looked at me and said, "Rose, move over."'

He was quoting a speech from *Gypsy*. It's one that Madam Rose makes when she finds that the act has been booked into a third-rate burlesque house and realizes that this is the end of the road.

'I'm sorry, Momma,' I replied, joining in the spirit of the game.

'Why? She didn't ask you to move over,' Hush said, laughing. 'Now pass us that Lucozade, wench, I'm parched.'

The author Mark Steyn states in his book *Broadway Babies Say Goodnight* that he was saddened by the banality of a farewell message on the Aids Memorial Quilt that read, 'I'm ready for my close-up now, Mr DeMille,' an oft-spoken line from *Sunset Boulevard*.

What had distressed him was that a man facing death could think of nothing else to sum up his life but a hand-me-down drag queen quote. As excellent as his book is, I'm afraid that I have to disagree with him.

To be able to summon up the spirit of camp even as the Grim Reaper is polishing his scythe, transforming tragedy into comedy, requires immense courage. Certainly, the circumstances are unbearably sad but the ability to put on an extremely brave face as death draws closer and go out with a quip, a wisecrack or a line from a favourite movie in a final bid to raise a smile for the benefit of loved ones is humbling, and I only hope that I can demonstrate such guts and nerve when my time comes.

As Hush's coffin slid through the curtains I muttered the line, 'Slow curtain, the end' from *All About Eve*. It seemed appropriate.

The drag queens mourned Hush's passing as he'd been their fairy godmother, especially towards those who were just starting out. His kitchen was normally full of queens having wigs set, show tapes put together, and costumes made out of 'this spare bit of material that I've got hanging about, wench'.

At the funeral tea, held as always at the Vauxhall Tavern, I had a fight. I kicked a tray of sandwiches out of the hands of a drunken, gobby queen who Hush and I had never liked and who I considered had no right to be there in the first place. Vera dragged me out of the pub before things got really out of hand and while I shook with rage, not from the fight but from anger at the senseless loss of another good friend, the tears finally fell.

\*

'What was it you said, Savage?' Murphy asked. 'You couldn't see yourself on the BBC at seven o'clock? Stick with me, kid, and I'll have your name up in lights.'

'The only way you'll ever get me name up in lights is if I changed it to Emergency Exit,' I replied, long before Woody Allen said something similar.

'Then tell me, what time is this show going out?' he asked triumphantly.

'I know, I know,' I admitted as I got out of the taxi at BBC Manchester where I'd been booked to appear on a show called *That's Showbusiness*, hosted by the late Mike Smith.

It was the frothiest of light entertainment, with two teams of two 'celebs' answering questions on film and television. It could get quite rowdy with four people showing off at once but Mike was a great ringmaster, effortlessly reining everyone in when things got too wild, which they usually did.

I did that show lots of times over the years, teaming up with Fionnuala Ellwood, Jill Summers, Bryan Mosley, Brian Glover, June Whitfield, Nicholas Parsons and a very young Simon Gregson.

Bryan Mosley, known to millions as *Corrie*'s Alf Roberts, was in an early episode of *The Avengers* and was happy to talk about his time with Steed and Mrs Peel. As he said, it made a change from constantly being asked about the *Street*.

They filmed two shows a night and after the show everyone got together at the hotel for drinks in the bar. This inevitably turned into a late one and at six o'clock one morning I found myself in the lobby with Jill Summers, knocking back whisky while the cleaners hovered around us.

Jill was another *Street* veteran, better known as the blue-rinsed battleaxe Phyllis Pearce, the bane of Percy Sugden's life. Fame had come late in life for Jill and she was making sure she enjoyed every moment of her success. She'd certainly worked hard for it as she'd been performing with her brother, 'touring the 'alls', since she was six years old. In her time she had also worked in the cotton mills of Lancashire and run a newsagent/barber's with her first husband, a man twenty years her senior.

I wanted to be Jill's best mate as she was feisty, outspoken and very, very funny and had more tales to tell than Aesop.

'My real name is Honor and at one time I used to sing like an angel,' she told me in that unmistakable gravel voice. 'Then one night when I was hitting a top note it cracked and that was the end of me singing career. Eh, I were heartbroken,' she said sadly, shaking her head at the memory of it.

'Betty Driver used to have a wonderful singing voice as well but then hers packed up. Women's vocal cords have a tendency to calcify as they get older, you see.'

I sat in silence as I listened to her, unusual for me but I didn't want to interrupt her mid-flow.

'They used to call Betty "the poor man's Gracie Fields", you know,' she went on. 'She sang with the big bands and I think she had a much sweeter voice than Gracie. I was on tour with her, you know.'

'Who? Betty Driver?'

'No, Gracie Fields,' she rasped.

'What was she like?' I pressed her, eager to hear these old tales.

'I don't really know,' she replied after giving the matter some thought. 'I thought she were stuck up at first as she kept herself to herself and never came to any of the parties with the cast. So on the last night I went to her dressing room to say goodbye and I asked her why she'd never bothered coming to any of the parties, and do you know what she said?'

'No, what?'

'She said, "Because nobody ever asked me." Isn't that sad?

It just goes to show you it's true what they say, it is lonely at the top.'

Jill had turned to comedy by accident. She was touring with ENSA during the war and tripped on stage as she made her entrance, letting rip with a few choice swearwords. The audience, believing it was all part of the act, laughed like drains and a new comic was born. She changed her name to Jill Summers and with comedy material written by her second husband she toured as Jill Summers, the Pin-up Girl of British Railways, dressed in a porter's outfit and lugging a trolley behind her.

I valued our friendship highly and looked forward to those late-night calls, crying with laughter as I listened to her rant on about certain members of the cast of *Corrie* who'd had the temerity to throw a hissy fit on the set or, worse, had dared to cross her.

I've got a feast of Jill Summers stories, but regrettably due to the laws of libel the majority of them are unprintable.

Once again Vera was left in charge of the flat and the moggies as we packed the car up and set off for the Edinburgh Festival. I was back at the Assembly Rooms only this time playing the three weeks in the Ballroom, the biggest space in the building. I was worried about filling it but thankfully ticket sales were great. Nevertheless, I had to get out there each day and do some loony stunt for a photoshoot or appear on any telly or radio show that would have me.

It was like I'd never been away, as I was working with the same crew as last year and hung out after the show with the same old gang. Mark was back in the UK and having ironed the crimplene safari suit and smoothed down the wig he was bobbing around in a venue across town and occasionally we'd pop in and out of each other's shows.

A new bar had opened next to the Playhouse Theatre called CC Blooms and it's where most of us gathered after our respective shows came down. Diane and Brian, who ran CC's, were the most generous hosts I've ever had the privilege to encounter, up there with Pat and Breda McConnon. They certainly knew how to run a bar. Their lock-ins were legendary and I learned to take dark glasses with me as I knew it would be daylight by the time I slid out the door like a pissed-up vampire.

Everyone went to CC's, you only had to mention its name on stage and you'd get a laugh. I took the late, great Jack Tinker, the theatre critic for the *Daily Mail*, there after the show one night and he stayed till dawn, entertaining an enthralled bar staff with stories of all the famous people he'd met. Jack loved the theatre and enjoyed the company of actors and entertainers from all areas of the profession. He was a tiny little man, with an elfin face and blessed with a sparkling wit. As a critic he was unique, neither a bitch nor a pretentious snob, and he attended first nights with genuine excitement and a desire to enjoy the performance.

The sun was coming up when we piled out of CC's that morning and for the first time ever Jack was late with his column, for which, as always, I was blamed. Sadly both Jack and Jill went up that hill a long time ago and recalling them now I wonder, where have all the characters of their stature gone? And who, if anyone, is going to replace them?

I always preferred a lock-in with good company and an obliging landlord to drinking during opening hours any day of the week, but late licensing mostly put paid to the lock-in. With the fast decline of the traditional British boozer it seems likely that in a not too distant future such traditions beloved of the late-night barfly will be ancient history.

\*

I was back again at the Hackney Empire every Saturday night, compèring a show that featured the comics who'd been at this year's festival. On the bill was a hilarious comic called Brenda Gilhooly who went out as 'Gayle Tuesday, Page Three Stunner', dressed in a blonde wig and miniskirt with her boobs oozing over her low-cut top. She was the public's idea of the archetypal would-be glamour model and got away with the most outrageous gags by delivering them with a naive innocence.

Lily: 'Where's the most unusual place you've ever had sex, Gayle?'

Gayle (after a moment's thought): 'Up the bum?'

Brenda was one of the few comics who genuinely made me roar with laughter and it was a change to work on this circuit with another act who wore a wig and costume besides Mark and me.

'How would you like to play the ghost of a drag queen who died from Aids and a Marlene Dietrich type who sings in a neo-Nazi Bierkeller?'

Not something you hear every day, particularly on a cold October morning when your only means of heating, a two-bar electric fire, has finally called it a day.

'I don't care what I do, Murphy, as long as it's warm,' I grumbled down the phone. 'You could hang meat in this dump today, it's so bloody cold.'

The two moggies were obviously of the same mind as they'd vanished under the duvet some time during the night. As they hadn't moved in hours I was beginning to feel some concern in case they'd suffocated. I searched the bed with my foot until I came across something furry and warm that wasn't a two-day-old sandwich that had got lost in the folds of the duvet. Giving it a rub with my foot, I was rewarded by a set of claws seizing my big toe.

'Get out of bed, you lazy whore,' Murphy said, ignoring my yelps as Dolly started to eat my foot. 'I'm coming round, I've got a couple of scripts for you.'

Shaking off the tiger under the bedclothes, I jumped out of bed and into the bathroom, crunching cat litter underfoot on the floor. The neighbours next door were arguing again. As I stood and peed I tried to decipher what had started them off this time, while admiring the ice crystals that had formed on the tiny bathroom window that always reminded me of the windows of the bedroom I grew up in back in Birkenhead.

'I wonder what these scripts are like?' I yawned at the cats, who, having followed me out of bed, were now sitting on top of their litter box expectantly, waiting for me to get my arse into the kitchen and open a tin of Whiskas for them. 'Maybe,' I said hopefully, 'they'll be well paid and then we can afford to move.'

The cats gave a pessimistic yowl in response. The woman next door seemed to be of the same opinion this morning as I listened to her exchanging terms of endearment with her husband.

'I wish I could pack me bags and get the feck out of here,' she screamed at him. 'Get the feck out and never feckin' come back.'

My sentiments entirely, I said to myself, and went off to feed the cats.

Just as my moggies had predicted, the fee for these jobs didn't enable me to go rushing off to the estate agent's. In fact, one of them only paid a fiver a night – not that it bothered me as it was a chance to be involved in a bit of 'legit theatre'.

*Elegies for Angels, Punks and Raging Queens* is a play about Aids that was inspired by the Aids Memorial Quilt. It requires a cast of over thirty actors and musicians to tell the story of a variety of people from all walks of life, ages and sexual orientations who had died from the disease. The play was opening at the King's Head in Islington, which is basically a pub with a small theatre space at the back and an even smaller stage. It has a lot of character, an excellent reputation and many West End productions appear at the King's Head first before transferring.

'How the bloody hell are they going to get all us lot on that stage at the King's Head?' I muttered to the young woman in the biker's jacket who sat next to me at the first read-through. 'It's no bigger than a coffin lid.'

'What I want to know is how we're all going to fit in the dressing room,' she replied, frowning. 'There's not enough room to swing a cat.'

'That's a shame as I was going to bring my two in and give them a little spin during the interval,' I told her.

The girl in the leather jacket laughed and someone behind told us to shush.

'That's your fault,' she said, sinking lower in her chair and jabbing me in the leg with her rolled-up script.

The room was overcrowded and the air thick with cigarette smoke as we sat and listened to the enthusiastic producers assuring us that after we'd opened at the theatre pub in Islington it wouldn't be long before we all transferred to the West End.

'Yes. Sure,' Miss Leather Jacket and I both said in cynical unison, setting the shusher behind us off again and sending us into that awful bout of sniggering that takes hold in the most inappropriate circumstances.

'Do you want a ciggie?' I whispered, offering her my fags.

'I'd kill for one, darling,' she replied and then, looking at the packet, she asked what they were.

'Lambert and Butler,' I told her. 'Cleaning ladies' fags.'

'Hard core,' she murmured, and with that a lifelong friendship was born.

Her name was Amanda Mealing and she'd been in the business since she was six years old, making her debut with Dame Julie Andrews on a BBC TV special. She was also devastatingly beautiful, a party animal extraordinaire and with her short curly hair, leather jacket and cat's eyes, a dead ringer for my favourite *Avenger* girl, Tara King. I could write an entire book about her and the trials, tribulations and tequila we've been through, but as she has her dicey lawyer on speed dial and has threatened to kneecap me I won't. Needless to say, we've been through good times and bad times together and I love her like a sister.

Her friend Andrea Oliver turned out to be the shusher behind us and the sulky little girl sitting with her was her daughter Miquita, also in the play. Who'd have thought this mardy little miss clinging on to her mam would go on to be the über-cool presenter of her own Channel 4 music show at the ripe old age of sixteen. God, I feel ancient.

Her mother Andrea was big, sassy, sexy and full of attitude, and by the time Murphy arrived to see what was happening an unholy trio had formed an allegiance.

'What did he just call you?' Amanda asked in response to Murphy's customary greeting.

'Savage,' I replied.

'Oh, I like that,' Andrea boomed, 'I like that very much indeed,' and from that day on they've never called me anything else.

The problem of staging a show with such a large cast was resolved by sitting us all on raised benches. The first actor came out, delivered his monologue and then sat down and the second actor followed suit, until by the end of the play the entire cast was on stage. It was tough if you were the first one out as you had to sit silent and motionless until the bitter end. I made my grand entrance somewhere in the middle and once or twice, when I was tired and the heat of the room made me drowsy or perhaps that glass of port that some of us had imbibed backstage – for *la voce*, of course – had had a soporific effect, I almost nodded off. I felt my eyelids growing heavier and before I knew it the chin would be heading downwards towards the chest and the mouth open and drooling. Thank God for Patrick Duggan, the actor sitting beside me, who would give me a surreptitious dig in the ribs the moment he saw the head bobbing and shock me back into consciousness.

Amanda had been right about the dressing room. It was like a narrow corridor with a very suspect toilet at one end. Those who got to change here were the lucky ones as the others had to change in the office and then climb across the roof in shifts and down a ladder into our dressing room – not much fun on a cold December night when it's lashing down and you're only wearing a small towel as Stewart, one of the cast, had to do.

*Elegies* was a very moving play and every night we'd hear sobbing from the audience, which, callous as it may sound, was music to our ears as it meant we'd got the message across and were doing our job. My character was called Roscoe. He was a drag queen who had wanted to go out with all the drama of *Camille* and in memory of Hush I wore the black sequin Rita Hayworth costume that he used to strip out of to 'Put The Blame On Mame'.

With Hush gone, finding somebody who could match him when it came to teasing up a wig was a big problem. Then Stuart, a former Barbette at Madame Jo-Jo's, offered his services and, genius that he was with a sheitel, kept Lily's platinum locks in pristine condition.

\*

It was a great cast of talented actors to be involved with and they were a lot of fun too. Brian Friel's play *Philadelphia Here I Come* had recently closed in the West End and many of the male cast had signed up for the Good Ship *Elegies*. There were always drinks in the pub after the show and then Amanda and I would hit Soho with a couple of the Irish lads from *Philadelphia* and carry on until the last illegal drinking club finally put the towels on.

Brendan Coyle, who went on to play Robert Timmins in *Lark Rise to Candleford* and Bates the valet in *Downton Abbey*, was also in the cast. Brendan was laid-back, charming and affable and last time I saw him, which was at an awards do somewhere, he hadn't gone all Hollywood and was exactly the same as he'd been in the King's Head.

I've great respect for actors who are prepared to work for a fiver a night. It's hardly what you'd call a living wage, is it? It was all right for me as I could go off and work a club after the show but it made me realize that actors, just like pub and club performers, would always rather be working, no matter how risible the fee, than sit at home waiting for the phone to ring. Success in the acting profession is achieved through hard work and if that means performing a play in a room over a pub for little or no money on the off-chance that a casting director or producer might come in and offer you a decent job, then that's what you have to do.

That other script Murphy had been sent was for an episode of *The New Statesman*. They were looking for a Marlene Dietrich type to play a cabaret singer in a Nazi Bierkeller. I didn't have to audition, thank God, as someone had seen me dragging that bloody lamp post around at the Edinburgh Festival.

I left the lamp post at home when I turned up for rehearsals in Acton as this time I'd be sitting on a barrel.

Rick Mayall had more energy than a bag of ferrets on crack cocaine. He was full of enthusiasm and would light up like the Champs-Elysées at Christmas at the discovery of a bit of business or a new gag as we rehearsed. I didn't have to do much, apart from act Germanic on a barrel, warble a song to a set full of neo-Nazi thugs and then sit on David Calder's knee, but for someone like me who didn't get the chance to appear on telly every day it was a joy.

Christmas came round quicker than a cold sore and I was preparing for another Christmas show at the Bloomsbury Theatre. This one was to be bigger than the last. It was called *A Spoonful of Savage* as I was to make my entrance as Mary Poppins hanging on the end of a wire.

Simon (Betty Legs)'s six boy dancers and I started rehearsing in a hall in Pimlico. You half expected to find *Dad's Army*'s Captain Mainwaring there drilling his hapless troop, it was so reminiscent of the war.

As Simon drilled the 'It's A Jolly Holiday With Lily' routine into the lads I stood idly reading a notice about an upcoming whist drive that was being held to raise funds for the upkeep of this shed. I fully agreed with this committee that was keen to preserve this little curio, tucked in at the end of a row of shops, stoic as ever among the council estates and mid-nineteenth-century houses in what is considered to be Belgravia's poor relation. I'd learned to be a Marine Cadet in a hut not unlike this and I'd eaten jelly off trestle tables covered in paper tablecloths at Christmas parties that the Union of Catholic Mothers held for the poorer kids of the parish.

('What d'you mean you don't like chicken, Paul? There's

children in Africa who'd kill for a nice chicken leg, now get it down you.')

I yawned from boredom, tiredness and too many Lambert and Butlers, and read the notice again, wondering for a moment if I'd be able to master whist and lend a bit of support.

*Like you've got time to learn whist*, the cynical voice in my ear scoffed. *You haven't washed your dishes for over a week and when did you last make your bed?* The voice was right, I didn't have time to wipe me bum. As well as getting this show together with limited resources I was still doing the rounds of the pubs up and down the country, making my usual trek around the hospitals, rehearsing, writing material and trying to get myself prepared for the ever-approaching threat that was bloody Christmas.

'Would you like to have another go at "Jolly Holiday" then?' Simon enquired, reminding me that I was here to rehearse after all. Simon, a superb dancer and choreographer, had drawn the short straw and ended up with the task of teaching me, with my limited terpsichorean talents, a complicated dance routine.

Stubbing my fag out I reluctantly joined the line of boys, feeling inadequate in front of these seasoned and quick-to-learn young dancers. I envied dancers, still do, particularly those who can tap-dance, making that lovely noise on a shiny black floor with the cleats on the bottom of their shoes while managing to make it all look completely effortless.

'OK, from the top,' Simon said. 'Five, six, seven, eight.' I always wondered what happened to one, two, three and four but this was no time to start questioning the ways and whys of choreographers. I set off as usual on completely the wrong foot and caused chaos.

'OK, from the top again,' Simon said patiently. 'Just

remember it's right foot first then back on the left then kick. Five, six, seven, eight.'

Oh God, the brain understood Simon's directions, it's just that they weren't quite getting through to my feet, and time, unlike me, was marching on.

'Don't panic,' Simon told me after we'd wrapped for the night. 'We've still got just over a week to go. I promise you'll have it way before then.'

I didn't hold my breath.

The show opened in Brighton at the Theatre Royal and I remembered my steps. Well, the majority of them anyway. After our stint there we moved on to the Bloomsbury for a week.

Martin Taylor, the guy who'd contacted me in Australia about making costumes, was now living in London and was he a wizard on a sewing machine. He was amazing. With the demise of Hush and Chrissie, he was a godsend and made all Lily's costumes from that moment on.

Thanks to him I made my descent from the flies to the theme from *Jaws*, resplendent as Mary Poppins.

I was looking forward to flying across the stage. I'd always wanted to do it ever since I'd seen Anita Harris swoop across the stage at the Royal Court Theatre in Liverpool as Peter Pan. The wires are attached to a leather flying harness, worn around the waist with thick straps buckled tightly around the tops of your thighs. On the sides of this contraption were two metal plates with hooks where the wires were attached. Nowadays the harnesses are much more lightweight and therefore more comfortable to wear but back then they were one step up from a torture instrument, a masochist's dream that left welts across the tops of my legs and slowly rubbed the flesh away on my hip bones. To ease the pressure one of the stage crew recommended shoving a few sanitary towels under the straps. 'The thick ones,' he said, so I sent my dresser out to buy a large packet of heavy-duty super-absorbent Dr White's.

They certainly did the trick and stopped any chafing. They also stopped the show on opening night as one fell out as I flew across the stage, much to the delight of the audience. I could hardly pretend it hadn't happened as this bloody towel was the size of a child's mattress, so I did the only thing possible.

'Luckily, they've got wings,' I ad-libbed and carried on. One problem I hadn't bargained for was trying to dance in the damn harness, as it restricted movement and made me walk like John Wayne. My thighs were in shreds by the time that show closed.

# CHAPTER 7

WE DIDN'T TAKE MANY HOLIDAYS THAT WEREN'T WORKING ones, mainly for financial reasons, but when we did it was usually close to home. Every January we either rented a house in the Outer Hebrides or took off for Brittany, regardless of the weather.

I wish I could summon up the same thrill of excitement that ran through me when I first caught sight of Mont Saint-Michel in the distance.

'What the hell is that?' I asked Murphy.

'That, sunshine,' he said, 'is the Mont Saint-Michel and it's where we're staying tonight.'

Mont Saint-Michel is a small craggy island with a magnificent Benedictine abbey on the top. It's a bit of a hike up a winding street full of cafés and shops selling a load of old tat, but when you get to the summit your thighs might be burning but you can see for miles and the abbey itself has a calming effect.

We stayed in the hotel and ate the famous omelettes served in La Mère Poulard restaurant and as it was the night of the full moon the tide rose to surround the island, temporarily cutting it off from the outside world. Magic.

Murphy and I went there many times and on one occasion

Vera and Regina Fong joined us. Reg ended up getting his passport and wallet stolen from his room, the culprit hiding undiscovered behind the long bedroom curtains unbeknown to Reg, who had gone back to his room after dinner to 'freshen up, daaarling'.

Realizing that he'd been robbed, he dashed into our room to rally the troops. On going to investigate we found the window open with a large set of muddy footprints on the carpet underneath and, bizarrely, a bar of chocolate placed neatly on his bed that certainly hadn't been left by the chambermaid.

'My God,' Reg gasped dramatically, 'he was in the room, daaarling, at the same time as me. I could've been attacked, murdered, raped.'

'Attacked and murdered I'll go with,' Murphy said, crouching down to examine the footprints in the manner of Columbo. 'But I don't think you need to worry about rape, not while there are sheep in the fields.'

'Cheeky bastard,' Reg sniffed, fanning his face with a brochure. 'And anyway, when you come to think of it, who's to say the thief was a he, it might have been a she.'

'Well, if it was then she had big feet,' Murphy replied. 'These prints are huge.'

'So then, Miss Marple,' Reg shouted, his voice no doubt echoing over the salt marshes, 'we have a clue. We're looking for a French woman with size sixteen feet running around fucking Normandy with my wallet and my passport. She'll probably be on the boat to England as we speak.'

'What are you going to do then, Regina?' Vera asked, holding on to the headboard to steady himself after the amount of wine we'd consumed at dinner. 'How are you going to get home without a passport?'

'Oh my God,' Regina screeched, 'how am I indeed?' Leaping off the bed, he stood motionless on the spot with one hand slapped on his forehead and the other on his hip. In less stressful circumstances one might have suspected that this was Reg positioning himself before he went into his interpretive dance, Martha Graham-style. However, tonight it meant high drama.

'I'm stranded, daaarling.' The hands moved swiftly to the face now, framing either side of his open mouth like the man in Munch's *The Scream*. Vera, propelled into action by the word 'stranded', slapped his hand over his gaping mouth in a display of sympathy and the pair of them looked like two brass monkeys hearing and speaking no evil.

'I can't live here, daaarling.' Reg was on one now. 'What would I do? I'd have to hustle in a dockside bar for a few francs . . .'

'Euros,' Murphy interrupted.

'Francs,' Reg went on, ignoring him. 'Hustle for francs as I play my accordion around the tables to an audience of ruffians and sailors singing melancholy tunes of old Paree before the war.'

'Didn't know you could play the accordion, Regina,' I piped up, knowing full well that he couldn't.

'Oh yes, dear,' he said matter-of-factly. 'I was with the Ivy Benson all-girl band for years, playing accordion and xylophone.'

'At the same time?' I asked.

'At the same time,' he replied. 'Now where's my fucking passport, daaarling!'

We searched the gardens around the hotel to see if we could find it. Reg was slightly apprehensive about this at first. Being one of these paranoid sorts who are terrified of revealing their true age, he was worried that I'd be the one to find the passport and expose the truth. We didn't find either the passport or the wallet so we went back to the room to drink the duty-free we'd bought on the boat and discuss the evening's events.

Reg got his passport and wallet back the next morning. They were found by a member of staff slung in a bin but minus the money.

'Oh well, daaarling,' Reg drawled philosophically once he'd calmed down. 'Not everyone can say they've been robbed blind by the Milk Tray man.'

Saint-Malo was almost becoming a second home, we went so many times, making the journey in the Citroën on the overnight boat from Portsmouth.

I once spent a very long weekend in Saint-Malo with someone I used to know. Her name was Fudd, a well-preserved woman of indeterminate age who, like my aunty Chris, would rather be shot at dawn in a flannelette nightie than appear in public without a full face of warpaint and an immaculate barnet. Late each morning after her daily ritual of worship at the altar of beauty Fudd would appear on the cobbles of Saint-Malo, painted up and perfectly coiffed, dressed in the smart little black skirt and jacket she always wore and trailing a mink coat, looking like a cross between a BOAC stewardess and Kay Kendall.

When she was riding on her imperious high horse she was inclined to be an insufferable know-all but then when she climbed down off it she was lots of fun, up for just about anything, very intelligent and spoke wonderful French. She very rarely complained at my constant demands in shops to 'Ask them how much that is, will you,' as my French is shamefully limited to 'bonjour', 'avoir' and 'je voudrais un chocolat chaud s'il vous plaît'.

We were the last guests to stay at the Hôtel France Chateaubriand as it was closing for renovations. Although the rooms, charming as they were, could do with a spruce-up, the view from our enormous bedroom windows overlooking the ramparts and the English Channel beyond was more than adequate compensation for the utilitarian bathroom and fading paintwork.

Fudd's pride and joy was her hair. The care that went into keeping the Raine Spencer style that she favoured bordered on the obsessive and a mild breeze would have her running for cover, while at the merest hint of rain she'd go into meltdown. With a phobia for water that rivalled the Wicked Witch of the West she never, ever left the house – regardless of whether the sun was cracking the flags and hosepipes were banned – without an enormous umbrella.

It was a beautiful sunny morning and I'd managed to persuade her to take a walk along the ramparts with me. For some unknown reason she didn't take her umbrella with her, a memory lapse that she was soon to regret. No sooner had we got to the middle of the ramparts, at a place where there was absolutely no shelter at all, when from out of nowhere a storm broke. Instantaneously we were hit by a torrential downpour accompanied by a gale force wind.

As we ran through the maelstrom in search of a flight of stairs to get us off the ramparts, all I could hear was Fudd's hysterical screams as she chanted repeatedly, 'Oh my hair, oh my hair.' Looking like she'd just been fished out of the sea, she was a gibbering wreck as we marched through the streets back to the hotel with her once perfect coiffure hanging in rat's-tails around her sodden shoulders.

The demons of mischief were on my side and even though I was soaked through to my underpants I was desperate to laugh but didn't dare to as she was in such a lather. In the lift going up to our rooms I had to pinch my thigh hard in an attempt to avoid exploding into hysterics. While I looked at her mournful, mascara-smudged face, her hair began to turn to frizz like an old doll's.

I got changed and then joined her in her room. The soup-can rollers were already in place, securely gripped by hairpins as big as javelins, and as she stood in her underskirt puffing on a fag to control her nerves she hit on a bright idea.

'Have you got a paper bag?' she asked.

'Why, are you hyperventilating?' I wouldn't have been surprised if she was as she was incredibly nesh.

'No, Savage,' she explained, 'if I ring down and get a hair-dryer I can pop a bag over my hair, put the hairdryer in and voilà, an instant hooded dryer.'

I didn't have a paper bag but I had a carrier bag from Sainsbury's that I'd wrapped my shoes in.

'That'll melt, Savage, from the heat of the dryer – but then you knew that, didn't you?' She rang down to see if they had a paper bag, ordering tea for two while she was at it.

While Fudd fussed around, I fiddled with the remote, changing channels on the TV, which, like the one in my room, sat on an unreachable shelf in a corner. Apart from BBC News all the channels were, not surprisingly, foreign but one of them, probably German, was showing hard porn. It featured an extremely verbal blonde of enormous proportions with a pair of hooters the size of buoys, who was treating her hirsute gentleman caller to what is known in the trade as a 'tit wank'.

Room service knocked on the door with the hairdryer.

'Turn that off, Savage,' Fudd said, rushing to answer the door.

Instead of turning it off, I turned it up to maximum volume

189

and taking the remote with me I locked myself in the bathroom.

I couldn't hear much over the grunts and moans of the fat blonde and her hairy paramour and in the absence of a key-hole I couldn't see what was happening either, but I could picture the scene and that was enough to have me bent over the bath sick with laughter. Eventually, after what seemed like an age, I heard Fudd shout a desperate '*Merci!*' as the room service guy beat a hasty retreat.

'You're warped, Savage,' she said when I fell out of the bathroom and turned the telly off. 'I could've died, God knows what he thought, and me a respectable married woman.'

She was a good sport about it though and we both ended up laughing like a pair of kids. To make amends, I bought her a fabulous dinner in Delaunay's, a gastronome's delight of a restaurant serving oysters from Cancale and the absolute best to be had in plain simple Breton fare.

'My, my, will you get a look at this,' I growled, moving in for the kill on Daniel Day-Lewis as I slid next to him on the sofa. 'Give us a ciggie and I might make it worth your while.'

Daniel stared at me, not quite a rabbit caught in the head-lights but a little wary nevertheless.

'You see, I can be very nice.' I carried on regardless, running my hand up his thigh towards his crotch. 'Very nice indeed, but then again I have been known to turn if I don't get my own way, so hand your ciggies over now before I ram my fist down your throat.'

Mr Day-Lewis, who up to that moment had been looking distinctly uncomfortable, suddenly started to laugh, as did the other two occupants of this Park Lane hotel suite that I'd found myself in late one afternoon.

I wasn't doing a bit of whoring on my way into the theatre, I was auditioning for a part in the film *In the Name of the Father* and the voyeurs were the director Jim Sheridan and the actor Pete Postlethwaite.

'That was great,' Jim Sheridan said, smiling, 'but this time can you make him more of a psycho?'

I was absolutely mortified at having to walk in off the street, plonk my bum on the sofa and chat up Daniel Day-Lewis, especially as I hadn't even taken my coat off and had a bag of Marks and Spencer's shopping in tow, but I channelled Chrissie and gave it my best menacing psycho shot, padding out my ad-libbed script for full effect.

'Great,' Jim Sheridan said again and a very solemn Pete Postlethwaite nodded in agreement. Daniel Day-Lewis remained impassive, with just a hint of mild amusement on his face.

Jim told me it was a three-week shoot in Dublin and that they'd be in touch as they still had other people to see.

Once outside the hotel I rang Murphy immediately to tell him how this strange audition had gone.

'I hope I get it, Murphy,' I said eagerly. 'I'd love to be in a film.'

'Savage,' he replied calmly, 'you'll walk it. Look at what they're looking for, a psychotic, hyper-violent queen. Have you never heard of typecasting?'

*Elegies* did transfer to the West End although it wasn't quite Shaftesbury Avenue. It was a bit further down the road, the Tottenham Court Road to be exact, at the Drill Hall, a venue with an excellent reputation and known for its more experimental and avant-garde productions.

The women who ran the Drill Hall were a little frosty at

first, as we were probably a bit rowdy compared to previous performers they'd been used to. The small bar ran dry after the first night and Andrea and Amanda had a quiet word with the woman in charge of that side of things, advising her to stock up.

'Particularly on Baileys,' Amanda added, as that was the latest craze. Needless to say, the bar broke all box office records during our run.

Being so close to Soho, some of us resumed our old habit of 'going on somewhere after the show'. We joined the rank and file of the night owls of Soho, becoming familiar faces to doormen, bar staff, cab drivers, the homeless and the working girls who hung around Walker's Court hoping to pick up a punter from among the tourists and the male audience coming out of the Revue Bar.

*Elegies* did well at the Drill Hall and because of this success there was now a strong likelihood that it would transfer to the Criterion Theatre on Piccadilly.

The cast had been extremely loyal staying with the show, and having worked for next to nothing at both the Drill Hall and the King's Head they deserved this transfer. As for me, I was just looking forward to making my debut in the West End in your actual legitimate theatre for a change, especially since it was the theatre I remembered standing outside when I emerged from the tube station on my very first morning in London en route to Virginia Water in the early 1970s.

Fate had other things in store for me though, and I never made it to the Criterion even though I'd been offered the part. The producers decided to replace some of the cast with what they considered to be 'names' and, appalled at this shoddy treatment of the superb actors who'd been elbowed out to make way for what we saw as usurpers, Amanda and I reluctantly withdrew.

I'm very loyal, sometimes to the point of stupidity, and I believe in fair play. I saw the replacement of actors who had brought life to their monologues and made their parts their own as nothing less than treacherous. Some of the newcomers gave distinctly inferior performances.

Regina Fong, who had occasionally stood in for me in *Elegies* on nights when I had club work that I was committed to, took my place.

'If you'd been around during the war, which you probably were considering your advancing years, you old bag, they'd have tarred and feathered you and paraded you through the streets for sleeping with the enemy,' I ranted at him down the phone.

'You turned it down, they offered it to me and I accepted, so what's your problem?' he replied haughtily. 'I also have lots of experience working in West End shows, unlike you, and as I know the piece I was the obvious choice to replace you.'

'They didn't offer it to you,' I shot back. 'You rang them up the moment I told you I'd walked and begged them for the part, and as for working in the West End, the last time you kicked up one of those varicose-vein-riddled legs in the back row of the chorus the Black and White Minstrels were appearing twice daily at the Victoria Palace.'

'How dare you!'

'And how dare you!'

Slam. I banged the phone down angrily and set about packing my gear for my monthly weekend stint in the clubs of Blackpool, Manchester and Sheffield.

'So much for the West End,' I said to one of the cats, giving the wig a good shake-out before putting it in its usual mode of transport, a bin liner. 'Plus I've heard nothing back about the film so it doesn't look like I'll be going anywhere apart from the Attercliffe bloody Road, Sheffield.'

To add to my frustration and misery, Murphy turned up telling me that the car was misbehaving and that he wouldn't bank on it making the journey north, so I'd better get the train. Oh God, four days trailing around the north of England on trains and buses with a suitcase and a wig in a bin liner for company, when I should be in the West End and making films. My cup runneth over.

I was optimistically planting fresh herbs in my window box as the last lot had withered up and died after a week – due, I surmised, to the traffic pollution on the South Lambeth Road – when Murphy rang and told me that casting director Patsy Pollock had been on the phone to tell him that they wanted me for *In the Name of the Father*. I was ecstatic at this news and when I heard how much money he'd managed to wrangle out of them I was rendered speechless.

I sat silently on the sofa chain-smoking as I contemplated my new-found fortune. Was this how Viv Nicholson felt on hearing she'd won the pools? I'd never earned so much money for three weeks' work in my entire life, plus I was going to be staying at the Berkeley Court Hotel and being given something called perdiums each day for my expenses. I couldn't believe it.

Before we started filming, the cast had to fly to Dublin for a read-through of the script. Considering I only had four lines in the entire film it hardly seemed worth the expense of flying me over. I'd been disappointed at my sparsity of dialogue when I'd first read the script and my character didn't even have a name, but Jim Sheridan told me to ignore the script as he was looking for actors who were good at improvisation and that was why he'd hired me. On hearing this I didn't feel like an imposter any more, in fact the way I constantly went on about my career in the movies anyone would think I'd been picked to play the next James Bond.

The early morning Aer Lingus flight to Dublin was full to capacity and I found myself sitting right at the back of the plane next to the galley. The stewardess was very chatty and kept me supplied with tea. I attempted to sound casual as I explained that I was flying to Dublin to make a movie, as if it was something I did every day.

We'd been in the air for about forty minutes when the captain made an announcement. He'd had a message from Heathrow to say they'd found something on the runway that had dropped off the plane when we'd taken off.

'Nothing to worry about though,' he reassured us, in the way that they do.

The something turned out to be a tyre and the next announcement was that we were going to make an emergency landing. Although it was nothing to worry about, could we all adopt the brace position?

'Could I have a word with you,' the stewardess asked anxiously and I left my seat and followed her into the galley.

'Are you willing to help?' she wanted to know. 'I need to show you how to open the emergency exit.'

'Why?' I asked.

'In case anything happens to me,' she replied hastily and proceeded to give me a very quick lesson.

The plane started to descend more rapidly than I'd have liked. Looking around the cabin, I could see every passenger had their head buried in a small pillow on their lap while the oxygen masks overhead, released from captivity, danced wildly with the violent shudders of the plane.

'Quick, strap yourself in that seat,' the stewardess shouted, 'and get blowing on that whistle and shouting "Brace" as loud as you can.'

So there I was, strapped in a cabin crew seat, blowing this whistle and roaring 'Brace' in a voice that could be heard on Mars, treating the whole experience as a game, not out of bravado but from a firm conviction that my destiny was not to die in a plane crash.

Patsy Pollock told me later that the actor John Lynch turned to her and above the noise of the plane's descent, the screams from passengers and the row from the galley he said to her resignedly, 'Am I going to my grave with "Brace" screamed in a Scouse accent as the last word I'll ever hear? God help me.'

After a succession of violent bumps as we hit the ground and bounced, to the relief of everyone on board the plane eventually drew safely to a halt in a field somewhere outside Dublin airport. Every passenger sighed as one, some laughing nervously while others cheered and applauded the successful landing.

However, as in all good or even not so good disaster movies, relief is predictably short-lived and such was the case here, for the cabin slowly started to fill up with smoke as the under-carriage caught fire.

'Remove your shoes, leave all personal items behind and make your way to the emergency exit,' came the order over the intercom, or words to that effect.

'Get the door open,' the stewardess commanded as she started to deal with the deluge of hysterical passengers piling into the galley. I pulled the lever as instructed but instead of the door swinging open as I'd imagined, it shot off with great force.

'I think I've broken the door,' I said apologetically to the stewardess, fully believing that I had.

'Never mind the feckin' door,' she screamed. 'Get this lot down the slide.'

With the speed of lightning a great chute had inflated. 'Shoes off, arms across your chest and then jump down the slide,' I told each passenger as I slung them out of the door and off the plane. I took no prisoners, if you dawdled at the exit then you were pushed, and in minutes the plane had been evacuated. Once you got to the bottom of the chute you had to hit the ground running, as the undercarriage was blazing away merrily and there was a real danger of the plane exploding.

It was a while before coaches turned up to take us to the airport. Tempers were fraying as we stood barefoot, without outdoor clothes, in a muddy field getting soaked through in the predictable Irish drizzle. I put my arm around a young actress called Beatie Edney who was shaking from a combination of the cold and fear, and for the first time I became aware of the enormity of the situation. This crash could've turned into a major disaster.

As we entered the airport a trio of musicians playing Country and Western music greeted us with Patsy Cline's 'Crazy' – ironic really given Ms Cline's unfortunate demise when her plane crashed into the side of a mountain.

We sat waiting for hours in the airport until someone eventually turned up with our belongings in individual plastic bags and dumped them unceremoniously in the middle of the lounge. Rooting through the enormous pile for the bag containing my shoes and coat, the thought crossed my mind that had I not survived the crash it would in all probability have been Murphy who performed this strangely unsettling task.

As we were so late, we rushed through the read-through at Dublin Castle in less than an hour before we had to leave to catch the last flight back to London. Not surprisingly, Beatie was terrified at the prospect of having to get on a plane again, specially at such short notice, after what had happened. I plied her with brandy at the airport and held her hand tightly on the flight home, which thankfully was uneventful.

I bumped into her years later at the Olivier Awards and the first thing she asked was 'Do you remember me?' Of course I did, how could I forget her after sharing such an experience? Laughing about it, we raised a few eyebrows when we explained to people with a nonchalant air that we 'survived a plane crash together'.

A month after our emergency landing I received a letter from Aer Lingus, apologizing for the inconvenience and offering me three free flights to Ireland as compensation.

Wot, no medal?

Even though I'd been to Ireland more times than I could remember, I knew very little of Dublin. We only ever passed through the city briefly after getting off the Liverpool boat en route to the station to catch the train to Castlerea, stopping off for the full Irish at Bewley's café in Grafton Street first.

*In the Name of the Father* tells the story of four innocent men who were framed by the police for the murder of five people in the IRA bombing of a Guildford pub. Daniel Day-Lewis played Gerry Conlon and Pete Postlethwaite his father, Giuseppe, and all our scenes were shot in Kilmainham Gaol, a grim fortress known as the Irish Bastille.

My cellmate and partner in crime was someone I already

198

knew. His name was Alan Amsby, aka Mr Pussy, Ireland's foremost and at the time only drag queen. During the sixties he'd been working on the flourishing drag scene in London as part of an established act called Pussy and Bow. The act split up and Alan accepted a solo booking in Dublin, and as drag queens were rare as hen's teeth in holy Ireland he caused a sensation and never came back. Alan is one of those rare human beings who hasn't got a bad bone in his body. I've never seen him lose his cool or blow his top, and he's incredibly generous and kind-hearted. He also loves to party and knows just about everyone in Dublin and together we shared a very small trailer, one in a row of them that had been set up in the prison yard.

Pete Postlethwaite was next door to us and he'd bang on the wall, wanting to know if we ever drew breath and stopped talking for a moment. He was also fond of playing 'Liverpool Housewife', starting the ball rolling each morning as he let himself into his trailer with a diatribe about me spoken in a thick Liverpool accent.

'I see she was out all night again,' he'd say in a voice loud enough for me to hear. 'Leaving her kids on their own, the dirty, filthy, drunken trollop, while she's out on the prowl, sleeping with anything for a half of Guinness.'

I'd duly oblige by flinging my door open and standing on the step, arms folded, in the traditional manner of affronted housewives of yore squaring up for battle.

'You want to be careful who you're making accusations about,' I'd hiss through pursed lips. 'I'll have you know I was at home all night on me knees saying a decade of the rosary with the parish priest for my poor dying mother.'

'Is that what you call it? You might have been down on your knees, madam, but you certainly weren't praying.'

'Are you accusing me of defiling my body with a man of the cloth?'

And so it went on, helping to ease the boredom of filming, which I'd gathered so far meant hanging around for the best part of the day waiting to be called on to the set.

On slow days Alan and I would explore the old part of the gaol, trying to visualize what it was like to be incarcerated in one of the inhospitable little cells and reading the heartbreaking graffiti on the walls, the handiwork of desperate men and women from a bygone age. On Easter Sunday we stood in the prison yard where so many had been executed by firing squad for their part in the Easter uprising of 1916. We lit a candle and placed it in a hole in the wall. I was becoming very aware of my Irish roots and heritage and bought lots of books on the history of Ireland.

It's not hard to fall in love with Dublin. We had quite a lively social life outside of filming and together with Frank Harper and John Benfield we usually started our evening rounds with a livener to kick things off at the Dockers, an ancient pub on the city quay overlooking the Liffey that was popular with film people. Sadly, it became yet another casualty of the declining pub trade and closed down some years ago.

Daniel Day-Lewis spoke in a Northern Irish accent for the entire duration of the shoot. Even when he wasn't filming and came clubbing with us to Lillie's Bordello (a club, not a brothel) he kept the accent up. To prepare for the big interrogation scene he insisted that he was kept locked up in his cell over-night and deprived of sleep – a little extreme, I thought, but it seemed to work for him. Pete Poss considered it unnecessary and a 'load of bollocks'. We were also frequently asked to ver-bally abuse him when we were on set, which didn't come easily when you'd only just shared a very pleasant lunch with the man on the dinner bus.

To pass the time away in our little trailer, Alan and I would invent an entire life story for our characters, whom we christened Stella and Rita. I was Rita, a vicious psychopath doing life for the murder of one of his customers when he was a young rent boy. That was some years ago and even though he was well past his sell-by date he still thought of himself as a highly desirable catch. Alan was Stella, a master forger who had been drawn into a con involving the Irish Sweepstakes.

On the days when we actually managed to get on the set and do some work we were encouraged to get into character and improvise. The riot scenes where we were chased along the landings by guards waving batons were my favourite, as were scenes where I was required to act crazy and sit at the dinner table flicking food at other prisoners. One afternoon Jim Sheridan told Alan and me to perform an impromptu cabaret on the landing, which went on for hours and ended up bluer than anything a stag night compère could deliver. As a result Alan and I were dragged off to our cells screaming abuse at the guards. Great fun.

Hours of film were shot over the three-week period we spent in that gaol. My scene ended up on the cutting-room floor and the only trace of me in the entire movie is when Gerry and Giuseppe first enter the prison and, looking up as they climb the stairs, they get to see me looking down from the number threes, the landing that is home to rapists, sex offenders and the like, licking my lips suggestively.

'Dahling,' Regina said over the phone after the film came out, 'I saw your little film at the cinema this afternoon but I couldn't see you in it apart from that blink-and-you'll-miss-it scene where you lean over the balcony.'

'Really?' I sighed.

'And that was a dreadful shot if you don't mind me saying, most unflattering, dear, jowls like a bloodhound. Still, I suppose that's the film industry for you. So what are you up to now that you're back in town?'

'Reading your reviews for *Elegies*,' I replied acidly. 'Fancy calling you a tired old pub drag queen, how awful for you.'

'Thank you, dear,' Regina snapped back archly. 'Kind of you to be so concerned.'

'How did you feel when you read the one in the *Standard*?' I asked in tones dripping with mock sympathy. 'I mean being described as the worst thing ever seen on a West End stage must take some getting over, especially when you consider that the *Evening Standard* is read by just about everyone in London . . .'

'Yes, I know, dear, thank you for pointing that out,' Regina almost screamed down the phone. 'Now let's talk about something else.'

We regularly had conversations like this over the phone. Although they might sound malicious and cruel there was no harm in them, as for Regina it was the sort of bitchery that Vera Charles and Aunty Mame might exchange and was the stuff of life to him.

I wasn't really that bothered that I didn't make it to the big screen as I'd had a wonderful time, made some decent money as well as a lot of new friends, gained a wealth of experience on a film set and fallen in love with Dublin into the bargain.

I became a regular visitor to Dublin and now that funds had improved I set up camp at the Shelbourne Hotel, even spending Christmas and New Year there with Murphy and Joan. Alan Amsby had gone into business with Bono and was now the front man of a trendy café called Pussy's Parlour that stayed open quite late and served up mugs of 'Whore-Licks' laced with Jameson's whiskey. On Christmas Eve, Murphy, Joan and I hired one of those open horse-drawn carriages to take us around the back streets. Snow started to fall and a party of hookers prowling the streets wished us a very merry Christmas. Afterwards we drank whiskey in the lounge of the hotel as we listened to the pianist in the dining room playing a selection of carols. I buried myself in the comfortable armchair, inhaling the smell of wood smoke and turf coming from the blazing fire in the grate and watching the snow falling outside, and for the first time in years I felt what normal people refer to as 'Christmassy'.

'Oh well, Savage,' Murphy said, shrugging his shoulders with his usual maddeningly idealistic attitude, 'you win some, you lose some. It's a crying shame but forget about it now and move on to more important matters.'

He was referring to the letter I'd received from the brewery turning down our application to become the new proprietors of the Royal Vauxhall Tavern.

Pat and Breda McConnon, the licensees at the time, had finally decided to call it a day. The staff, artistes and clientele of the most famous pub on south London's Barbary Coast were devastated at the news, but we sent Pat and Breda off in grand style with a big party on their final night so everyone had a chance to say goodbye and thank you to this hugely popular couple. Almost all the acts turned up to do a number and every single regular had come out in support. The pub was packed but even though the atmosphere resembled the night they ended prohibition, it was tinged with an air of sadness.

I didn't want this pub to fall into the hands of someone who didn't understand it. I was too fond of the old place to let it go and after discussing it with Pat, who promised to put in a good word for us, Murphy and I had applied to the brewery to take it over.

We were going to become publicans, the licensees of the Royal Vauxhall Tavern. It was all we talked about.

I had big plans for transforming the interior of the pub into a palace of kitsch, a homage to Lily's front room in a riot of leopard print, fake fur, family photos and the gaudiest of religious icons. We'd live over the shop and were prepared to give it our all to make the place a big success, with the best cabaret, live music and Lily compèring every night. Sadly it wasn't to happen and our dreams had been shot down in flames by a letter that began, 'It is with regret that we have to inform you that your application has been unsuccessful.'

'Their loss,' Murphy said. 'We'd have turned that place into a little gold mine,' and with that he never mentioned it again.

The pub closed after Pat and Breda left while the brewery appointed a new manager, and by the time it reopened unfortunately most of the punters had drifted away.*

Reg was back working there on a Monday night and around 3 a.m. if he was still coherent I'd get the phone call.

'You won't believe what it's like having to perform there now,' he'd moan as he slugged brandy and smoked a spliff. 'There's no fucker coming in these days. I worked to twenty-five tonight, twenty-five, dahling! It's utter torture.'

I had lots of phone calls like this from Reg. On a Tuesday after he'd worked the Black Cap he'd get home and always phone me for a good moan.

---

* Pat and Breda were sorely missed.

'I don't know how much longer I can stick it, dear. The security is absolutely useless, three times I shouted for him to come down to the stage because there were a group of lairy dykes in front causing trouble. Three times, and did he come? Did he fuck.'

I never stood on the stage of the Vauxhall Tavern again after Pat and Breda's final night. It was the end of an era and it just wasn't the same without them. The snub from the brewery, who weren't even prepared to give us a chance, still stung and I resolved that if I couldn't run the place then business between us was over, and I certainly wasn't about to swell their profits by working for them ever again.

Inevitably there were cries that I had sold out and that I'd forgotten my roots but I had good reason for walking away. As Murphy said, 'If they can't recognize a golden opportunity when it's offered to them on a plate, then it's time to move on and leave the bastards to stew in their own juice.'

Despite my regrets over the Vauxhall, the future was looking bright as all sorts of weird and wonderful jobs started coming in. I was a regular in a series called *Viva Cabaret* along with Bob Downe and Gayle Tuesday. Tom Jones hosted the first show and considering his international fame he was every inch the down-to-earth Welshman, even going to a local pub after the show and getting up with the small band for an impromptu session. The locals couldn't believe it.

'He's the best bloody Tom Jones impersonator I've ever seen,' one of the regulars told me.

For the forthcoming Edinburgh Festival I was booked into the Playhouse Theatre for three nights, a prospect that I found daunting. I was dubious about selling enough tickets considering the theatre is a three-thousand-seater.

'I'll never fill that,' I moaned as Murphy made the deal with Addison Cresswell.

'Of course you will,' Addison said, rubbing his hands together. 'They can't get enough of you at the moment.'

I wasn't in the least convinced but in the end I didn't get a chance to find out as there was a fire backstage at the Playhouse and all shows were cancelled.

'Never mind,' Murphy said. 'You're doing the show at the Usher Hall instead.'

'How many does that seat?' I asked tentatively.

'Well, it has a smaller seating capacity than the Playhouse,' he began to explain.

'That's all right then,' I said, relieved.

'It holds about two and a half thousand,' he said, as if it was nothing at all. 'It's got a massive pipe organ and usually only holds classical concerts. Wonderful acoustics apparently.'

'Oh great,' I gulped. 'In that case I'd better polish up on me Mozart's Missae and see if our Vera's available to work the bellows.'

Imposing as the Usher Hall was and despite it being possibly the most incongruous venue to find a drag queen in, I had a great three nights there and, as Addison had so confidently predicted, we sold out.

Two days after my last show at the Usher Hall I worked a pub in a grim northern town that I've long since obliterated from memory. After the majesty of the Usher Hall I was brought back down to earth with a bang when faced with the lavs to change in and a sound system that packed up halfway through the act, leaving me to shout for the rest of it as two tough lesbians battered each other in front of me because one of them had allegedly looked at the other's girlfriend. Much as I hate that old adage, there certainly is no business like show business.

'Keeps your feet on the ground,' Murphy said cheerfully as we drove home. 'It doesn't do you no harm to work a boozer, it keeps your rough edge and anyway, I doubt if you'll be doing them for much longer.'

Around that time I was also making regular trips to a studio cellar in Carnaby Street as the sometime television and video critic for Mariella Frostrup's *The Little Picture Show*, filmed in a garage in north London singing 'Trouble' with a mixed bag of Elvis impersonators and a very young but extremely bright Caitlin Moran for a show called *Naked City*, and presented *It's A Queer World* for Channel 4. This was filmed in what was supposed to be Lily's house where she lived with her nephew, and took a look at gay TV from around the world. It was all low-budget telly that invariably went out at some late hour, but at least it was telly, and I never turned anything down no matter how lousy the pay.

'The King's Head want you to do a benefit for them to raise money for a new roof,' Murphy said as we drove up to Blackpool to work the Flamingo Club. 'What do you think?'

'I don't see why not,' I told him as I ate a bag of crisps and flicked through the *TV Times* to see how often I was on that week. 'Where are they having it? In the pub?'

'No, it's at the London Palladium,' he said nonchalantly, 'sharing the bill with Victoria Wood.'

I stared at him mid-crisp, open-mouthed. 'Come again? You mean THE London Palladium?'

'Yes, the London Palladium,' he replied, laughing. 'Now do you want to do it or not?'

'Nah,' I replied, carrying on reading my mag. 'Why would I want to appear at the Palladium with Victoria Wood, Murphy, when I'm quite happy trailing up and down the motorway?'

Murphy looked at me incredulously and before he could go into a lecture about how foolish it would be to turn such a proposal down, I chipped in.

'What do you think, you soft sod? Of course I bloody do. Get on the blower first thing and tell them yes please.'

I spent a fortnight writing new material that catered to the fact that I, Lily Savage from the pubs, was playing one of the most important theatres in the world. I went over and over it, adding, tweaking and improving until I was satisfied that I had a good forty-five minutes' worth of strong and, more importantly, brand new patter under my belt. I dragged the Marlene and the lamp-post routine out as it always went down well, and roped Irish singer Rose-Marie into doing a duet with me of a number called 'The Grass Is Always Greener'.

The last time I'd appeared at the Palladium had been for *The Jonathan Ross Show* and I hadn't come across very well. This time though, I told myself as I walked down the stairs to the stage door carrying the wig in the bin liner, I was determined to nail it.

The show had sold out and people were queuing at the box office for returns. 'Shame we're doing this for free,' Murphy muttered as he examined the contents of my dressing-room fridge for something to drink. 'We'd have cleaned up. Never mind, we'll know better next time.'

'I think you'll find that the majority of punters have come to see Victoria Wood,' I told him. 'She's a comedy goddess, don't forget.'

'Don't be so sure of that, Savage. They've come to watch a battle between the two of you and to see which one comes out on top.'

It was no contest as far as I was concerned. Victoria was the undisputed queen of comedy, a multi-award-winning genius who was currently selling out the Royal Albert Hall. I was just the support act and quite content to be so.

Victoria was friendly but businesslike. Comedy was no laughing matter to her and she took it very seriously. She asked me if I would be touching on any topics that might be in her repertoire, explaining that her act was set and she couldn't change it. There were a few royal family gags I was doing but I was more than happy to drop them and she went away satisfied. I admired her as she had a brilliant mind and an enviable ability to consistently produce a wealth of astounding comedy material.

A friend of mine from the Vauxhall Tavern called Andy had the task of dressing me. He was and is a chirpy Glaswegian whom we quickly christened Agnes.

'Are you nervous, dear?' he asked as he pottered about the dressing room checking off all the items on his list that he needed for the quick change into Marlene and the lamp post.

'Don't forget the lacquer so I can spray the fringe on that Marlene wig,' I reminded him, 'and the small hairbrush. If I don't give it a quick squirt it hangs over my face like a broken wing.'

'I know, I know, dear,' he replied. 'But are you nervous?'

I thought for a moment and realized that surprisingly I wasn't. I was excited. I knew the patter off by heart and couldn't wait to get out there to see how it went down. My new wig had come straight from Stuart's that morning and was a towering mass of perfection, and the new biker slut outfit that Martin Taylor had made me was comfortable and suitably irreverent for the surroundings. I had nothing to be nervous about, I reassured myself, refusing to allow even the smallest of gremlins to creep in and disturb my self-confidence.

The Palladium was built by the architect Frank Matcham, a man responsible for some of the most beautiful theatres in the country. He certainly knew what he was doing when it came to designing variety houses, as standing centre stage at the Palladium is not a scary experience in the least. On the contrary, it's a warm, magical spot to find yourself in, where you feel that you're in total control of the entire house.

That hour and fifteen I spent on the stage flew by. It was exhilarating and despite the advice of an old comic who said that your one aim when walking out on stage was to 'Get off if you're dying and get off if it's going well' and 'Don't over-stay your welcome', I still went over my allotted time as both the audience and I were having such good fun.

After the show my dressing room filled up with people. Murphy was like the cat who'd got not just the cream but the whole bloody dairy.

'Well, you won that battle, Savage,' he crowed. 'You want to hear them in the bar. The general consensus is you won it hands down.'

I've never been cocky if I think that a show's gone well. I've seen comics come off stage after a mediocre set puffed up like a turkey cock and I've always looked down on them for their arrogance. False modesty is just as bad, as is the needy comic who pleads, 'Was I funny? Did you hear that gag I told . . .' I see going on stage as akin to a boxing match. You win some, you lose some – that's the nature of the beast, as no matter how prepared you are you can never tell when you're going to be floored or if you're going to come away feeling like you've won the heavyweight title bout.

Even so, success is fleeting and it can easily lead you into a false sense of security if you allow it to go to your head. You can never, ever afford to relax and sit back on your laurels as there are more fights to win and you'll find they grow even more taxing and demanding with time. That's how I've always seen it, anyway. Comedy is a time-consuming pain in the neck but as laughter is highly addictive and as necessary as oxygen you keep on striving to keep it going.

I was back at the Palladium again later on in the year for another benefit, only this time it wasn't for a pub roof, it was for Stonewall, the charity who fight for LGBT rights, and not for needy farmers who want to repair ancient boundary walls. The bill was packed with a host of starry names and I was opening the show as one of the legendary Tiller Girls, joining them in the line-up.

Having worked with the Tillers at the Royal Festival Hall in another post-Edinburgh show and fallen in love with them, I'd confessed that they were the stuff of legend to me. I'd been fascinated by them as a kid as I watched them on our black and white telly on *Sunday Night at the London Palladium*.

Strange how things turn out, for now here I was sharing a dressing room with more or less the same gang, all of them high-kicking with the same precision years later.

I vowed to them that if I ever got a telly programme of my own then they'd be the first people I'd call up. I think they'll testify that it was a promise I kept. In fact I can't bloody get rid of them as they've ended up appearing on almost everything I've ever done since, and I half expect to find them one day kicking the legs up in a kennel in Battersea Dogs Home.

That night we gathered on stage waiting for the tabs (curtains) to go up, the girls warming up and chattering like a flock of excited budgies. They were dressed in matching turquoise and black outfits, the skirts of which were extremely short even for me, and in the one they'd had made for me I felt and looked like a slightly gormless and extremely ungainly giraffe.

The curtain went up to a roar of applause as the audience caught sight of this legendary troupe back on their home turf, high-kicking to 'Variety', a tune that those of a certain age had no trouble recalling. It took a few moments for it to sink in that the tall skinny one just off centre wasn't quite in sync with the others. In fact she was way out . . . way, way out.

It was another unbelievable night. I'd been given a ten-minute spot in the second half that I didn't want to end as I was enjoying myself more than I would lying on the couch back home wolfing a box of Turkish Delight. I left the stage high as a kite, loving that theatre more than ever.

The Palladium held no fear for me. Oddly enough, considering its awesome reputation and the fact that I'd only set foot on the stage a few times, I felt immediately at home there. It occurred to me as I stood centre stage that it was really not that different from the Vauxhall Tavern, apart from being much more civilized and a great deal bigger, that is. Far from being intimidating, I discovered that standing alone on that big empty stage in the warmth of the follow spot prattling away to a full house was the most comfortable place in the world to be.

'We'll book the Palladium and put on our own show next year,' Murphy said conspiratorially as we necked champagne at the Stonewall after-show party. 'You up for it?'

At that moment I'd have done anything to get on that stage again. Even though I was a little teeny bit wary of chancing my arm and breaking my run of good luck, I threw caution to the wind and agreed on the spot.

'I can't go back to pubs, Murphy,' I said. 'Not after a taster of what it's like working in these theatres. It's heaven going on at 7.30 instead of one in the morning and it's . . .' I struggled to find words to describe such an experience. 'It's . . . it's the real McCoy. It's what I want to do, work in the theatre. Sod the telly, it's the theatre where I belong,' I said grandly, sounding like Dame Edith Evans. 'Tell you what, why don't you organize a tour?'

'Hang on, Savage,' he said, taken aback by my sudden enthusiasm. 'If you want to sell a tour then you've got to be on telly. How else is a mainstream audience going to know who you are? You won't be going back to the pubs, sunshine – not if I can help it. Just leave it all to me.'

I laughed at his confidence and helped myself to another glass of champagne.

'I love you when you're happy and want to take the world by the balls,' he said, grabbing me violently by the back of my head and kissing me forcibly on the mouth in a gesture that Murphy considered romantic.

'How disgusting,' Mig Kimpton said as he wafted by. 'Oh and Savage, why are you blushing?'

At Christmas I usually did the rounds of the circuit with Adrella, but he'd more or less retired due to a painful back condition that on a bad day left him barely able to move. I did the usual tour of the clubs up north and the pubs around London on my own.

I also got involved in a programme called *Camp Christmas*. In it, the presenters Andy Bell of Erasure and Melissa Etheridge invited a host of famous gay and lesbian faces to their beautiful log cabin in the snow for a Christmas party. The set was magnificent and the cast was a veritable who's who of the LGBT world, with everyone from Pedro Almodóvar to Quentin Crisp 'popping in'. There was an impressive stone-effect fireplace in this cabin and on it hung a talking reindeer's head, complete with a bulbous red nose, that was voiced by Julian Clary.

I played one half of the caterers. They were called, appropriately enough, 'Savage Caterers – You'll Remember Us in the Morning', a tag-line thought up by Bob Downe who was also in the show. My partner in crime was Polly Perkins, a brilliant singer and comic who went on to star in the short-lived soap *Eldorado* (they should've given it more time) and later as Dot Cotton's sister Rose in *EastEnders*. We had quite a lengthy scene, with a lot of dialogue and complicated business as we arrived in the kitchen laden down with trays of food. Both Polly and I fluffed a few lines and had to quickly improvise and when it was over we both thought we could do it a damn sight better.

'We'll go again,' Polly said. 'Don't worry.'

But we didn't go for another take. Instead the director shouted, 'Moving quickly on,' leaving a bemused Polly and me standing behind the set in a gloomy mood. It was like this all through the show, this recording at breakneck speed, except for the music items which seemed to take for ever.

Derek Jarman put in an appearance despite being very ill and frail. He sat quietly in a chair on the set putting an incredibly brave face on and probably wondering what he was doing there. The rest of the cast were obviously of the same mind as once the presents were distributed nobody seemed to know what to do with him. To make conversation, I asked him if he'd like a sandwich.

'No thank you,' he replied, grinning.

'OK then, love,' I said in motherly tones. 'I'll save you a bit of cake for later.' This not particularly funny bit of ad-libbed dialogue tickled Vera as it was reminiscent of the kind of line those fierce matriarchs of our childhood would come out with.

I didn't have high hopes for this show. Among other things, I thought it mawkish and a bit worthy at times but it came good in the edit and turned out to be a decent programme. The press mauled it. No surprise there.

# CHAPTER 8

I STOOD ON THE SIDEWALK IN GREENWICH VILLAGE, captivated by the clouds of steam belching out of a manhole cover in the middle of a street and excitedly repeating the line that has undoubtedly been spoken by trillions of first-time visitors to New York before me.

'It's exactly like the movies.'

'I know, Savage, I know,' Murphy sighed, having heard me make the same remark quite a few times since we got here.

I couldn't sleep in New York. It had nothing to do with Murphy refusing to sleep with the air conditioning on in the studio apartment we'd borrowed off Luke Cresswell of Stomp and thereby turning it into an oven, it was all down to excitement. I felt like I'd been plugged into the mains all the time I was in NYC, fizzing all over and bursting with energy. Just as well, as in the week Murphy and I were there we covered miles on foot exploring the city.

Ian McKellen had invited us to come over for the opening of his one-man show, *A Knight Out on Broadway*. I'd worked relentlessly up till now, so a bit of a break and the chance to not have to think about Lily Savage before I set off on tour again wouldn't come amiss.

New York is not the place to go to relax, particularly in the

**Below:** Amanda Mealing and me – the fortieth.

**Above:** Murphy, LA.

**Below:** Sam Beckinsale, Andrea Oliver and Amanda. The fortieth.

**Left:** Harry Hill, Mark (Bob), Brenda (Gayle), Al Murray, me and unknown redhead on tour somewhere.

**Left and below right:** What a way to earn a living. Mary Poppins, the Bloomsbury Theatre.

**Below:** The actress today.

**Left:** Backstage at the number one dressing room at the Palladium. Lil, Gayle, Vera, Mark (Bob).

**Above:** All Tillered up backstage at the Palladium.

**Below:** Rehearsals with the Tillers at the Palladium.

**Above:** They dyed my hair and eyelashes. With Pete Postlethwaite, *In the Name of the Father.*

**Left:** Two hardbitten old lags – *In the Name of the Father* with Alan Amsby.

**Right:** On location at Kilmainham Gaol, Dublin, with Alan Amsby for *In the Name of the Father.*

**Above:** Easter Sunday, the Palladium. Vera, Gayle, Bob, me and Betty, who joined us on the revolve with her shopping for the finale.

**Left:** Murphy and me, NYC.

**Below:** With Mark (Bob), NYC.

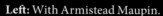

**Left:** With Armistead Maupin.

**Below:** Ian McKellen, *Live at The LilyDrome*.

**Above:** Stonewall Equity Show, Royal Albert Hall, with some fellah I picked up.

**Above:** *Live at The LilyDrome* with Cheryl Murray, who played the feisty Suzie Birchall on *Corrie* and who was my only choice to play the bitchy barmaid.

**Above:** Mark Little, Lily Savage, Claudia Schiffer and Gaby Roslin.

**Above:** My favourite nephews, Zig and Zag, *Big Breakfast*.

**Right:** Kenny Rogers, 'Islands In The Stream'.

_Fred Hayman_ BEVERLY HILLS

**Left:** LA. Shopping with Jackie.

**Below:** Harry Winston's, shoplifting with Jackie.

**Left:** Golden Girl Betty White in LA.

**Below left:** With Robin Williams.

**Below:** Whoring on Rodeo Drive.

ROBIN + LILY'S DANCE REVIEW

**Far left:** *Prisoner Cell Block H the Musical.*

**Left:** Backstage, *Prisoner* on tour. Obviously a matinee.

**Below:** 'Got any smokes on yer?' Backstage at the Queens, *Prisoner Cell Block.*

BUSTER

**Left:** Buster as a puppy.

**Top:** Oh, those leather pants!

**Above:** Mig and Murphy, Blackpool.

**Right:** Murph at Raffles, Singapore.

**Above:** That bracing Blackpool sea breeze.

**Right:** Murphy recovering on the Eastern and Oriental Express.

heat of June when the city was celebrating the 4th Gay Olympic Games. I never really did stop thinking about Lily Savage as I was always on the lookout for new sources of comedy material. Nevertheless, I found time to occupy my mind in plenty of other ways. A whole gang of us had congregated for the week: Mark (Bob Downe), Mig Kimpton who was working with Ian, and Michael Cashman and his partner Paul Cottingham.

My first Broadway show was *Guys and Dolls* and to walk out on to Times Square in all its illuminated glory after seeing a musical set in the very same place was like stepping out into an extension of the show. The same happened with *Damn Yankees*, another musical, only this time it was about baseball. I went to a matinee of that with Michael and Paul and that night we sat in the Yankee Stadium not watching baseball but the opening ceremony of the gay games, roaring our heads off as the British team paraded by.

Ian and Mig took me to see *Beauty and the Beast*, but apart from the impressive special effects the show left me cold. It was like sitting through a very beautiful panto but one that lacked soul and I was desperate for one of the cast to break through the fourth wall and talk to the audience.

Times Square before it was cleaned up and sanitized was still a risky area after dark and it was not advisable to walk around on your own. To be honest, I preferred it the way it used to be. It's lost its edge now, although there are still a few old Times Square bars to be found where things are basically unchanged.

At a very trendy party just off Times Square that I remember being held in a white space – either a fashion house, an art gallery, somebody's apartment or perhaps all three – I had an encounter with Madonna.

If this party had been held in London then those nonentities who misguidedly considered themselves the height of importance, the type who would show their bare arse in Selfridge's window for an invitation, would undoubtedly spend the evening either gliding about like storks on ether or stood on the sidelines affecting a 'too cool for school' manner. Here in New York there was a different buzz, as they say, and the atmosphere despite the glaring white decor was warm, laid-back and friendly.

The guests were an eclectic mix of supermodels and drag queens, politicos and activists, artists and athletes, actors whose faces I recognized but couldn't put a name to and the most beautiful waiters I'd ever seen. To quote Shirley MacLaine in *Sweet Charity*, I was the only person in the room I didn't recognize.

The porn star Jeff Stryker stood at one end of the room smiling slyly, obviously well aware that every male, as well as quite a few women, who passed by sneaked a surreptitious glance at his crotch. Mr Stryker's gimmick was his enormous willy. At the other end of the room Elaine Stritch held court surrounded by a gaggle of enraptured middle-aged queens hanging on to her every word as she related one of her tried and true theatrical anecdotes.

Suddenly the mood in the room changed, the atmosphere grew tense and the crowd parted as one to make way for a new arrival. She swept into the room like the evil fairy at the christening, only instead of a spinning wheel this latecomer came armed with an entire film crew and a retinue of flunkeys who proceeded to take over.

'Oh God, Madonna's here,' I heard someone say. 'There goes the neighbourhood.'

'I'd have thought that Madonna turning up at a party

would've been cause for celebration,' I said to the singer Gabrielle, a big fan of the great lady. 'But this lot don't seem very pleased.'

As we stood watching this performance I was beginning to see why. The lighting from the cameras was very intrusive as she charged around the room in her bare feet, filming herself with the beautiful people for a documentary she was making and rapidly turning a great party into a circus.

Murphy was equally unimpressed by Madge's arrival, which wasn't surprising as celebrity failed to make an impact on him. He was far more interested in the clean-cut young athlete he was talking to, pulling out all the seduction stops as he focused him in the full beam of his 'Marlon Brando stare'. This effect was achieved by removing his glasses and squinting myopically but it was guaranteed nevertheless to floor the impressionable and unsuspecting.

'Seen who's in, Savage?' he shouted over to me in the same tone of voice he'd use if Vera had just walked into the Vauxhall Tavern. Then he turned his attentions back to the javelin thrower or whatever he was.

I went and sat next to the author Armistead Maupin on a very long, very white leather sofa. Then the lady plonked herself down the far end.

'Look who's here,' I said to Armistead in the voice my mum used when she spoke about cancer. 'It's Madonna!' Yes, I'll admit it, I was excited – well, it's not every day a global superstar sits next to you. Following Armistead's lead, I looked over and gave her a feeble wave. Armistead's was more heartfelt, but Madonna was playing at being world-weary and completely ignored us.

She wouldn't know me from a sack of spuds but she could've

at least acknowledged Armistead, who apart from being a good-natured fellah was also an internationally famous writer. Armistead took no offence at her rebuttal, that's if he even noticed it, but privately I thought she was downright rude.

Dressed as she was in a grubby vest and combat trousers, she wouldn't have looked out of place at a bus stop eating chips, but when you're a star of that magnitude I expect you believe you can wear anything and still look cool. Lowering her aviator dark glasses over her eyes, she curled up on the sofa tucking her feet underneath her. The soles of her feet were filthy, dirtier than a potato-picker's who'd forgotten to bring their wellies to work.

She threw her head back dramatically and let out a long sigh.

'You know what I want?' she said imperiously, presumably either to me and Armistead, or possibly to herself since there was nobody else on the couch.

'A fucking good wash?' I offered.

It came out before I had time to stop it and I sat frozen with bated breath to see her reaction, but none came. She clearly hadn't heard me or if she had then she was ignoring me.

'I need some air,' she announced suddenly to nobody in particular and with that earth-shattering statement she took off, presumably in search of a canister of oxygen or, failing that, a window.

'I could live in New York,' I said to Murphy as we sat in the back of a taxi on our way to JFK airport.

'You say that about everywhere,' he replied. 'I remember you saying the same thing about Hull.'

'Well, it was a nice row of terraced houses.'

'They were slums, Savage,' he said, dismissing my nonsense. 'What you need to be thinking about is getting out of that bloody rats' nest and buying yourself a nice place to live in.'

'Vicky Mansions isn't a rats' nest,' I protested, defending my place of abode.

'It is, Savage, it's a bloody tip. The place is falling to bits and you've got no room to put anything. You should get out. You're going to be earning some decent money so it's high time you started thinking about moving.'

I had a love-hate relationship with my flat. Murphy was right, it was cramped and falling to bits but the rent was cheap, it was central and I'd lived there for over a decade. The thought of packing up costumes, wigs and the junk I'd accumulated over the years gave me the horrors, as did spending every penny I'd managed to save on a flat.

What if the work dried up? I'd saved a fair bit now and whenever I panicked and started worrying about the future, which I was prone to do, I'd drag the Halifax savings book out from under the mattress and reassure myself that for the time being I wouldn't starve.

Costumes and wigs were a big expenditure and the more I was doing the more new outfits I needed. The thigh-length boots were made on the Holloway Road, the wigs came from Hairaisers and Martin Taylor was kept extremely busy on the sewing machine, inventing outrageous creations with the fabrics that I'd bought from sources I'd been using since I'd first started this game.

Moving was inevitable but the idea of flat-hunting was daunting for one as indecisive as me, and the issue was avoided for the moment. However, as often happens, a series of events was about to force my hand.

\*

I had two weeks off in the whole of 1994 and the amount of work I got through is staggering. Two national tours, a fairly short one around the smaller theatres first with Bob Downe, followed by a much longer one with Caroline Aherne and Gayle Tuesday that took me into the next year. It coincided with the launch of a video I'd made one Sunday at the Fortune Theatre called *Paying the Rent*.

The company who made the video normally made adult movies and I was most put out when I sat down to watch it and found that the trailers advertising forthcoming attractions were of hard gay porn. I complained about this, reasoning that if they wanted the video to sell to a wider audience then why was it being marketed as a gay video? It wasn't a happy relationship and I hated having to sit in the local HMV in whatever town I'd rocked up in on the never-ending tour dressed in full drag in an attempt to flog the bloody thing.

In one shop they put me in the window one afternoon and I sat there mortified as a gang of football supporters banged on the glass shouting, 'Show us yer tits,' and other such original inanities. I could empathize with those Amsterdam hookers who plied their trade in dimly lit windows.

*Lifeswaps* was a series for BBC North with a very simple premise in which people from different backgrounds traded places with each other. A copper from Washington swapped with a village bobby, an Essex girl with a debutante, a barman from Heaven nightclub with the barman of a pub in the remote Yorkshire village of Middlesmoor, and so the list went on. The possibilities were endless and Lily presided over the proceedings as a sort of fairy godmother figure.

It was an interesting experiment seeing how people coped in an alien environment way outside their comfort zones and the outcome was often surprising. The cop from Washington loved village life, and his swap adapted remarkably well to finding himself on one of the most dangerous beats in the USA. The Essex girl, defying all stereotypes, held her own and won everyone over with her quiet charm and grace, while the debutante had the Essex lads eating out of her hand as she proved that she was most definitely no snob.

The barman from Heaven didn't fare quite so well. His idea of hell on earth was the quiet hamlet of Middlesmoor. Forced to go without make-up and put on a shirt and tie instead of his usual lairy garb, he pulled pints of bitter behind the bar of the Crown with a broken heart. His counterpart, on the other hand, once he'd got over the initial shock of finding himself serving drinks in one of Europe's biggest gay discos, overcame his shyness and took to life in the Big Smoke like a duck to water. I think he was sorry when his girlfriend arrived to take him back home.

We filmed the series every weekend and each Friday I'd take the train up to Manchester as I'd been doing for years, although this time I was filming instead of working Rockies club. Rockies was definitely the easier option as I now found myself in drag for the best part of the day and in all sorts of absurd locations. I was supposed to be travelling around the country overseeing my swaps in a battered old caravan and I changed in this jalopy. When that wasn't available, I changed in the back room of pubs, people's homes, public toilets and once behind a hedge in a field. On one occasion I found myself in the middle of the Welsh mountains dressed as Snow White.

On Saturday mornings I became a familiar sight clacking through the deserted Palace Hotel at the crack of dawn in a wide variety of whorey outfits. The hotel, a former insurance office, hadn't been open very long and even though it was an impressive building it still wasn't very busy. Neil Crombie, the producer, called it 'The Shining' and what regular guests there were got used to having their breakfast with Lily Savage, hardly batting an eyelid.

I enjoyed making *Lifeswaps*. Neil was great fun to work with and apart from suffering the indignities of parading through the streets in full drag I had a great time of it.

One of my ambitions was finally fulfilled that year and that was to present *Top of the Pops*. E17 were number one and it was still shot in the same old way that it had been for years. You stood surrounded by teenagers bopping away as you introduced the next guest and while the act sang to backing tracks (well, some of them did but there was also a lot of miming going on) you charged across the studio to the next location and stood among a different group of teenagers, who were either trying to look nonchalant or gurning at the camera and waving at their mates back home.

It was all filmed live so there was no room for error and the time just sped by, and I can safely report that nobody tried to touch me up.

Another memorable job was filming *Late Licence* with Gayle Tuesday. In a tiny studio in the basement of Channel 4 on Horseferry Road we recorded links for the shows that were shown throughout the night, in other words, the graveyard shift. Brenda (Gayle) and I ad-libbed the entire thing, and what were supposed to be brief links became twenty-minute epics, invariably ending up with Lily blind drunk and Gayle apologizing for her. We flew very close to the wind with some of the stuff we came out with, but as it was going out in the wee small hours of the morning it didn't matter.

We had a ball making these and eventually they became so popular the channel would occasionally drop the scheduled repeat and leave us to ramble on instead.

*Late Licence* became a cult among students and Brenda and I were amazed when we were approached and had whole scenarios quoted at us word for word that neither of us could remember saying as we'd simply improvised. I worked well with Brenda. The character of Gayle Tuesday, Page Three Stunner, was extremely funny and an ideal foil for Lily and these links were a great opportunity for us both to allow our imaginations to run riot as we bounced off each other with increasingly absurd dialogue.

Murphy thought performing at the Royal Albert Hall as part of the bill for a Stonewall fundraiser alongside the likes of Elton John and Sting would be the most memorable occasion of my career so far, but it wasn't. It was an unbelievable experience, to say the least, but despite sitting in a dressing room alone with a shirtless Sting strumming on a guitar as he sang 'I've Got A Crush On You', that honour belongs to another night.

'He's into tantric sex,' Agnes, my dresser, had said knowingly at the time. 'He goes all night.'

'I don't care if he's into Irish dancing,' I murmured in reply, still dazed by the effect of being in such close proximity to the pure animal sexuality of the beautiful Sting, 'and he can go for as long as he wants.'

The icing on the cake of '94 belongs to the London Palladium. As promised, Murphy had booked it for Easter Sunday and I was the busiest person in London preparing for it. I had new costumes made and some of the flashier ones that Hush had left me when he died taken in and altered to fit. Simon (Betty Legs Diamond) came on board as choreographer again. As I wanted to do a send-up of Torville and Dean with Bob Downe, he set us to work on a complicated routine to *Boléro* that made us look as if we were skating. Brenda was heavily pregnant with her first child and it didn't help that she was suffering from permanent morning sickness, but she wasn't going to let that stop her. Along with Jimmy Somerville and the Tiller Girls (of course) she joined the troupe.

We had very little time for an actual rehearsal on the stage of the Palladium, just a few hours before the show, but the old revolve was still in place. Simon put it to good use as part of the Torville and Dean routine, changing a few of the well-rehearsed steps to accommodate this new bit of business, which panicked me slightly in case I messed it up.

'You're not nervous, are you, dear?' Agnes asked as he always did.

'No, I'm fine,' I lied as I stared into the mirror of the number one dressing room, the same room where Judy Garland, Frank Sinatra, Marlene Dietrich and just about every other great star who'd ever appeared here had done at one time or another.

Our brief dress rehearsal had been disastrous. Brenda was chucking up into a bucket with the force of the kid from *The Exorcist*, and a fiery club manager from Wolverhampton, who was not amused at having his Easter Sunday act cancel on him as somehow I'd been double-booked, was threatening to come down and disrupt the show.

Murphy had promised to 'lay him out' if he so much as put his foot in the door, which did nothing to alleviate my nerves.

'Never mind, dear, you know what they say,' Agnes said, wincing as a curl of smoke dangling from his lip caught his eye, 'a good dress rehearsal makes for a bad show.'

'It's the other way round, you dozy mare,' I told him.

'You know what I mean, hen.' He was gathering up my costume for the quick change. 'I'll just take these up to the wings, dear. Will you be all right on your own? You're not going to lock yourself in the bathroom like Judy, are you?'

'No, I'm going to hang from the light fitting like Bela Lugosi. Now will you please bugger off?'

It was good to be on my own. As I'd been too preoccupied worrying about the show to have time to gather my thoughts, at that moment I allowed panic to set in.

'Pack it up,' I said to the reflection in the mirror. 'It's a bit late to start bloody fretting now, so get a grip and get on with it.'

'Who are you talking to?' Murphy asked, strolling into the room.

'Myself, and you're supposed to knock.'

'Bollocks, and what were you talking about?'

'I was giving myself a pep talk,' I told him, turning from the mirror to face him. 'I'm a bit worried about how this show is going to go, to be honest.'

'Budge up.' He pulled up a chair next to mine. 'You've nothing to worry about, Savage, believe me. The fates won't allow it.'

This made me laugh. 'Since when did you believe in fate?' I asked him.

'Since now,' he said, gripping my shoulder to grab my full attention. 'Listen to me. This is your Gypsy Rose Lee moment.'

'How d'ya mean?' I asked, bemused by this as Murphy didn't have a camp bone in his body and was most certainly not into musicals, preferring football, Joni Mitchell and *The Teachings of Don Juan* by Carlos Castaneda to people bursting into song mid-sentence.

'This is it. This is your Minsky's,' he explained patiently. 'You've done it, Savage, just as she did. You've achieved the unattainable and worked your way up from being a drag queen in gay pubs to topping the bill at the London Palladium. Didn't she do the same? Work her way up from humble origins in what is considered by some a dubious profession to star at the most famous theatre in the world?'

This analogy tickled me pink and I was amazed that he'd even thought along these lines. Normally he was so pragmatic and not fanciful in the least, but knowing that I was a big fan of both the musical and Miss Lee herself he'd made this tenuous link.

'You must treasure moments like this,' he said, 'as they don't come along for everybody.'

I understood and nodded in agreement.

'Now go out there and show that full house just what you're made of, kid,' he said as he was leaving, in a mock-American accent. 'Are you ready?'

'Open the cage, Murphy,' I replied, as always with false bravado, 'and let me out.'

Before you enter the wings of the Palladium there is an enormous mirror with an elaborate frame in the hallway that

I think they built the theatre around. I stopped to check myself as thousands of others had done before me, and, satisfied with what I saw, I took my place on stage at the top of a flight of stairs ready to make my descent to 'I'll Build A Stairway To Paradise'.

'Break a leg, dear,' Agnes hissed from the wings and before I knew it we were off.

Despite my worries, the show went without a hitch, everyone went down a storm and the Torville and Dean routine brought the house down. Brenda managed not to throw up and despite her advanced stage of pregnancy squeezed into her Miss Electra outfit and caused hysterics as her bits lit up when she joined Betty Legs and myself for the ubiquitous 'You Gotta Have A Gimmick'.

As Tessie Tura the Texas Twirler, Simon (Betty) executed a perpetual spin at breakneck speed from one side of the stage to the other. What with Gayle's light bulbs and the Texas Twirler my poor old bugle dance had some heavy competition. Nothing I couldn't handle though . . .

We ended the show in the traditional Palladium way, with the Tillers going round one way on the revolve and the cast going round the other on the inner revolve. I'd stuck Vera on it dressed in an old coat and headscarf. He was in seventh heaven as he went round and round clutching a carrier bag from Bejams and waving to the audience. I came up on the drum that rose slowly from the centre wearing an elaborate turquoise creation of Hush's to which Martin and I had gone cross-eyed glueing thousands of small diamantés.

Going around on the revolve at the London Palladium should be available on the NHS as a cure for depression. As I stood there spinning slowly to Val Parnell's familiar finale music and a standing ovation I remember thinking that Murphy was right. It doesn't get any better than this. Whatever happened from here on in, I would never forget this magical night.

# CHAPTER 9

'**Y**OU WOULDN'T BELIEVE WHAT'S GOING ON UP HERE,' I fumed down the phone to Regina from my room at the Imperial Hotel, Blackpool.

'Well, it can't be any worse than Tuesday night at the Cap, darling,' Reg moaned. 'Count your blessings, Miss Saveloy, you haven't got drunken dykes to deal with.'

'I'll swap with you,' I groaned. 'Gimme the lairy dykes any night of the week. I've got a sound man who doesn't know what he's doing, a floor manager who's never floor-managed before, a director who's very young and has only worked on regional news previous to this epic, the lighting stinks and—'

'William!' Reg shouted, interrupting me mid-moan. 'Sorry, dahling, but William's about to jump out of the window. William! Will you please come down, dear.'

William wasn't a suicidal partner about to take a death leap. William was Reg's cat. He had another one who lived under the bed because she mistrusted the world and everyone in it, and only came out to eat and use the litter tray.

'Sorry, dahling, where were we?' Reg continued, William having obviously been talked down from the windowsill. 'Oh, yes, the LilyDrome, tell me all about it, dear, Mother Fong's all ears.'

*Live at The LilyDrome* was an hour-long production for Granada filmed in the Leyton Institute Club, Blackpool, a social club of the old school that, like so many of its ilk, has now sadly closed down.

The *Wheeltappers and Shunters Social Club* had been a big TV hit in its day and we were trying to recreate the atmosphere of a genuine northern working-class club complete with pies, peas, bingo and cabaret. To give it a twist there was a flimsy backstage plotline involving Lily's attempts to run an ailing working-men's club after inheriting it from her aunty.

The Leyton was a perfect venue and I really enjoyed my time there, working to an audience of club regulars, even if the crowd was a bit thin on school nights. I had hoped Granada might've hired a coach and brought a gang over from Manchester, but then I'd hoped for quite a few things on this show that had so far failed to materialize.

We had some great guests on that show: Boy George, The Three Degrees, and one of my idols, Mr George Melly, with John Chilton's Feetwarmers. I got to join him in a duet of his immortal version of 'Frankie And Johnny'.

We had singers and speciality acts and a host of comics, including the old faithfuls Bob Downe and Gayle Tuesday, and Jayne Tunnicliffe who, as her alter ego the slutty, ukulele-strumming Mary Unfaithful, I was to work a lot with in the future. Like Jayne, another comic I admired was Blackpool's Johnnie Casson, a traditionalist who'd cut his teeth in the working-men's clubs. To watch the man work was to see a master class in comedy.

Some of the London comics didn't go down too well with the Leyton crowd. Mark Lamarr had a lousy time with them. Even though he was on top form his material wasn't to the regulars' taste. It's what I meant by getting a coach party over – a bit of audience diversity wouldn't have gone amiss.

Although I didn't think much of the production values, I've got happy memories of that show. Ian McKellen agreed to play the parish priest who officiated at Lily's daughter's wedding. He later excommunicated her from the Union of Catholic Mothers for her drunken behaviour, but that didn't stop him from imbibing himself and taking to the dance floor with Liz Dawn, Vera from *Corrie*, wearing a biker's jacket over his cassock.

An old friend from Liverpool, the actress Jackie Downey, together with another *Corrie* stalwart, Cheryl Murray, better known as Elsie Tanner's lodger Suzie Birchall, played the cleaner and the bitchy barmaid respectively. Cheryl was great but she didn't do stairs. She wasn't being awkward; she genuinely suffered from a condition called bathmophobia (a fear of stairs), which meant rewriting a few scenes, although she did brave the cellar steps for a scene that we couldn't relocate.

The series was filmed over two weeks of long days, long nights and a lot of writing, frustration, fish and chips and cider. When it eventually went to air I was disappointed as it hadn't lived up to my original expectations and I was so embarrassed by it I didn't want to go out and have to face people. Until, that is, I received a phone call from a certain comedy legend.

'I'm a head-shaking-in-admiring-wonder, gurgling-deep-down-with-laughter-and-whisky-going-down-my-nose-type Lily Savage fan,' he told me as I stood holding the receiver to my ear, open-mouthed in disbelief as I listened to the unmistakable voice of Mr Bob Monkhouse. Bob was a friend of Jayne Tunnicliffe's and I suspected she might have said something to him about how despondent I was over the series. For Bob, comedy wasn't just an occupation, it was a vocation and he loved to encourage any new comedy talent that he rated.

'I agree with you about the production side of things, which isn't right,' he said, but don't you worry as Lily shines through and I adore her.'

I was fortunate to get to work alongside Bob over the years and unusually for a comedian he was an especially generous performer, always making sure that you got your fair share of the laughs.

For a night owl like me who wasn't and isn't at his best at the crack of dawn, signing up for a job that required getting up at 4 a.m. might seem strange. The job in question was replacing Paula Yates interviewing celebs on a bed in the hugely popular *Big Breakfast*.

I'd previously appeared on the show once or twice to plug the tours and, apart from the unholy hour, I'd really had a good time. Paula was very giggly throughout the interview, which was conducted lying down on The Bed, but she was a great interviewer and very smart and I liked her a lot. We shared a love for a writer who went by the name of Miss Read, who wrote a series of books about life in the fictional villages of Thrush Green and Fairacre. Surprising bedtime reading for a wild child who had achieved an enormous amount of notoriety. I'm talking about Paula here, of course, not me, you under-stand, and so keen was she on these absorbing tales of the life of a country headmistress that she'd gone and written her own account of her experiences of living in a village community, called *Village People*, even dedicating the book to Miss Read.

It seemed common knowledge that although married to Bob Geldof she was having a sexually charged affair with Michael Hutchence. 'Torrid' was what Barbara Cartland would have called it; my ma would have described it with far stronger words.

Getting changed in the tiny make-up room after the show,

Paula was surprisingly indiscreet. She spoke enthusiastically of her affair with Hutchence, treating both me and the make-up girl to a graphic description of just how wonderful he was in bed.

'Aren't you worried about Bob finding out?' I asked her, wondering if in fact that was exactly what she wanted to happen.

'He wouldn't care anyway,' she replied, shrugging her shoulders, 'and neither do I. I just want to be with Mr X.' I don't know why she gave him a pseudonym. Apparently everyone apart from Bob was fully aware of who Mr X was.

Inevitably Bob and Paula split up, their acrimonious separation played out each day on the front pages of the tabloids and, given the circumstances, Paula had to go, even though *The Big Breakfast* was a show that her husband had originally conceived of as a vehicle for her.

I dithered at first when I was asked to take over. I didn't want to be seen stepping into a job on the back of someone else's misfortune, and then there was the little matter of having to get up in the middle of the night and put all the gear on before the sun had even risen.

Murphy was having none of it. 'Are you mad, Savage?' he argued. 'This is a fabulous opportunity for you. If they like you, then they want to sign you up for a year.'

'A year?' I squawked. 'A year of getting up at that hour of the morning? I'm a nightclub act, I don't do days.'

'The money's good. Well, their original offer wasn't, but it is now after a bit of hard-nosed negotiating on my part.'

I sympathized with the producers of the show. I knew Murphy didn't pull his punches when it came to negotiating fees.

'I've also got you a costume allowance as I should imagine you're going to need at least three new ones a week,' he went on, highly delighted with himself but trying hard to conceal it.

'Plus you get picked up every morning by car and taken home again when you finish.'

'But the hours, Murphy, I'll never be able to get up,' I moaned, even though I knew that the deal had been done and dusted and my protests fell on deaf ears.

'You'll just have to go to bed early then, won't you?' he said, a note of impatience in his tone. 'Turn your body clock around and train yourself to get up earlier.'

'Train myself? What do you think I am? A performing seal?'

'It'd be a lot easier if you were,' he said, picking up the phone and ringing the producers. 'Now you'd best get to bed early tonight in training for Monday morning.'

'And what will you be doing?' I asked.

'Going out, of course,' he replied.

Bloody typical.

*The Big Breakfast* greeted the public live at 7 a.m., five mornings a week. The house where the show was filmed had been a couple of lock-keepers' cottages on Fish Island in Bow, East London, knocked into one. Its former occupants wouldn't recognize it if they came back, not unless they too had a penchant for decorating in psychedelic colours.

The interior of the house always reminded me of the Joker's headquarters in the 1960s *Batman* series. As well as the alarming decor, the camera angles were often shot in the same crazy fashion. The show was fast-paced, loud and brash, with the emphasis on Fun, Fun, Fun!

Lily was dressed accordingly, thanks to Martin, who was spending most of the day and night chained to his sewing machine churning out a variety of pyjamas, basques, dressing gowns and other such creations suitable for an early morning Lily. He also made me a bright yellow frock adorned with appliqué fried eggs, and a fake fur and bright pink Lycra poodle outfit complete with a tail and ears. All the garments were made out of suitably lurid fabrics with a slightly cartoonish feel to suit the mood and decor of the show. On some mornings my outfits clashed so violently with the set you needed sunglasses to watch in comfort.

Getting up was a nightmare. Even though I went to bed every night in the week at 8 p.m. it never got any easier. The show came off air at 9 a.m. and if I wasn't doing anything, which wasn't very often, then all I wanted to do was crawl back into the sack and drift off into a coma. But I'd learned that if I did that then I wouldn't sleep at night, so I made every effort to keep busy and out of the bed. I went around in a permanent state similar to jet lag. Even if I was desperate to go out and see people and have a drink, I never did. I was always terrified that I'd sleep in the next morning.

The two main presenters were Mark Little and Gaby Roslin. Mark I knew well from the Edinburgh Festival, and Gaby, the girl next door, couldn't be more welcoming. I love Gaby Roslin. She's one of the good guys and we've been friends ever since.

Gaby was warm and encouraging, constantly hassling the producers to give me more air time, as quite often all I did was the ten-minute interview on the bed. I was more than keen to join in the insanity – I didn't feel I was giving value for money or being used to my full potential just doing the interviews. Eventually they got the message and started to use me more.

Some mornings I'd appear at the top of the show crashing about in the kitchen area in a wig full of soup-can rollers and dark glasses looking as if I'd been out on the lash all night, while Mark and Gaby tried to do the opening link over the racket.

There were various insane competitions, one of them called Beat the Banger. This involved running around the day's celebrity guest as they stood in the garden while holding a sausage and singing the 'Beat the Banger' theme song. One damp cold morning I found myself doing this with Cher, who gamely shrugged the drizzle off and acted as if she got involved in this sort of nonsense every day.

The lighting in the bedroom where the interviews took place was not in the least bit flattering. In fact, it would make a fresh-faced 16-year-old look like a 60-year-old ravaged by time and heroin. Jacqueline Bisset was less than impressed when she saw it.

'Is this the lighting?' she asked, in the same tone of voice Marie Antoinette might have employed on seeing her cell in the Bastille. 'Oh my dear God,' she moaned softly when I told her it was, and resignedly she shouted for make-up before she climbed on the bed.

Dora Bryan was an actress I'd always loved and together we teamed up for a slot in which we acted as a pair of agony aunts, reading out the viewers' messages and answering their questions when they phoned in. Dora was a naturally funny lady; she was also an accomplished actress who could switch from heartbreaking pathos to comedy in a flash. She had it all: the face, the mannerisms and that unmistakable voice, and some of the advice that Dora handed out was priceless, if rather near the knuckle. Delivered as it was in her vague manner, she got away with murder.

Mickey Rooney, on the other hand, was not very nice when he appeared on the show. He came across as an angry little turkey cock of a man, who could turn it on for the camera at the drop of a hat, transforming himself into the warm, humble old pro I'd naively assumed this multi-talented Hollywood legend was like in 'real life'. Perhaps his circumstances had a lot to do with his mean disposition. Whatever it was, I was to hear many Mickey Rooney stories, none of them favourable, from people who appeared with him in panto some time later.

Robin Williams was the exact opposite. His first words on seeing me sprawled out on the bed were: 'What have we got here? A ten-dollar whore in a two-dollar joint?' I told him that I didn't do Greek and to wash his bits in the sink before we got down to business and off we went, Robin giving a great interview. Superb at improvisation, he got the whole Lily gag and really enjoyed himself playing along with me.

Later on he told me that he loved performers who adopted different personas and developed them until they became fully rounded individuals in their own right. When the time came for him to promote his film *The Birdcage*, it was Lily he asked to join him in Germany for an interview. I flew over with Murphy and a small film crew and got to spend the day with him. After the filming was over we had dinner in the hotel restaurant.

He spoke mainly of his early days as a stand-up in San Francisco. He was full of fun and seemed genuinely content with his life. He certainly gave no indication that one sad day in the future he would take his own life.

I've long forgotten most of the stars I interviewed during my twelve-month stint on the show, but I do remember that there were some impressive names on that list. I lay on that bed with Pierce Brosnan, Bob Geldof, Patrick Swayze, Cher, Robert Downey Junior, Claudia Schiffer, Kate Moss, to name but a few. I'd sung 'Falling In Love Again' with Neil Sedaka accompanying me on the piano, done the nanananananas for James Brown as he sang 'It Feels Good', and joined Kenny Rogers for a duet of 'Islands In The Stream'. It was an exciting time. Along the way I got to meet some of my idols from the world of music, stage and screen, and I wasn't disappointed.

\*

239

*This Morning with Richard and Judy* was at the height of its popularity. The show was still being filmed in Liverpool at the Albert Dock studios and if you were appearing on it then you were flown up from London in the Richard and Judy jet, which seemed all very glamorous.

A car was waiting for you when you landed on the runway at the John Lennon airport to whisk you to the studio, and champagne and canapés were served on board. Ah, the good old days of telly when they had money to spend, and did. I usually went straight from the *Big Breakfast* studio to the airport in full drag, riding pillion on a motorbike with my holdall strapped on the back, and the wig in its usual bin liner so I could get the helmet on.

I'd made my debut on the show earlier in the year and to everyone's amazement, including my own, I slotted into *This Morning* with ease, becoming a regular guest over the years. I loved making Judy laugh, which wasn't hard to do. I knew she could get quite nervous in front of the cameras so I would quite often hold her hand and talk nonsense until she finally cracked up, calling me a fool.

I never turned down a request to join Richard and Judy on the sofa. The show was a perfect vehicle for Lily, and I was, and am, very fond of the pair of them. The show's agony aunt Denise Robinson is bliss. That lady, apart from being a beautiful human being, is a comic's dream. She can play the perfect straight man (or should that be woman?), managing to maintain a deadpan expression whatever you throw at her, no matter how outrageous or obscure.

We'd answer some of the viewers' problems together, which was normally fairly light-hearted stuff and nothing that heavy – until one morning a woman who was a long-term victim of domestic abuse rang in.

We listened in horror as she told the sickening tale of how

her husband came home from work and used her as a punchbag. Denise gave sound advice but I, of course, went the other way. Lily advocated waiting until this drunken yob had gone to bed and then, when the woman was sure he was sound asleep, setting about him with a baseball bat, letting him know that each time he hit *her* this was what would happen, reminding him that he always had to go to sleep at some point.

There was a bit of a stink over that one, as you can imagine, but many of the viewers got in touch to say how much they agreed with me.

Personally I'd have murdered him and fed him to the pigs, but it's not advisable to say that sort of thing on daytime telly, especially when you're slotted in between an item on mohair sweaters and the parents of a little boy with hydrocephalus.

Then there was the oft-repeated wine-tasting incident in which Lily got maudlin drunk, sang the Russian lament 'Dark Eyes' and threw glasses with gay abandon into the Albert Dock before collapsing. I thought Judy was going to have a seizure, she was laughing so much. The crew were pretty much in hysterics as well, although I don't think that Charles, the well-informed wine expert, was very happy at being upstaged. However, I'd like to say here and now that not a drop passed my lips that morning and I was sober as a judge. It was all just an act.

I was about to turn forty and not happy about it. Forty not only seemed so old but it had come round far too quickly. I didn't want to know. I preferred to pretend it hadn't happened. Not a chance there when you worked with Zig and Zag, though, as they made sure they announced it. 'Aunty Lily is forty today,' they chanted gleefully, and to rub it in even further there was a party on the bed, with a banner hanging above it proclaiming *Happy Fortieth Birthday, Lily* for all the world to see.

Zig and Zag were two extra-terrestrials from the planet Zog who were in reality a couple of puppets, although I never treated them as such. To me they were real, and that was the secret when working alongside them – even though I had Ciaran Morrison and Mick O'Hara, the puppeteers, sitting on the floor with their heads wedged beneath my legs.

As a birthday treat Murphy had booked me into a suite at the Savoy for the weekend and one of the first things I did was to get on the phone and invite Regina round for tea.

'What are you doing this evening then?' he asked casually, daintily dabbing at the corners of his mouth with a snowy white linen napkin in case any crumbs from the cucumber sandwich he'd just demolished were lurking there. 'Any plans?'

'We're going for a meal somewhere,' I told him. 'I don't know where. Murphy's arranged it.'

'Oh,' he said, staring out of the window, unable to meet my eyes. He seemed on edge and I wondered if perhaps it was because he felt uncomfortable in the plush surroundings of the Savoy, being waited on by my own personal butler.

After an initial shyness at finding myself in such opulent surroundings and an uncomfortable feeling that at any moment the management might unmask me as a fraud and throw me out, I took to life at the Savoy like a duck to water.

For me, who'd never stayed in a hotel as grand as this before, it was as if I'd been transported into another world. Unable to resist the splendour of the film-star bathroom, I must have taken at least four baths in less than 24 hours. This magnificent marble art deco bathroom was the stuff of dreams, and a million light years away from my own humble bathing facilities back at Vicky Mansions. To be able to stretch right out in a sandalwood-scented bath that went up to my chin and then step out on to a warm marble floor and envelop myself in one of the many carpet-thick towels on offer was the best present of all.

Murphy had said that he'd arranged for a Rolls-Royce to pick me up to take me to the restaurant. 'The chauffeur is an extremely handsome Russian,' he told me, 'and he'll be coming up to the room to get you.' I prayed that he hadn't gone and got me an 'escort', no matter how stunningly good-looking he was. After having taken another bath and got dressed in my brand new Giorgio Armani suit, bought that day in Harvey Nichols at what I considered to be enormous expense, I'd hate to have to take it all off again for a quick Rumble with the Russian. At 8 p.m. exactly the phone rang. It was the Russian, telling me in a thick accent that reeked of samovars and troikas that he was coming up to my room and was looking forward to 'getting to know' me.

The bastard. He did get me a prozzie. I'll kill him. These were the thoughts that raced through my mind as I replaced the receiver and threw back a glass of champagne in one, shuddering violently as it hit the back of my throat, for champagne was a taste I'd yet to acquire.

There was a loud knock on the door and, bracing myself for the ravaging, I opened it, only not to Ivan the Terrible, but to Ian McKellen.

'*Privyet!*' he shouted. 'Happy birthday, darling.'

Thank God I didn't have to take the suit off.

Outside the Savoy a Rolls-Royce was waiting to take us to dinner. However, as we approached the Playhouse Theatre I saw a woman who looked just like my cousin Marje, then there was a woman who was the dead ringer for my sister, then the penny dropped. It *was* my sister as well as my entire family and all of my friends.

'Surprise!' they all shouted as two youths clad only in leather jockstraps hauled me out of the back of the Roller.

'You bastard, Murphy,' I hissed, embarrassed, confused, and not amused that I'd had a surprise sprung on me.

I loathe surprises. When they were going to do a *This is Your Life* on me, I found out and quickly put the kibosh on it, refusing point blank to participate if Michael Aspel jumped out from behind a bush with his big red book and tried to persuade me to accompany him to the studio. I couldn't think of anything worse than having to sit there wearing a fixed rictus grin as people from my past that I don't know or more importantly don't want to know were paraded out to pay phoney homage. I feel the same way about surprise birthday parties, but I was touched that Murphy had gone to all this trouble, and it was great to see everyone. So what the hell – instead of running I joined the throng, played mine host and got suitably bladdered, and a good time was had by all.

The party continued back at the Savoy after the Playhouse had turfed us out and my suite was like a scene out of *The Great Gatsby*. Lines of coke were being racked out on top of the marble dresser, a couple were locked in my beautiful bath-room going at it hammer and tongs, up against my sink no doubt, and the booze, courtesy of an overworked room service, just kept on coming. Thank God my sister had gone back to her hotel.

The last time I was at the Edinburgh Festival, with a few drinks inside me, I'd collared Mal Young, the producer of the Scouse soap *Brookside*, and cheekily asked him when he was going to offer me a part in it. He promised he would, and true to his word a year later he rang to ask if Lily would like to open Barry Grant's new restaurant. The premise was that the stuttering gangster Sizzler had arranged with Barry to send a celebrity to do the honours, that celebrity being a 'big blonde from Birkenhead'.

Jimmy Corkhill was roped in to play chauffeur for the day, driving Lily in the back of one of those embarrassing-to-be-seen-in-unless-you're-on-a-hen-night stretch limos, and as Jimmy's current storyline had him addicted to coke – the drug, not the smokeless fuel – I thought it might be very funny and completely in character if, when we pulled up outside the restaurant, I should get out of the car, sniff, wipe my nose with the back of my hands and say, 'Thanks for that, Jimmy.' Well, if Jimmy was snorting his brains out at the wheel, then Lily, if offered, wouldn't be averse to taking a toot off the side of her handbag as a little livener either.

Unfortunately the director didn't agree with this bit of method acting and so we went for another take, only this time without the sniff and the nod to Jimmy's addiction. I was over the moon at being asked to appear in *Brookie*, but then it seemed that these days I was being offered all sorts of jobs that I'd never have imagined Vauxhall Lily doing.

'You'll be on kids' programmes next,' Murphy said, making me wonder for a moment if he was trying to get me on *Blue Peter*. 'Talking of which, I've got a script here . . .'

'I wouldn't mind being in that,' Liz Smith said to me during a break in filming some weeks later. 'I've always fancied being in a West End musical.'

Liz is a versatile actress who is equally at home in a Pinter play or sitting on the sofa as Nan in *The Royle Family*. She'd come into acting quite late in life, fifty to be exact, having spent her time raising two children on her own in extremely difficult circumstances, and this talented lady hasn't stopped working ever since. I always thought that if they were ever considering a woman to play Doctor Who then they'd do no better than casting the wonderfully eccentric Liz.

'Yes, I wouldn't mind being in a nice musical,' she said, staring into space as she absent-mindedly adjusted her tricorne hat. 'Be a nice change.'

Liz suited her costume for Grandma Blood, the matriarch of a family of pirates who had forsaken a life at sea and settled on dry land in a council house. Based on the popular children's book, *Pirates* had been turned into a BBC children's sitcom that was as anarchic as it was bizarre with a variety of wacky characters, such as a luminous baby in a pram who glowed green, and the Man in the Sack who was, well, a man in a sack.

I was playing a character called Bang Bang Chicken, an old nemesis of Grandma Blood's, an eastern procuress who had turned up with a Girl in a Bag as an appropriate mate for the Man in the Sack. Well, every pan has a lid and that was a perfect pairing.

There were lots of laughs on that set because the dialogue was so ridiculous. Imagine trying to keep a straight face while sitting on a chaise longue dressed as a particularly oddball geisha seducing the actor Paul Bown and spouting lines like: 'You can call me Miss Chicken. May I call you Mr Enormous?'

My particular episode ended with Bang Bang, Granny Blood and Rebecca Stevens as the foul-mouthed Grog Blossom Kate playing mah-jong, smoking our heads off and getting blind drunk. Alcohol abuse? Tobacco? Gambling? And on a children's programme? Compliance would fill their knickers these days and OFCOM would no doubt be inundated with complaints from those extra-sensitive parents demanding that the licence fee be abolished etc, etc. Of course, the kids the programme was aimed at loved it.

Liz had been very interested when I told her that my next venture was going to be *Prisoner Cell Block H the Musical*.

Ashley Herman, an experienced producer of West End musicals, was keen to find a show for Lily, but what? I could hardly see her as Maria von Trapp or Fanny Brice. Besides, don't you have to be able to sing to be in musical theatre? I'd rather be horsewhipped naked down Oxford Street than stand in front of a packed house and attempt to 'sing' a straight ballad. In the end we decided to write a musical of our own called *Tales of Tinseltown*, a story not dissimilar to *42nd Street* and *Sunset Boulevard*, about an ageing bitchy star (Lily) and a young fresh ingénue (to be played by Helena Bonham Carter).

I wrote some scenes and even a song but the appeal of this idea began to wane, and so did our initial enthusiasm. Eventually we abandoned the project.

'The only musical I'd be interested in doing is *Prisoner Cell Block H*,' I remember saying at a meeting in Ashley's office, only half joking because I was a massive fan of the show. 'I wish there was a script for that.' Be careful what you wish for . . .

It turned out that over in Australia there just so happened to be such a thing. What little I saw of this script wasn't up to much. They'd sent over a brief outline and a sample of the music and I wasn't impressed. There was a raunchy shower scene involving the women, and a sexy hunk of a doctor, none of which bore any relation to the original show. My heart sank.

Looking on the positive side, there were some interesting

plot ideas that could be developed, and quite a few of the songs were outstanding, in particular a raunchy rock number for the Freak, and a beautiful ballad for the Top Dog.

'It's got possibilities,' Ashley said hopefully, 'and we can always tweak it until we've got it just right.'

I nodded in agreement, without considering that tweaking a corpse isn't easy.

I'd been looking at flats for some time now. It's a miserable task. The places you can just about afford you don't like, while the ones you do like are well outside your price range.

I was keen to move now. I'd outgrown my little flat and, having been held up by a guy with a knife one night as I entered the block, I no longer felt the same affection for the area that I used to. He'd cornered me on the stairs demanding money while waving a knife around. I'd worked a private party in Bath and still had the cash fee in my back pocket but I was buggered if I was letting this piece of shit have it. There was some loose change in another pocket and a five-pound note which I offered him, explaining calmly that that was all I had, while all the time desperately trying to work out how to get the knife out of his hand. He didn't believe me and insisted that we go up to my flat for some money. I'd been to the shop on the way back and was carrying a carrier bag with two pints of milk in it, and an idea hit me. I explained that that wouldn't be a good idea as we were having a Tenants' Association meeting and my flat was full of neighbours.

'Hence the milk,' I added.

For a moment I thought he was going to stab me but instead he turned and ran off, muttering threats about how I shouldn't call the police if I wanted to live.

Of course the first thing I did was call the police as soon as

I got in, but the copper who eventually turned up wasn't much use, nor was the woman from Victim Support who 'popped in' to see how I was doing.

'It's really bad around here,' she said, perched on the end of the couch stirring the cup of tea I'd made her. 'You'd be safer walking through Harlem in the dead of night than down Dorset Road, and as for South Lambeth Road, well –' she paused to take a sip of her tea before continuing with her words of comfort – 'there's been more stabbings, muggings and break-ins along here than I'd care to mention.' I can't tell you how reassured I felt after her visit.

Lambeth Council had erected scaffolding around the block some years ago, where it had remained ever since. They'd covered it with a mesh which cast a greenish hue over the front room whenever the sun hit it. I called it the *Little Mermaid* effect and, despite the Wicked Witch complexion the mesh gave me, I enjoyed the scaffolding outside the window. I treated it as a balcony to hang washing on as well as a convenient walkway for dropping in on the neighbours.

Thanks to *The Big Breakfast*, there was some interest in the press to find out what the man behind Lily Savage really looked like. Consequently I came out of the bathroom one afternoon wrapped in a towel to find a gentleman of the paparazzi on the scaffolding, snapping away. Yes, it was time to change lodgings.

I wasn't prepared for such press intrusion, nor was my daughter, who was hounded by them. The *Sunday Mirror* in particular was for years unnaturally obsessed with my having a daughter. I'd never kept her a secret, but sitting outside a café in Turkey on a rare holiday I happened to glance over to the newsagent's next door to see a copy of that paper hanging outside and a front page that screamed out 'Lily Savage's Secret Daughter!!' Inside was a full-page article and a box at the bottom offering their readers a cash reward if they knew who Lily's secret daughter was, and if they did to 'ring this number'. Shameful. To make matters worse, a hack from the *Sunday Mirror* set up camp in the old Holiday Inn in Liverpool and went through all my family, friends and old workmates with a fine-tooth comb looking for some scandal about me and my daughter that they could use to hang us out to dry.

The press office for *The Big Breakfast* rang to say that the *Sunday Mirror* was cobbling together a story for the following week that was designed to blacken both my daughter's name and mine. So much for my holiday. After three days in Turkey I was back home again. Together my daughter and I gave an honest interview to *The Sun*, thereby scuppering the story the *Sunday Mirror* had planned, which they then had to withdraw.

I met the journalist responsible for this years later and he asked me if I hated him for what he'd done.

'Not at all,' I told him. 'You've got a job to do, if you can call it that.'

'Do you believe in reincarnation and the rule of karma,' he asked me, 'and do you think that if there is a next life I'll probably come back as a pile of dog shit for what I've done in this one?'

'Don't worry, you won't,' I told him. 'You see, you have to come back as something different in the next life.' And with that I moved swiftly on to where the air was purer.

After futile attempts at house hunting around south London, a friend finally pointed me in the direction of the area around Tower Bridge, where at last I found a suitable and, more importantly, affordable little house not far from the river.

I should've been delighted that I was getting out of the Mansions to go and live in a two-bedroomed house with central heating, endless wall sockets, a garage for the drag and a small back garden, but instead I packed away my belongings with a heavy heart, feeling as if I was deserting an old friend. I'm the type who can get attached to a hotel room after an overnight stay, and as I'd had connections with these Mansions since the seventies, having lived in various flats here over the years, saying goodbye to the tatty little hovel with all its memories that had been my home for over a decade was never going to be easy.

The cats had gone to live with Vera ages ago, as he finally had a flat of his own now, and one with a garden, no less. I was away touring so much that they spent more time with him than me. He was happy to take them, but parting was hard and I missed having them around.

My first night in the new house was spent sleeping on the front-room floor with no curtains on the window and surrounded by boxes and packing cases, an experience no doubt familiar to every first-time house buyer.

'What have I done, Murphy?' I whined out loud in the semi dark as I tried to get comfortable on my makeshift bed of pillows and coats. 'I want to go home.'

'What the bloody hell are you banging on about, Savage,' Murphy snapped back, in no mood for counselling at 3 a.m. 'This is your home. You've got a lovely house here, not a flat. A house, and one with a garden and in a great area to boot, so what's your problem?'

I didn't quite know what the problem was, except that the responsibility of being a home-owner after years of squatting and living in rented accommodation was a bit of a worry.

'I don't know,' I said after a while. 'I just feel . . . unsettled.'

'Then be like dust and settle, will you, and get to sleep,' he replied. 'You should be over the moon at getting out of Vicky Mansions, not bloody moaning.'

I lay quietly for a while before picking up the thread again.

'I hate that upstairs bathroom,' I said calmly.

Murphy exploded. 'You what? You've just come from a grade-A dump with a bathroom straight out of Ten Rillington Place and you're giving out about the one here? It's got a shower, for Christ's sake.'

'I don't like showers and I don't like those brown and beige tiles either,' I went on relentlessly.

'Then we'll get someone in to redecorate,' he roared. 'We'll knock walls down, make the kitchen and living room one big space, strip the bathroom out, lay wooden floors, build the hanging gardens of Babylon in the back yard if you like. Just get to fucking sleep, will you!'

'Garden,' I corrected him. 'It's not a back yard, it's a back garden with a patio.'

'Well, be careful I don't bury you under it, Savage,' he warned. 'Now get to bloody sleep and in the morning I'll introduce you to the joys of showering.'

The next morning I got on to my friend James, who is a builder, and set about revamping the gaff without even considering the expense, inconvenience and chaos involved. I just wanted the job done and I wanted it done yesterday.

In the end I lived in a building site for over a year. Not a good idea when you're working all the hours God sends and you have nowhere to relax when you get home. But it was worth it when it was finally finished, even if it did cost me a fortune and had me semi-demented.

\*

The script for *Prisoner* needed more than tweaking, it needed a major bypass. When the cast assembled in a rehearsal room in Waterloo for the first read-through of the script it became apparent that in its present state this show wasn't just a turkey, it was Mr Bernard Matthews's entire flock.

'I came all this way to appear on the West End stage in this?' Maggie Kirkpatrick complained bitterly, shaking her head angrily. 'What a load of bloody rubbish.'

I squirmed in my seat as she let off steam to the director. I'd been instrumental in getting her over here to recreate her role as the evil prison officer, Joan 'the Freak' Ferguson.

The call came as a surprise to Maggie. Back in Oz as far as she was concerned *Prisoner* was old news. It hadn't been on air for years and was remembered only by the diehard fans. It was a different story in the UK, though. *Prisoner* was still showing on Channel 4 and had a huge fan base of loyal enthusiasts, myself and Murphy among them.

'You can't do *Prisoner* without the Freak,' I'd argued. 'We need an original cast member, preferably a good villain, and as far as I'm concerned there's only one woman for the job, and that's the Freak. She's the driving force behind the show, and more importantly she'll get the punters in.'

The prospect of a season in the West End was too promising an offer for Maggie to turn down. She was unemployed and had nothing to lose so she packed her bags and hotfooted it over to Blighty. Now here she was, living in a basement flat in Doughty Street and about to make her West End debut in a 'load of bloody rubbish'.

I was in my element, getting a chance to work alongside my favourite screen villainess. She really was magnificent and compelling viewing in the part. The producers arranged for us to have dinner together at the Ivy so we could get to know each other. I picked her up in a cab at her basement flat, quivering in anticipation at getting to meet the notorious Joan Ferguson in the flesh. My ma and my aunty Annie, both *Prisoner* fanatics when they'd been alive, would never have believed it.

Apart from height and a commanding presence, Maggie turned out to be nothing like her television counterpart. I was greeted at the door by a charming, well-spoken lady elegantly dressed in black. Both of us had adopted our best party manners for the occasion, but thankfully as the night and the booze progressed we dropped the genteel act and allowed our true colours to shine through.

Maggie was a complex character, a typical old-school Aussie, blunt, outspoken and opinionated, who could come across as hard as nails when in reality she was quite a vulnerable soul. She became very emotional after a few drinks, especially when the conversation turned to her daughter and grandchildren, whom she missed and constantly worried about. She spoke very fondly of 'that old bugger' her ex-husband Fitzpatrick, a sailor from Northern Ireland whom she'd divorced some years ago. She had nothing but good to say about him.

Maggie and I got along just fine and I was looking forward to getting on stage with her. Now all we needed was a workable script.

'Right then,' said Maggie, sucking the end of her pencil as she studied the script in rehearsals. 'Let's see if we can't make something of this.'

We all pulled together. We wanted this show to work, and thankfully the cast were a multi-talented lot. They went home after rehearsals each night and wrote songs and dialogue – a highly unorthodox way of putting on a West End musical, I know, but there was no other option.

Apart from myself, and I was in drag, the only other male member of the cast was Jeff Perry, playing 'the Man from the Department'. Jeff was a talented songwriter and he came up with a witty duet for himself and Penny Morrell, the wife of actor George Cole, who'd been perfectly cast as Mrs Davidson, the Governor, who always brought the roof in.

As there was no mention of Lily in the original script, I had to find a way to write her in and find a reason to explain what she was doing banged up in a women's prison in Australia. I'd long sussed out that if this show was to be a success then we had to play it straight. Playing it for laughs with knowing winks to the gallery was strictly out, and if we stuck to this rule then the plot lines and dialogue could be as camp and implausible as we liked, which as it happened they were.

Lily had won a holiday in Australia for two after finding the winning ring-pull on a can of Fosters. Taking her sister Vera along to carry the cases, she'd ended up in court charged with shoplifting, soliciting and the murder of Vera, who had gone missing in mysterious circumstances after the pair of them had taken a trip to the beach.

Of course Lily was innocent, of killing Vera anyway, but the evidence against her was damning and she was committed to Wentworth Detention Centre for life.

Lily's first encounter with the Freak occurs in the reception area of the prison. The exchange between them set the tone for their relationship, as the battle lines were drawn.

The Freak, eyeing Lily up and down contemptuously as she checks the list on her clipboard: 'And you are?'

Lily: 'A lot taller than you, love.'

There had to be a Top Dog. Val Lehman, whose portrayal

of Bea Smith, the hard-bitten Top Dog in the telly show, had won her many accolades, was miffed at not being asked to recreate her role. The producers had never even considered using her, but when asked what she thought Miss Lehman had declared that the musical was making a mockery of the show and that having a drag queen in it was beyond ludicrous. Maggie was less than impressed by her old colleague's broadsides but, ever the pro, she kept her counsel with the press, only letting her real feelings be known in private, and there was certainly no love lost between those two.

We managed to cope without Bea Smith on the steam press thanks to a glorious Scottish actress by the name of Terri Neason, who made Steph, our formidable Top Dog, her own.

Terri was blessed with a voice that could break your heart, and this she did with each performance when she sang Don Battye and Peter Pinne's beautiful ballad 'I Never Told Him I Love Him', which she sang about her dead brother. She played Steph as a rock-hard, territorial thug who wasn't putting up with some Pom newcomer who might be after her crown. Terri was much shorter than me and of a bigger build. We made a comical pair as she swaggered across the stage with fists clenched, reminiscent of Popeye's arch enemy Bluto, and squared up to me.

Rehearsals were frantic. We had less than a month before we were due to open at the Queen's Theatre. There was no luxury of an out-of-town try-out for us. It was straight in with a matinee that was really a dress rehearsal and then the press night. Not even the benefit of a week's previews.

Tempers were frayed during rehearsals, to say the least. Tears were shed and more wobbles were thrown than during an earthquake in a jelly factory. The director, a creative but sensitive man who was better known for his work in opera and classical theatre, had quite a few divas to deal with, myself included. We'd have put any of the prima donnas at La Scala to shame.

One night, after a day that had begun when I left the house at 4 a.m., the director wanted to run through the fight scene between the Top Dog and Lily. A stunt coordinator had been brought in to choreograph this brawl in the laundry as it was pretty full on.

We were all exhausted, having been rehearsing since 10 a.m. As it was now nine at night and judgement was impaired because of tiredness, it was probably not a good idea to go through the fight scene again. However, we did, and through no fault of her own, Terri, wearing an enormous prop knuckleduster, mistimed a punch and I got it full force in the mouth, splitting my lip.

I ended up in A&E that night getting my lip stitched up, and a few hours later I lay slumped on the *Big Breakfast* bed with a lip like a fluke's gob.

I was tired, no, not tired, knackered. Getting up each morning at 4 a.m., doing *The Big Breakfast* and then spending all day in rehearsals followed by a night at home writing material was pretty exhausting. Grim determination to make this show work, fuelled by that dangerous drug adrenalin, somehow kept me firing on all cylinders.

I'd sit up fighting sleep in the rubble of what was once my new house writing scenes, mainly for me and Maggie. Inspired by the creative juices flowing in the rehearsal rooms I even wrote a couple of songs, one for me called 'I'm Innocent', and another little ditty entitled 'I Like You' for the old lag Minnie, played by Liz Smith, who'd meant what she said that time in the *Pirates* rehearsals about wanting to be in a West End musical. Most of the cast had great voices, and among them, playing 'the nice prisoner officer', was Alison Jiear, who has possibly one of the best voices in the business yet she didn't have a song in the show. So I wrote one for her, called 'Life's Not Easy When You're Nice', but I never took it in. I didn't think it was good enough for such a superb singer.

The set was exactly like what you saw on the television show: bare brick walls and iron bars, and even though I'd never seen the set wobble in all the time I'd been watching the programme – it was more than likely an urban myth, probably started by TV critics – to appease the punters we allowed one of our walls to wobble once; other than that the set was pretty solid. The costumes certainly didn't break the budget, just a few prison warder outfits and denim dungarees worn with yellow shirts for the women. The Lily outfits I supplied myself.

In the second act of the show the Freak, thanks to devious, underhand measures, has managed to achieve her ultimate goal, to rule supreme as the Governor. Dressed now in jodhpurs and leather boots, with her mannish haircut slicked back, she bumped and grinded her way through 'Gloves', a raucous homage to her fondness for slipping on her black leather gloves when conducting 'a full body search' of her latest victim. It was hilarious to watch Maggie giving 'Gloves' her all, one of the highlights of the show.

In an attempt to escape Governor Ferguson's fascist regime (she had a copy of *Mein Kampf* on her desk) the women decided to dig a tunnel. Ridiculous, I know, but bear with me here. To enable the women to engineer this escape, a diversion was needed. This came in the form of 'The Wentworth Follies', a low-rent Ziegfeld parade of women dressed in costumes made from whatever had come to hand in the prison.

Miss Infirmary wore an ingenious ensemble created out of bandages and sheets with a bed pan balanced on her head and a necklace of syringes draped around her throat. Miss Allotment wore a confection of astro turf, sacking and artificial fruit and veg. Miss Laundry had panniers on her hips made from plastic washing baskets and an astonishing headdress of washing powder packets complete with an artful arrangement of plastic bubbles.

Lily acted as MC, but once the parade of women was over the tempo changed. She went into a striptease, shedding the pale pink beaded outfit (don't ask how she acquired such a costume – the answer is far too convoluted), her modesty covered at the denouement by two cons holding a pair of battered feather fans that weren't quite big enough for my liking.

On opening night I'd been to work in the morning as usual on *The Big Breakfast*, heading straight to the theatre afterwards. The billboards had been up outside the theatre for a week now but I still couldn't get over the enormity of the head-and-shoulder shot of Lily in prison uniform behind bars that covered most of the frontage. I must have used up an entire roll of film taking photos of it.

Agnes had been roped in as dresser again and was busy in the dressing room laying out costumes on the single bed.

'Hello, hen,' he said, wincing from the smoke emanating from the fag wedged in the corner of his gob. 'Are you ready for this?'

Surprisingly – since I was about to make my West End theatre debut – I was. After the battleground of rehearsals and the struggle to get here I was ready for world war three, let alone a show. I was bored with talking about it now and eager to get on the stage and run the show in front of an audience.

'Open the cage, Agnes, and let me out there,' I said, and meant it.

The matinee performance before the press seemed to fly by and even though I wouldn't say I was completely relaxed, preoccupied as I was with concentrating on timing, lines and moves, I managed to enjoy myself.

The positive reception from the audience raised the cast's spirits. They laughed in all the right places as well as in quite a few where they weren't supposed to, and we got a standing ovation at the end, something we most definitely hadn't expected. Elated by the enthusiastic response, we felt that with just a little bit of luck this former turkey might metamorphose into a swan.

*The Biggest Blonde Star since Marilyn Monroe*, the *Independent* screamed. *A Huge Hit*, said the *Observer*. *An Absolute Hoot!* the *Guardian* declared. Jack Tinker in the *Mail* went overboard with his review and we even had an accompanying cartoon by Jak of Maggie and Lily.

'Bugger me,' Maggie gasped as she read the *Evening Standard*'s review. 'Looks like we got a hit on our hands, kid.'

'Maybe they felt sorry for us, Maggie,' I said, 'and gave us ten out of ten for trying.'

'What? These sharks?' she scoffed. 'They wouldn't give a drop of sympathy to a dying child. No, they liked it all right.'

I'd been completely bowled over by the reaction of the first-night audience. I've since learned from experience that first-nighters are normally a reserved lot. The presence of a coven of critics tends to create an atmosphere of tension both on and off the stage. Our audience was anything but and, relieved that we'd somehow pulled it off, Murphy and I, with a little help from Agnes, polished off two bottles of champagne in less than twenty minutes as soon as the curtain came down.

It felt good to be in a hit. It made all the worry and hard work worthwhile, and at the same time it wiped the smug expressions off the faces of the Doubting Thomases who either wanted the show to flop or were convinced that it would from the onset. Reassured but not made complacent by the glowing notices outside the theatre, we settled in for our twelve-week run.

What would you think was the last thing a person working virtually twenty-four hours a day and living in a bomb site needed? You're quite right, a dog.

One late November morning there was an item on *The Big Breakfast* involving dogs and I arrived to find the studio crawling with puppies. One in particular, a bichon frisé/shih tzu cross who was nothing more than a yapping ball of fluff, abandoned the lively game he was playing with his companions, marched confidently across the studio floor and plonked himself down on my foot.

'I'm going to keep this puppy,' I said to Barbara Windsor, who was dressed as a fairy and on the show to plug her forthcoming panto.

'How are you going to manage a dog with two shows on the go and a tour coming up?' she asked. 'Are you sure about this, darlin'?'

'Easy,' I told her. 'I'll put him in my handbag.'

I called him Buster Elvis Savage, and for the next twelve years he rarely left my side, accompanying me on tours and on every television job I ever did.

That night I took him into the theatre and let him wander around the stage before the curtain went up. He mooched about as if to the manner born and after a good sniff of the proscenium arch he cocked his leg and left his mark.

'Everyone's a critic,' remarked Maggie, who had gathered along with the rest of the cast to worship at the paws of the new arrival. Terri Neason, our fearsome Top Dog, cooed and aahed over Buster like a fairy godmother at a christening, offering her services as a babysitter any time I needed.

Murphy was less than impressed when he walked into the dressing room and found Buster sprawled out on the bed. 'That,' he said grimly, 'is not stopping. Get rid of it.'

Of course I ignored him completely and after a few days Murphy, like the rest of us, became one of Buster's, or the Todge as he called him for some unfathomable reason, most devoted followers.

Buster was born to lead a theatrical life. He loved touring; he was in his element backstage. When he wasn't ensconced in a cast member's dressing room poncing biscuits, he sat quietly next to the stage manager in the wings, watching the action on stage with a bored indifference before sloping off to my dressing room for a kip under the make-up shelf or in the velvet folds of a Wicked Queen's cloak.

Cher was another member of the Buster fan club. The evening after she'd appeared on the *Big Breakfast* show she came down to see *Prisoner*, providing, she claimed, that she could get her fix of Buster in the dressing room after the show.

Having Cher in the audience caused quite a stir among the cast. As promised, she came back after the show and set about enchanting Buster, who was more than happy to sit in her arms and bury his head in her armpit. Not very gentlemanly behaviour, but Cher didn't seem to mind. The stage-door man rang to tell me that I had visitors and did I want to see them? I did. I wanted the whole of Shaftesbury Avenue to drop in so I could show off my new best friend. It's not every day that a star of Cher's stature is sitting on your bed while you scrape the slap off.

Stephen Tompkinson was my first visitor and I was happy to see that he was suitably gobsmacked to find her swigging champagne and stroking my dog, but Regina Fong's reaction was priceless.

'The real Cher?' he asked her after I'd introduced them, completely dumbfounded.

'No, the artificial one,' she replied, enjoying the expression of sheer disbelief on his face.

'Well, fuck me,' was all he could think of saying by way of a response.

'Thanks for the offer, baby,' she came back with. 'But if you don't mind I'd rather not.'

*Prisoner* came to the end of its twelve-week run. Although I'd found the process of being in a West End show, as well as the work involved in getting the show up and running, as alarming as it was thrilling, I was grateful that the pace of life was slowing down a little. Three months without sufficient sleep had taken its toll and getting up on a cold winter's morning having only had four hours' sleep was getting harder each day, especially as I no longer had a staircase and had to make the descent down a ladder with Buster in a carrier bag. One morning, waiting in the middle of what was once a kitchen for the kettle to boil, I sat down on a bin liner full of rubble and promptly fell into a deep sleep, waking in a fit of panic some hours later to find that I'd missed the show. When I rang to explain and apologize, the executive producer didn't seem the least bit bothered, which made me question if I'd even been missed.

Just as well that I'd made the decision to go on tour instead of renewing my contract for another year. I loved *The Big Breakfast* and was grateful for the exposure but it was time to move on and, besides, another year of dragging up at the crack of dawn would turn me into a basket case.

I was beginning to think that I was sharing my new house with three builders who seemed hell bent on systematically demolishing the interior of the place day after noisy, dusty, nerve-jangling day. I'd started to go straight from *The Big Breakfast* to the theatre to try and grab a few hours' kip and was spending more time there than I was at home, sleeping the afternoon away in my single bed with Buster tucked behind my knees while above me on Shaftesbury Avenue the world went about its business.

Gaby had left *The Big Breakfast* some months before I did and been replaced by Zoë Ball who, when she first joined the show, was already committed to two shows a day as Cinderella in panto, which meant she was getting even less sleep than me. Not that she let it show on camera – she always managed to appear bright and perky.

The chemistry that seems so vital between presenters just wasn't there between Zoë and Mark and squabbles often broke out during the ad breaks. On one occasion after one of these rows, Mark stormed off the set to 'have words' with the producers and inconsolable Zoë, in floods of tears, was in no fit state to be in front of the camera. Which meant the job of presenting the next part of the show fell to me. There was no autocue or earpiece with a director guiding you from the gallery, just a script which, if you didn't want to look like a bumbling amateur, you had to quickly memorize so that when you came back after the ad break you looked relaxed and confident as if you knew what you were doing.

It's exciting flying by the seat of your pants, especially when you're blagging your way through it as blue murder is breaking out off camera. It's what live telly is all about, having to cope with the unexpected, and that's why I prefer it any day of the week to pre-recorded shows.

I liked both Mark and Zoë, they were both great fun to work with, and apart from Zoë getting upset, their rows didn't bother me. On the contrary: I looked upon them as a bit of diversion that gave me something to chew over with the make-up girls.

*Big Breakfast* flew me out for the Oscars and just as I had done in Edinburgh I spent more time in drag than I did in mufti. Golden Girl Betty White was the first star I interviewed when I got to LA, and she was a delight. Betty is one of the original pioneers of American television, having started out in 1939, and she was the first woman to produce a sitcom. She described herself as 'Jurassic' and jokingly claimed that it wouldn't be long before she'd be playing canasta in an old folk's home. When I protested that she belied her years, she asked me how old I was, then replied that in 1954, the year before I was born, she had her own chat show on television, and there was the proof that she'd been around too long. Although she spoke fondly of her co-stars in *The Golden Girls*, she admitted that Bea Arthur didn't like her.

'Why?' I asked, finding it hard that anybody could dislike this enchanting lady.

'Because she said I was always so damn positive,' she replied, 'and she found my happiness annoying.'

*

Jackie Collins is the greatest good sport in Hollywood. She's the Queen of Hollywood who knows just about everybody who's worth knowing in that town, and nothing, and I mean nothing, fazes her, which was just as well as she'd agreed to accompany Lily on a shopping trip down the exclusive Rodeo Drive. I had thought that I'd stand out like a sore thumb, dressed as I was in fake Chanel trimmed in faux leopard skin, but compared to some of the women on the drive, Lily looked understated.

Jackie swanned confidently into Harry Winston's the jeweller's with me and the film crew trailing behind her.

'This is my friend Lily,' she said pleasantly to the startled staff, 'and we've come to look at some watches.'

No sooner had Jackie laid her hands on the most beautiful art deco, diamond-encrusted timepiece, which had reputedly once belonged to Billie Holiday's pimp and which she was trying to persuade me to buy, than the film star Mena Suvari sailed in with her entourage. It's the custom at the Oscars for the big stars to borrow jewellery for the occasion and Ms Suvari was here for just that purpose. Giving me and Jackie the once-over, she muttered something to the manager of the shop and within seconds the shutters on the window came down and we found ourselves out on the street.

'Well,' a flabbergasted Jackie exclaimed, 'I've never been thrown out of a shop before, especially Harry Winston's. That's the last time I set foot in there.'

However, as Jackie is not the type to bear a grudge, I do know she went back some time later and bought the watch.

I never got to go to the Oscars ceremony itself, which I was very grateful for. There's nothing more boring than sitting for hours listening to those interminable thank-you speeches, even if you are surrounded by the crème de la crème of the film industry. I went to the after-show party though, where I met up with Robin Williams again, who greeted me like an old friend. I confessed to him that I felt very self-conscious in full drag among the glitterati of Hollywood. 'Relax, baby,' he reassured me. 'They probably think you're Sharon Stone.'

As I was going on to Elton's party after this (the name-dropping is hideous and I apologize) and then to report back live to the *Big Breakfast* house, I didn't want to get hammered. I was here to work after all, I reminded myself, and doing the sensible thing for a change I thought about eating something to soak up the booze.

'What's a nice girl like you doing in a place like this?' a male voice said from behind me. Turning to see who the wise guy was, I came face-to-face with Ben-Hur himself, Charlton Heston.

'I didn't recognize you without your chariot,' I told him cheekily – which made me realize that lining my stomach against the booze was something I should've thought of a bit earlier.

'It's parked outside,' he responded deadpan. 'I might give you a ride in it later.'

'It's not a ride I'm looking for,' I said. 'It's something to eat. You haven't got anything to eat on you, have you?'

'I've got a hot dog in my pocket,' he said, grinning.

Although Robin had greeted Charlton Heston effusively, he said very little except to smile slyly as I chatted briefly with this Hollywood legend. After he'd kissed my hand and said his farewells, going off in search of his wife Lydia, Robin started cackling.

'He thought you were a woman,' he said delightedly. 'That old right-wing Republican thought you were a woman!'

'Surely he didn't.' I couldn't believe that he thought I was for real. Admittedly there were quite a lot of women in the room who had big hair and as much, if not more, slap on, but he must've known I was drag.

'Believe me,' Robin laughed, 'he wouldn't have kissed your hand like that if he thought you were a guy. He'd have run a mile. Oh, that has really made my night,' he added, rubbing his hands with glee, 'but I don't think he mistook you for Sharon Stone.'

'Who then?' I asked.

'Mae West,' he replied, and laughed even more.

Punch-drunk on film stars (Elton's party had been crawling with 'em) and on the large Scotch and Cokes that the waitress at the restaurant we were recording the live broadcast from had been plying me with, I went on air. Lippy smeared and speech slurred, I broadcast live to the nation back home as they ate their breakfast, pissed as a fart.

Being in the thick of things makes such a difference when you're in LA. Last time we were here there'd been a riot. This time round it had been equally riotous but for entirely different reasons, and both Murphy and I were reluctant to go home after our five days in Tinsel Town during the insanity of the Oscars.

On the day before we left, we spent the afternoon at David Hockney's beach house in Malibu. It was far from grand. It had been nothing more than a tumbledown shack when he'd first bought it but instead of tearing it down and rebuilding he'd lovingly restored it, and if I ignored the breathtaking view of the Pacific Ocean, the living room was strangely reminiscent of Aunty Annie's in Lowther Street. The first thing David said was that he was deaf and I'd have to speak up, which I did, my voice perfectly audible down the beach at Goldie Hawn's house, according to Murphy.

We spoke mainly about Bridlington and his dislike of restaurants, but it was Murphy that he took a shine to, the pair of them sitting for hours deep in conversation while I took a walk along the beach with a very handsome young man who pointed out the homes of the famous like a guide on one of those bus tours around Hollywood.

'You know, Murphy,' I said on the plane home as I clutched the Oscar as if it were the Holy Grail, 'I'm beginning to regret leaving *The Big Breakfast*. When I think about it, this past year has been surreal. I mean, just look at the last five days.'

Nick Park was anxiously wringing his hands as he waited to get back the Oscar he'd won for *Wallace and Gromit*. He'd let me hold it for a moment and I was reluctant to hand it over as right now I wanted to lock myself in the toilets with it and make my acceptance speech in the mirror to see how I looked.

'Savage, give the man his Oscar back, will you,' Murphy said, sighing, and adding after a moment's thought: 'Now, there's something I never thought I'd hear myself saying. You're right, Savage, life suddenly is surreal.'

When Gaby left the *Big Breakfast* they brought in Dean Friedman, one of her favourite singers, who sang that song 'Lucky Stars'. Of course, Gaby was beside herself at meeting her idol. I wondered if I was going to get a surprise guest on my final morning. I'd sniffed around for any clues to no avail, and even my trusted sources of information drew a blank under the severest interrogation.

Although I was pretending to be not the least bit bothered by the lack of fuss on this my final bloody day, in reality I was sulking and feeling very hard done by, barely able to speak to the crew, who seemed more concerned about a broken French window than my departure.

Just as I was about to interview Bob Downe, Mark Little interrupted to ask me if I recognized the woman on the monitor running full pelt down the towpath. She was too far away for me to get a good look at her face and for a moment I wondered if they'd got me a famous athlete, and if so, why? Athletics is not my forte. I can rarely be found glued to the telly fascinated by the sight of someone chucking a javelin. Ask me to name three female athletes and I'd say Dame Kelly Holmes, Mary Rand and Olga Korbut, such is my knowledge of the field.

The reason we'd been constantly warned not to go near the French windows became apparent when the woman on the towpath kicked the sugar glass and balsa wood replacement in to make a spectacular entrance.

They had got me a surprise after all and here she was, my favourite Avenger, Linda Thorson, aka Tara King. If Gaby was beside herself then I was hanging off the pelmet after finally getting to meet the woman I'd been crazy about since I was twelve. Looking around at the cheering crew laughing and applauding, I felt a massive rush of affection for them all and wondered if I was making the right decision by leaving.

Too late for regrets now. I waved bye bye to the viewers hanging from a crane dressed as Mary Poppins with Bob Downe serenading from below as Linda looked on.

Any regrets quickly evaporated when the clock didn't go off at 4 a.m. and for the first time in a year I got to lie in bed of a weekday, providing the builders weren't at it, as well as go out clubbing again on a school night, which took quite a bit of getting used to after a year of early nights.

I didn't get to lie in my pit for very long though, and leaving the builders to it I went on a tour of one-night-stands up and down the country with Gayle and Buster in tow.

God bless the Little Chef and their all-day breakfasts, our chief source of sustenance on the road. We ate there so often we even had favourite branches. We never failed to stop at the ones in Doncaster, Crewe and Norwich.

It was interesting, if not puzzling, to see how different audiences reacted to us. In Cheltenham, the respectable Sunday audience looked upon Gayle and Lily in the same way they might had a pack of travellers descended upon the town, while in Cambridge they studied us as if we were speaking Aramaic. However, in places like Liverpool, Sunderland, Glasgow and Swansea it was a different story, and we were always guaranteed an enthusiastic audience, well up for a bit of salacious humour from a hard-boiled Birkenhead slapper and a dim-witted page-three stunner.

The work on the house was finally finished and at last I had the place to myself, but before I had time to enjoy it I was off again. Martin Witts, a producer, entrepreneur and very brave man, saw that there was plenty of mileage left in *Prisoner the Musical* and wanted to take it on tour. Maggie was hastily brought back from the Antipodes and I, saying goodbye to my new wooden floors and brand new Savoy-bathroom-on-a-budget, packed the bags, the costumes, the wigs, the electric frying pan and the Baby Belling oven and, together with Buster and Vera, who had a job dressing on the show, we hit the road.

We were due to open at the Lyceum in Sheffield and it wasn't looking very promising. The dress rehearsal had been an unmitigated disaster. The set was too big for the Lyceum's stage for a start, and making an exit or an entrance was damn near impossible. The band were under-rehearsed, as was the cast, and we had quite a lot of new numbers in this touring production. Linda Nolan had replaced Penny Morrell as the Governor, and in a scene set in the Governor's office she was to burst into a rousing rendition of 'I'm In The Mood For Dancing' after drinking tea from an urn that had been laced with a hallucinogenic drug by the Freak, stripping off her clothes and ending up on top of her desk in her bra and stockings and suspenders.

Maggie didn't approve of this. It wasn't an original number conceived for the show and she considered the strip was a step too far. I knew what she meant about adding popular songs to the show, but I said nothing, having included Elvis's 'Trouble' for myself in the laundry. *Prisoner* had definitely needed tweaking before we took it on the road. There were parts of the show that always needled me, and here was the chance to change it. My only regret was that the person who wrote the iconic theme tune for the TV show wouldn't let us use it in the West End or on the tour. That would've been the cherry on the cake for both me and the punters.

Maggie and I rewrote the penultimate scene in which Ferguson has Lily tied to a chair in her office and, before she packs her off to a life in solitary and inevitable insanity, she does what all villains do at a time like this: she reveals everything about her evil schemes. Lily, meanwhile, has a bit of business trying to flick the switch on the tannoy on the desk next to her. She eventually achieves this by use of her tongue, enabling the entire prison, and more importantly the Man from the Department, to hear the Freak's damning confession.

It was great fun to do and it became my favourite part of the show. Maggie didn't mind if I ad-libbed. In fact, I suspect she encouraged it. Lily having been saved, the nice prison officer – played on the tour by Lisa George, who went on to become a regular on the *Street* as gobby Beth Tinker – arrives as Ferguson is being dragged off to a cell. She announces that Vera has been found washed up in a fisherman's net and that Lily is free to go.

Apparently Vera had been swept out to sea but was rescued by a school of dolphins who treated her as if she was one of their own. When, as she lay on the sand after being recovered, she was asked by Channel Five news if she had anything to say about her experience, Vera replied: 'Squeak, squeak, squeak, squeal!' and jumped up in the air to catch a sardine that someone had thrown from the pier.

Michelle, the wardrobe mistress, and Agnes my dresser, as well as a member of the crew, hadn't been able to find lodgings, so as I had a suite in my hotel, and by that I mean a bedroom with a smaller room off it with a sofa in it and a bathroom that Norman Bates would've felt at home in, the three of them moved in with me, making that four of us and a dog. The hotel management were very obliging and sent up extra blankets and pillows without me even having to ask. They were also very decent about me cooking in the room, though Agnes said you could smell bacon frying all the way down the hall. When you're on tour, food is a problem, and you invariably end up living on Marks and Spencer's sandwiches and room service.

Usually after a show you go out to the pub or perhaps the local Chinese restaurant, and frequently these after-show 'quick drinks' end up as a full-blown night on the lash, rolling into your hotel at all hours. When you're on tour you don't want to go back to a lonely hotel room or your miserable digs so you end up doing something after the show. Not everyone is like that, of course. Some are quite happy to go home after the show, have a cup of Horlicks and go to bed, but I never could as I needed some time to wind down.

Following a day of two shows and a late night, you might want to lie in and not have to fall out of bed at the ridiculous hour of 8.30, hungover and looking like a war crime, to face a greasy full English among the businessmen and other lone travellers. The electric frying pan was a godsend because it meant I could have a cooked breakfast in the privacy of my own room at whatever time I liked and it didn't cost me a fortune.

I'd clear out the mini bar (only a fool or someone very drunk uses anything from the mini bar – have you seen the prices?) and fill it with milk, bacon, bread and other assorted goodies from a supermarket, cover the smoke detector with a plastic shower cap and rustle myself and Buster up a decent breakfast.

The Baby Belling oven was for dressing-room use, and later in the tour I made Maggie and myself a roast dinner in it between shows at the Birmingham Hippodrome. The manager had complained so I went up to his office with a counter-attack: why was the heating turned on full blast all over the theatre?

'The entire cast is sweating like a pack of whores at confession,' I fumed. 'It's roasting in those dressing rooms.'

'The reason the heating is on is because we have members of the Royal Ballet rehearsing in the studio,' he replied curtly. 'There's nothing I can do about it.'

'Well, in case you haven't noticed, it says *Prisoner Cell Block H the Musical* outside this theatre, and not *Swan* friggin' *Lake*, so turn the bloody heating off,' and with that Buster, being the intuitive little dog he was, cocked his leg and peed up the filing cabinet.

*

Mig Kimpton, our company manager, had tried to reassure me with the old theatrical comforter about how a bad dress rehearsal meant a good first night, but I wasn't convinced. How could anything possibly transform last night's cock-up into something that was fit to be seen by a paying public?

Well, something happened, and Mig was right. The show magically came together and ran like clockwork. *Prisoner* on tour was a better show in many respects than it had been in the West End, not that I could've foreseen that after the shocking dress rehearsal.

The audience treated it as a sort of adult panto, cheering and hooting, as well as booing Maggie to the rafters each time she made an appearance. Maggie loathed being booed. She couldn't understand that in British theatre, especially pantos, though probably never in *Coriolanus* at the National, the audience show their appreciation towards the villain by booing. The louder the hisses and boos, the bigger the compliment.

'I think it's fuckin' rude,' was all she had to say on the matter.

I did a lot of walking with Buster on that tour. Whenever I had to go out in the day he was happy to sit in the room and flirt with the housekeeping staff, who'd come supposedly to 'do' my room but had really come to play with Buster.

In Nottingham the night porter of the hotel fell in love with him and would quietly let himself into my room each morning and take him for a walk. How's that for service?

Swansea is a city I love and as the weather was glorious for the week that we were there I went to the beach each day, taking Buster with me. He spent the time we were there lying on a towel next to a bowl of water, protected from the heat of the sun by a child's umbrella I'd bought from Mothercare. To the uninitiated he looked like he was sleeping, but I was well aware that he had one beady eye firmly fixed on the wedge of delicious corned beef pie I'd bought from the café around the corner from the theatre. That dog was ruined, but I had no trouble in finding hotels that would accept him. Except for one.

The hotel we'd been booked into in Edinburgh had a no-dogs policy. As we'd arrived in the city late and couldn't be bothered with the hassle of changing hotels at that hour, I popped Buster in a holdall, telling him to be quiet. Like the pro he was, he didn't make a sound as I checked in.

The guy behind reception was French with a serious attitude problem. He looked down upon Maggie and me, dishevelled after a day's travelling and laden with carrier bags. Eventually he disapprovingly slid our room keys across the counter top, but only after checking our registration with the thoroughness of a Bootle tax inspector bearing a grudge.

Each day I smuggled Buster out of the hotel, right under the nose of the snooty Frenchman, with nobody any the wiser. Each night I went through the same rigmarole when I returned and went through the painful process of collecting my room key.

'Can I have my key please.'

'Room number?'

'Sorry, I've forgotten.'

'Name?'

'Paul O'Grady.'

'Do you have any ID?'

I could never remember my bloody room number. I'm dyslexic with numbers and find it impossible to retain them. The Frenchman saw me on a regular basis and knew full well who I was, but the officious little creep preferred to put me through this routine each time I wanted my key, and I had to allow myself to be interrogated like this each night because of Buster.

Eventually things came to a head. After a night when both Maggie and I had enjoyed the hospitality of CC Blooms, we returned to our hotel in the wee small hours, steaming drunk.

'Can I have my key pleesh,' I managed to blurt out, hanging on to the reception desk for support but still swaying slightly.

'Room number?' the French one asked imperiously as he always did, without even bothering to look up from his computer.

'It's that one over there,' I slurred, pointing in the direction of my key in its pigeon hole behind the desk.

'Room number?' he persisted.

'Aah, just give him the fuckin' key, will ya,' Maggie snarled, lurching towards him menacingly, 'and quit' horsin' around.'

'You heard her,' I said, spurred on by Maggie's bravery in the face of the enemy. 'I've been staying here for the lasht five days and every night it's the same performance when I ashk for my key. What is your problem?'

'I need your room number,' he replied, maddeningly calm.

'I need your room number,' Maggie mimicked from behind me. 'He's like a bloody parrot.' And with that, curious to see what the commotion was all about, Buster popped out of the bag and did his trick of standing on his hind legs and barking. The Frenchman wasn't impressed.

'You have a dog?' he screeched.

'Well, it's not a bleedin' penguin, sunshine, is it?'

This was it, the cat, or should I say dog, was out of the bag, so there was no point in pleasantries. 'Now can I have my key before I come and get it myself?'

'Tell him, Sav,' Maggie muttered from the armchair she'd slumped into.

'But you have a dog,' he said again, horrified and pointing at Buster like he was a freshly hatched dinosaur. 'Dogs are not allowed in here.'

'He's a very well-behaved little dog,' I said self-righteously, trying not to slur my words. 'He's a damn sight better behaved than a lot of your guests.'

Maggie belched long and loud and the Frenchman, who looked like he was about to cry at any moment, stared at her opened-mouthed in disgust.

Suddenly it came to me, the number of my room. 'Two-one-eight!' I shouted. 'That's the number of my room.'

'But the dog.'

'Never mind the dog. Hand the key over before I kill you.'

I got my key and there was no more mention of Buster, who now trotted freely in and out of the hotel each day, undisturbed but under the baleful glare of the Frenchman.

All seemed well until the morning when my nemesis left the safety of his desk and confronted me in the lobby.

'Mr O'Grady,' he said, in a voice that could be heard on the top floor, 'I must have a word with you. Your dog has urinated in the lift.'

'My dog has not,' I replied, outraged at this slur on Buster's exemplary bladder control. 'Buster would never do a thing like that.'

'The carpet was wet through this morning,' he ranted on, ignoring my protests, 'which can only mean that your dog is the one responsible.'

'How do you know someone hasn't spilled a drink?' I queried.

'Because it smelt of dog urine,' he replied smugly.

'So you're familiar with the smell of dog piss then?' I asked, my blood pressure starting to rise. 'Where did you train? Battersea Dogs' Home?'

'Your dog has urinated in the lift,' he persisted, refusing to be drawn into a discussion.

'He didn't.'

'He did.'

'He didn't. It was me.'

That silenced the Frenchman for the moment. Stuck for a suitable reply, he turned on his heel and returned to his post.

'Round two to us, I think, Buster,' I murmured as we sailed triumphantly out of the hotel and to the safety of the theatre.

# CHAPTER 10

I WAS SORRY WHEN THE TOUR CAME TO AN END. I WAS FINDING civilian life a bit dull after being itinerant. Each night at 7.30 I looked at the clock and told myself the curtain would just be going up to a packed house, and here I was eating spaghetti hoops on toast and watching *Corrie* instead.

I especially missed the cast and crew. They become your family when you're touring. As well as seeing them each night in the theatre, there was also the usual after-show socializing. Not having Maggie around was strange. That woman was a force of nature, and I missed having her pop her head around my dressing-room door to report on the day's menu.

'I had a beeeeeautiful lunch today, two beeeeeautiful little lamb chops served with some beeeeautiful new potatoes and a few little peas. Delicious, and all for under four quid. Beeeeeautiful.'

Even Buster was showing signs of suffering post-tour-matic stress. He'd sit on the top staircase (yes, I finally had stairs) peering down at me mournfully, waiting for a tell-tale sign, such as a suitcase or an electric frying pan, to indicate that we might be off on our travels again. He especially missed Linda Nolan and her husband Brian as he spent most of his time in their dressing room, where, I suspect, Linda gave him biscuits.

'I don't know what you're moaning about,' Murphy said. 'You'll be off again soon. Just think, four months of eight shows a week on the end of the North Pier. Do you the world of good, all that sea air – put a bit of colour in those sallow jowls.'

I'd had reservations about accepting a summer season in Blackpool, all of them down to prejudice, as so many people had advised me not to touch it with a ten-foot pole. 'End-of-pier shows are naff,' they said. 'Only has-beens at the end of their careers work on piers and you're just starting out. It'll damage your reputation.'

'Well, you won't miss what you never had,' Murphy had said, dodging the blow I'd misjudged to the back of his head. 'Don't let these media types cloud your judgement, Savage. What do they know? Some might say it's a sign that you've made it, topping the bill in a big summer season show.'

'Years ago they might have said that,' I replied. 'But it's sort of had its day now, don't you think?'

'No, I don't think,' he said, getting quite animated about the subject. 'You're following in the tradition of a long line of great performers, people you love and respect, by the way, who've worked in that theatre many times over the years, and anyway,' he added as an afterthought, 'two years ago you were working in a club up the road so when did you become so high and mighty?'

'I'm not,' I protested. 'It's just, well, I don't know what to do.'

'You never do, Savage,' he said, 'but if you want my advice, then you should do it. You like Blackpool, the type who go to Blackpool are your audience and it'll be an experience.'

'Are you going to come up and stay for the season?' I asked him.

'Am I shite,' he said. 'A weekend up there is quite enough, thank you very much. I'll stay and look after your house.'

Murphy was right as usual. There was nothing to be ashamed of, working on the end of a pier, and if it was good enough for the likes of Bruce Forsyth, Hylda Baker, Frankie Vaughan, Morecambe and Wise et al, then it was certainly good enough for me. Ignoring the detractors, I went ahead and signed up for *The Lily Savage Show*, starring Sonia, speciality act Pete Matthews, the Kim Gavin Dancers and a new young singer by the name of Russ Watson. Once I'd finally stopped prevaricating, stuck two fingers up to the snobs and taken the plunge, I began to warm to the idea and couldn't wait to get started and join the seaside fraternity for a season.

I was becoming a regular on the BBC show *Clive James on Television*. It was a job with plenty of scope for comedy as I was expected to comment on events of any interest that had occurred during the week.

Clive was and is a very charismatic man with a biting wit who had an eye for the slightly offkey. His latest discovery was the irrepressible camp Cuban singer Margarita Pracatan, who accompanied herself on an electric organ as she sang a selection of pop standards in strangled English. She was very endearing and the public took to her at once, and I had the pleasure of accompanying her on a pair of maracas as she sang something unintelligible from Carmen Miranda's repertoire.

Clive would show clips of bizarre television shows from around the world. One of his favourite targets was a Japanese programme called, aptly enough, *Endurance*, which basically did what it said on the tin: a group of Japanese punters would be made to take part in torturous trials, which included eating a variety of unimaginable animal parts. We'd all laugh smugly and say, 'Only in Japan, eh? Imagine that happening here?', unaware that *I'm a Celebrity* was just around the corner.

Clive had mentioned something about wanting to do a show with me as we were having a drink one night. There's lots of talk like this at the after-show drinks gathering in the green rooms of television studios – though only if the show you've just appeared on has gone well for you, I hasten to add. I thought no more of our conversation until someone from his company, Watchmaker, rang to ask if I'd be interested in making an *An Audience With* . . . show for ITV.

Lots of famous names have appeared on *An Audience With* . . . in the past and it was normally shown on prime-time TV on Saturday night, but as it turned out I wasn't grand enough to sail under that banner so mine was demoted to *An Evening With Lily Savage*, and as the network didn't consider it prime-time weekend viewing it went out on a Wednesday night. Not that I cared whether it was called *An Audience With* or *An Evening With* or *The Mother Teresa Ice Cavalcade*, it was the same format whatever way you looked at it: an audience of celebrities ask pre-planned questions that you have well-prepared answers for concocted out of your best material. Not that difficult really, and as they didn't want to film it until the end of the year I'd have plenty of time to work the show out while I was in Blackpool.

Things seldom go to plan, or at least that's what I've found out in life, and so it was with the *Evening With* show.

'Now, don't start, when I tell you this,' Murphy said cautiously. He had wisely chosen a café in Covent Garden to break whatever news he was about to impart, believing that I'd be less likely to raise my voice in public. Wrong.

'They wondered if they could film the *Evening With* sooner than planned,' he said, calmly stirring his coffee.

283

'How soon?' I asked hesitantly.

'At the end of the month.'

'But that only gives me two and a half weeks!'

'Now, Savage, don't kick off.'

I didn't kick off, I panicked at the thought of only having a fortnight to get such an important show together. I'll never do it, I told myself, wasting a week by fretting about it until I calmed down and stopped worrying and got to work instead. I came to the conclusion that this show, far from being intimidating, was in fact quite the opposite. There was no pressure to remember an hour's material because the audience prompted you with their questions. There was plenty of scope for ad-lib and audience interaction, and with all this in mind I worked through the night with confident vigour and by morning I had a show.

For musical numbers Barbara Dickson gamely agreed to join me in a duet of 'I Know Him So Well', a number I'd done on the odd occasion in the pubs with Dave Lynn and one that had always worked well for us.

Marlene and her lamp got dragged out of semi-retirement but as the song was a parody of 'The Laziest Gal In Town', the Cole Porter estate wouldn't allow me to use it. Panic, until Laurie Holloway, the musical director, stepped in and simply rewrote the music. Learning to do the number to a different melody after the original had been ingrained in my mind for so long was extremely difficult. The only way to get it to sink in was to go over and over it until the original version had been annihilated from memory, nearly driving me barmy in the process.

As usual I provided my own costumes, wigs and even the lamp post, did my own slap and wrote all the material for the show myself. Why would I let anybody else do it? Having been self-sufficient for so long I wasn't about to change now.

'Have you seen who's in the audience?' Murphy asked, coming into the dressing room with a pint of cider. 'It's like a who's who of showbiz out there. Even Yuri Geller's here.'

'I should hope so,' I said. 'I'm going to tell him how I went to see him once at the Fairfield Halls and as he was bending a spoon on stage my coil straightened out and buckled me to the seat like a staple in the middle of an exercise book.'

'You're looking forward to this, aren't you, Savage?' Murphy asked, amused at my attitude. 'Aren't you the slightest bit nervous?'

'No, not really,' I replied. 'I'm more curious to see how it goes down than anything else.'

'Most acts having to go out there and face an audience of famous faces and keep them entertained for an hour would be shaking in their shoes, but you, well, you're not natural.'

'Listen,' I started, 'when you've worked some of the places I have, this lot out here are a piece of piss. Don't forget, Murphy, I was trained at the Royal Vauxhall Tavern School of Dramatic Arts, so I'm able for anything.'

It wasn't false bravado, nor was it arrogance. It was simply that on occasions like this, as it was with the Palladium and all the theatres I'd toured in, if I was confident at what I was doing and had some fresh material and bits of business that I was keen to try out, then excitement genuinely overcame fear and I couldn't wait to get out on that stage.

'Open the cage, Murphy, and let me out,' I said, as I always did these days. This corny expression had morphed from a throwaway line said for camp theatrical effect into something far more important. Just like whistling in a dressing room or mentioning the Scottish play, omitting to say 'Open the cage, Murph' was to tempt fate and invite disaster. I really get annoyed at myself for being so superstitious. It places so many restrictions on me and can complicate life. Don't look at the full moon through glass. Never walk under a ladder, walk around it and into the gutter instead and face a barrage of abuse from a cyclist or sudden death by a passing bus. Never put new shoes on a table, or spill ink, or cut your nails on a Sunday, or pass a magpie without spitting . . . the list is as pathetic as it is endless, and I blame my mother entirely for it.

The show was recorded as live, which meant there were to be no stop–starts and all my quick changes had to be done in the length of the commercial breaks, which wasn't a lot of time. Still, the show ran like clockwork and there were no pick-ups afterwards to reshoot anything. Taking my bows at the end with Buster, who had been reluctant to climb down the stairs and had to be carried, I was amazed at how quickly time had passed.

Clive, who had been in the audience, was delighted with the way things had gone, and as we tried to talk over the noise of the amount of people at the after-show in the green room, he asked me what I was doing next.

'A season on the North Pier, Blackpool,' I told him, waiting to see his reaction.

'Really? How wonderful – congratulations,' he said warmly. 'Genuine variety in its spiritual home like a pier theatre is the very root of what it's all about, yet, like pantomime, it is all too often looked down upon. It's a dying art, but thankfully entertainers like you are breathing new life into it. You're a "Turn", O'Grady, aren't you?' he added with a sly smile. 'A branch of the business that commentators like me envy and respect.'

I felt like a pioneer, fighting to keep vent acts and jugglers, plate-spinners and poodle acts to the forefront of entertainment, hearing it put like this by Clive. Flushed with success, but more probably by the amount of red wine I'd put back out of sheer relief that the show had been a success, I began to look at my forthcoming season in a completely different light.

I was a soldier now, out to do battle with cinema and television and bring the holiday crowds down the pier and into the theatre again.

I explained as much to Murphy in the car going home.

'Don't talk bollocks,' was his succinct reply. 'You're going to add another string to your bow, have a good time and hopefully earn a lot of dosh in the process. How much have you drunk?'

I shrugged happily.

'Well done tonight,' he said after a while, as if he'd been summing up the show privately. 'You certainly left the cage with a roar this time. Now let's get Blackpool out of the way and see what transpires at the end of the year once this show goes out. Something big just might happen.'

Prophetic words indeed, for something very big did come along, and it was to become our biggest challenge yet.

Considering it was the beginning of July it was, to use that optimistic northern expression, 'bracing'. In other words, it was bloody freezing.

'Jesus,' I moaned, shivering each time the 'light breeze' (another optimistic northern euphemism) blasted across the North Pier. 'If it's like this now what's it going to be like in November?'

'Aye, it's a bit blowy, I'll give you that,' Murphy agreed, grimacing in the biting wind. Buster, following behind me on his lead, looked exactly the way he did whenever he stuck his head out of the car window, and I contemplated picking him up just in case he took off like a kite.

The less than tropical climate hadn't stop two stoic old girls from sitting on one of the benches that lined the pier and enjoying an ice cream. They'd come prepared for anything the weather could throw at them, their beige BHS macs covered in those clear plastic raincoats – what my mother used to call a Pac-a-mac – with matching plastic rain hoods that were doing their best to escape in the wind, lifting up from the ladies' permed heads like miniature parachutes each time a gust caught them. The ladies were undeterred by the icy blast coming off the Irish Sea. Scowling in the face of it, they sat there licking in contented silence, wrapped in their outer shell of plastic, making me think of two beige armchairs in a DFS showroom.

There was and still is a beautiful carousel outside the theatre, as well as a pub called the Merrie England Bar, which would prove to be handy, and a sun lounge jam-packed with pensioners in deckchairs in rows, humming contentedly like a colony of bees as they listened to the organist playing melodies from yesteryear.

The area around the theatre fire doors stank from a combination of piss and stale booze, as did the theatre once we'd got inside. It wasn't a promising start.

'The drains are up,' one of the crew explained. 'They've been up all week.'

My spirits certainly weren't and I left Murphy to sort out how the luggage was going to be transported down the pier. At the moment it was dumped in the back of his jeep, which he'd parked on the pavement outside the amusement arcade. There'd been a bit of argy-bargy between Murphy and a security guard who wouldn't let him park there, resulting in strong words being exchanged, which attracted a crowd who, welcoming this diversion, more than likely hoped they would come to blows.

'You're a jobsworth, mate,' I heard Murphy shouting as I sank lower in my seat of the jeep, 'a grade A wanker. I've just explained, we've got a car full of costumes and wigs that need to be transported down the pier, and since I can't drive down, someone from the theatre will have to come and get them, which is where I'm going this very minute. Got it?'

'I've told you, rules are rules and you can't park your car here,' the security guard said for the tenth time, refusing to give way.

'Well, tough shit,' Murphy growled. 'It's staying here and you're going to keep an eye on it for me.'

The guard looked at him, went to speak but then thought better of it.

'You see that billboard? And those posters and that advert down the side of that tram?' Murphy roared, pointing to the hoarding above the arcade as well as at a passing tram with the legend *The Lily Savage Show* running along the side of it. 'Well, I've got the star of the bloody show in the car and they're his costumes.'

The crowd, which had grown by now, craned their necks to get a good look at this star inside the car. I wanted to crawl inside the engine.

'Savage!' Murphy shouted. 'C'mon, we're going down to the theatre, I haven't got all day to waste explaining to Blakey here.'

The punters parted as I made my way through them smiling sheepishly and apologizing out of embarrassment while they stared at me in what I suspected was disappointment.

'Is that that Lily Savage then?' I heard a woman say. 'Well I never. I had no idea she was a fellah.'

The North Pier Theatre had been built as a temporary structure after the original theatre had burned down in the thirties. For a venue that was once considered to be number one on the variety/summer season circuit, it'd seen better days and was showing signs of neglect.

The dressing-room floor was littered with feathers that certainly didn't look like they'd belonged to Danny La Rue, not unless he was into pigeon feathers these days, and the stench of sewage made me gag. Danny had been appearing on the pier before me in old-time music hall and I refused to believe that he'd put up with this.

'Don't, dear,' Agnes said as I started to retch, 'it's disgusting. The place is full of dead pigeons and the lav's blocked and overflowing. I've been here half an hour and if you think this is bad then you should've seen it before I started clearing up.'

I opened the window to try and get rid of the stench and noticed for the first time just how spectacular the view was across the Irish Sea. This seascape more than compensated for the effluent and feathered corpses inside.

The costumes arrived on the back of a trailer pulled by a small tractor. When Murphy saw the conditions in the dressing room he went down and had words with the company manager, putting the fear of God into the poor man. I left this temple to Thespis, or should it be Cesspit, and returned to my rented house on North Park Drive, the posh part of Blackpool, with a dirty great black cloud of gloom hanging over my head and a sinking feeling in my gut at what I'd let myself in for.

'You're always the same before a show opens,' Murphy said as he examined the oak-panelled front room and seventies sofa. 'Remember what you were like before *Prisoner*?'

Putting his head around the dining-room door, he made one comment. 'Nasty.'

'What, me before *Prisoner* or the dining room?'

'Both,' he replied, moving on to inspect the vast open-plan kitchen extension, an expanse of lino and glass sliding doors that was completely at odds with Morticia's oaken front room.

The garden was expansive with a small swimming pool that I snorkelled in until the water began to look suspicious and algae formed along the sides. The pool was then abandoned and all that ever went in there again was a Vespa scooter during a particularly rowdy party, of which there were quite a few over the season.

On opening night, an invited audience made up of local dignitaries, business people and bed-and-breakfast landladies made the journey down the pier as they'd done with every other show that had appeared here. It was a tradition to invite the 'nobs', while the landladies were considered to be the most important as they recommended shows to their guests.

It was common knowledge among the Blackpool acts that a local audience was a notoriously tough crowd, in particular the 'first-nighters', who had the reputation of sitting through a show hyper-critical and with faces like smacked arses.

Forewarned is forearmed, but none of us were prepared for our first-night reception. Talk about an evening of torture – there was not a laugh, not a titter, not even a weak grin, and the applause, what there was of it, was lukewarm and begrudging.

Sonia, who has a real belter of a voice, walked off after her set to virtually the sound of her own footsteps, as did Russ Watson, who would go on, with a slight name change to Russell Watson, to become an international star. Pete Matthews, our speciality act, sweated as he balanced on his 6-foot unicycle, grinning like a maniac and juggling wooden clubs and daggers in a brave attempt to get this crowd of stuffed corpses going, but like the rest of us he failed to get a decent reaction out of them.

'Sod 'em,' I said to Sonia as we watched from the tiny wing space, dodging Pete's wooden daggers, painted silver to look like the real thing, as he slung them offstage from the top of his bike.

'I've never worked to a crowd like this before. Who the bloody hell do they think they are?'

'Shhhh,' Sonia laughed. 'They'll hear you out front.'

'They'll hear me all right at the after-show party,' I told her grimly. 'Loud and bloody clear.'

The after-show party was held in the Merrie England Bar and the producers who'd made the journey up from London gave charming speeches before I was asked if I would like to say a few words.

'Oh no, here we go,' I heard Murphy mutter as I stomped towards the dance floor and took the mike.

'I'll keep what I have to say short,' I announced as I glared at the assembled gathering, the majority of whom were decked out in chains of office, badges and the assorted shiny paraphernalia that denoted which guild or organization they belonged to.

'I can forgive you for the reception you just gave me,' I began, 'but not for your treatment of Sonia, Russ, Pete, the dancers and the band, who gave it their all out there tonight.'

The crowd stared back at me in disbelief but there was no going back now even if I wanted to, which I didn't. I'd been looking forward to this all evening.

'I've never come across such a pig-ignorant bunch of free-loaders as you lot in my life,' I carried on, no longer able to control my mouth. 'Look at you, draped in your bits of brass and tin like overdressed brewery dray horses. You're nowt but a load of parochial, provincial, mean-spirited snobs.'

The crowd were speechless and I could hear a few of their chains rattling with indignation.

'You've obviously only come for the free booze and the buffet, as your contempt for the show was palpable from the outset, so I won't keep you from stuffing your jowls at the trough. I'll just say goodnight and let's not keep in touch,' and with that I marched out of the bar with Murphy and the producers in hot pursuit.

Murphy was grinning like the Cheshire Cat, despite his pretence at being horrified.

'Don't sit on the fence, Savage,' he said. 'Say what you mean, why don't you?'

The producers were naturally worrying about business and were going on about damage-limitation but I was having none of it.

'You'll have more luck finding somewhere decent to eat in this town than getting an apology out of me,' I told them. 'If they'd been a paying audience I'd have kept my mouth shut and got on with it. You know the score as well as I do in this game. You win some, you lose some. But that shower in there, well, they were just being plain ignorant, and seeing that they're all on freebies I believe that I'm entitled to return the compliment by letting them know just how little I thought of them.'

I was livid. I rued the day I ever agreed to come to Blackpool. If tonight's show was anything to go by, it was evident that I wasn't Kiss-Me-Quick hats and seaside-sodding-rock enough for them, and I questioned how the hell I was going to get through the season.

'Savage Savages VIPs' screamed the headlines of the local paper. The *Stage* newspaper, the rag for the industry, also jumped on the bandwagon, both of them reporting the story as if I'd just burned down an orphanage.

In the cold light of day I felt ashamed of my outburst and the negative press that understandably followed and wondered if I should issue a grovelling apology in the paper, claiming that I was on prescription drugs or suffered from Tourette's syndrome to explain my behaviour. I retold the whole sorry episode on stage, repeating more or less exactly what I'd said apart from a few comic embellishments to enhance the tale, and instead of being greeted with disapproval as I'd half expected the audience cheered long and loud.

At the stage door a woman confided in me that her landlady was 'a right old battleaxe, exactly like the postcards, and it needed saying'.

My fall from grace (it wasn't a long drop) in the eyes of Blackpool society certainly didn't do the box office any harm. Business was booming. We sold out almost every show and at the end of the season I was presented with a gold disc by First Leisure for ticket sales in excess of 100,000 and for breaking all box-office records. Sweet music after that first night – although I'd long made my peace with the landladies, and become friends with the mayor and his wife, taking tea with this jolly, down-to-earth couple in their mayoral parlour one riotous afternoon.

The North Pier Theatre now has new management. I visited it again a few years ago when I was making a documentary for the BBC, and it has certainly been transformed since my day. The dressing rooms are well equipped and extremely comfortable and the new owners are enthusiastic and passionate about the old place, determined to bring back the hordes who once tramped down the 1,650-foot pier to see a show. Good luck to them. Such commitment deserves to succeed.

Our crew were mostly young but experienced, having worked on a lot of previous pier shows. 'You've been short-changed,' one of them told me when he came up to unblock the loo in the dressing room. 'All the other big names have the place decorated before they move in and they have a fridge stocked with booze, courtesy of the management. They've given you sweet FA.'

Red rag to a bull. I'd decorated the room myself courtesy of the tat souvenir shops along the North Shore. An Elvis carpet covered one wall, assorted cheap novelty lamps provided a relaxing light, a leopard-print fake fur throw covered the battered old sofa, and with the kettle, tea service, nicked hotel towels, CD player (bought from the back of a van outside the Metropole Hotel) and the ubiquitous Baby Belling and electric frying pan, the place looked quite homey.

Even so, I wasn't about to let First Leisure off the hook quite so easily. One of their representatives eventually graced us with his presence, but unfortunately for him it was just as I was practising my knife-throwing by hurling a blade at the dressing-room door from my prone position on the sofa. Pete Matthews had been giving me lessons and for once the knife had actually stuck in the open door, dangerously close to Our Man From First Leisure's hand as he knocked.

'Beg your pardon,' I said casually. 'I was just trying out a new act.' I'd been wondering when I was going to get a visit and now he was here I wasn't about to adopt my party manners.

'Sorry I haven't been down to see you before,' the poor man stammered, examining the knife embedded in the door, 'but you know.'

'Oh yes, I know,' I replied with mock sympathy. 'It's such an awful long walk down that pier.'

He laughed nervously and handed me a bunch of well-past-their-sell-by-date flowers that had clearly been wilting their lives away in a plastic bucket on the forecourt of a garage. The price was still on the cellophane wrapper. *Reduced to 99p* the sticker said.

'I brought you these,' he said, handing the offending flora over as if he were giving me a Cartier watch.

'Thanks. I'll just put them in water,' I said politely, taking them off him and dropping them out of the window and into the sea.

Nobody else from the company came near after that but they did send down a couple of cases of cheap lager, which I put in the communal hall for anyone to help themselves.

After the bad start I began to really enjoy myself as the season got going and the punters started rolling in. On Saturday matinees we usually had a couple of drunken hen nights in, the bride-to-be adorned with net curtains, prophylactics and an L-plate. They were a lively crowd and desperate to be torn to pieces and sent up, and I was more than happy to oblige.

Wednesday matinee audiences were an older and gentler crowd

but who, at the same time, enjoyed a dirty joke or two. I remember three old ladies one afternoon in the front row dividing out their lunch, oblivious to what was happening on stage.

'Do you want a cheese and pickle sandwich, Kath?' one shouted to her mate on the end of the row.

'No thanks, Joyce. Cheese repeats on me,' Kath shouted back. 'I've got some boiled egg and salad cream here if you want one.'

'I can't get the lid off this flask,' the third party in the middle piped up.

'Give it here,' Joyce ordered, evidently the self-appointed leader of this trio. 'All it needs is a good twist. Here, hold my Tupperware.'

Joyce's good twist was ineffective. No matter how hard she struggled the lid remained firmly in place.

'No good asking me,' Kath offered, nibbling on her egg and salad cream sarnie like a gerbil. 'Not with my arthritis in me wrists.'

This interaction didn't annoy me, even if I was risking third-degree burns with my fire-eating routine. Far from it. I found this treble act hilarious.

'Hang on,' Joyce said, finally. 'I know what I'll do.' And getting out of her seat she walked to the front of the stage and offered the flask up to me.

'Do me a favour, will you, love,' she said in all seriousness. 'Put those things out and see if you can get the lid of this flask for me, will you?'

I enjoyed walking down the pier to work on a sunny day and so did Buster, making a beeline for the ice cream booth where he knew that if he stood on his hind legs and barked, the woman inside would hand him down the tiny end of a cone with a blob of ice cream on it, making her his best friend for life.

Gypsy Petulengro had a booth on the pier and occasionally if she was standing outside I'd stop and say hello to her. The Petulengros have lived in Blackpool for generations and they are a much-respected family. Sara Petulengro had been reading palms and consulting the cards and crystal ball on the North Pier for over twenty years. The display cases outside her booth were full of glowing testimonials from satisfied customers, arranged around a selection of fading black and white photos of her reading the palms of the Beverley Sisters, Frankie Vaughan, Bruce Forsyth and a very young Shirley Bassey.

I hinted one day when I got to know her better that I wouldn't mind having my photo preserved for posterity in her window, and she readily agreed. Later that night she came to the theatre bringing a photographer with her, and she read my palm for me too. I was excited at having a true Romany gypsy give me a palm-reading. Her prediction was spot on.

'You'll work hard and achieve great success,' she said, 'but look after your heart.' If only I'd heeded that good lady's advice, then that poor battered organ might not be full of stents today. I've got so many now I don't need a cardiologist, I'm better off with a welder.

Betty Legs Diamond was causing a sensation at the Funny Girls cabaret bar up the road from Blackpool pier. Simon (Betty) conceived, choreographed and starred in the shows, all of which were of an extremely high standard, and consequently Funny Girls was a huge success.

The press, together with most of the queens in the Flamingo Club, assumed that once I'd turned up on what was seen as

Betty's territory there would be bitter rivalry between us and gleefully anticipated cat fights and bitching sessions. Unfortunately as we were best of friends we had to disappoint them, teaming up instead and terrorizing the town between us.

The town was jumping, the prom and the piers lively with holidaymakers. Blackpool has its very own eau de parfum. North Park Drive smelt of clipped privet hedges, but down on the North Shore the air was thick with a heady combination of frying chips, candyfloss, booze and sweet sticky rock, all whipped together by that 'invigorating' sea breeze.

London seemed so far away, almost as if it were in a different country. I had planned to go back home on my day off but as travelling by rail on a Sunday can be a long, complicated journey fraught with delays and work on the lines I never bothered. Neither did I complete the course of driving lessons that I'd signed up for. I only took four lessons before giving up, frustrated by the mysteries of gears and clutches and trying to drive at 30 miles an hour, and I came to the conclusion that perhaps the roads would be safer without me tearing them up.

I went back to London just once and that was for another Stonewall Benefit, held this time at the Royal Albert Hall. I dragged the entire cast down with me, who were very excited at appearing there. I remember Russ Watson modestly telling me that he wasn't turning down the opportunity to sing in the Albert Hall as it was the only chance he'd ever get. How was he to predict that in a few short years he'd be selling the place out with a string of solo concerts?

Among the big names appearing we held our own and it was probably the first time that an End of the Pier Show had ever appeared at the Albert Hall.

The soprano Lesley Garrett was on the bill and unbelievably (she must have had a funny turn that day) asked if I'd like to do a duet with her. Lily Savage sings opera? Why not? Lesley is a warm, unpretentious Yorkshire lass who believes that opera is for everyone and not just the stuffed shirts of the Royal Opera House. The piece she chose for me to crucify was Rossini's Cat Duet, a musical duel between two rival sopranos that I vaguely knew of. There are no lyrics to this duet, just a series of meows and growls, and after listening to a tape she'd sent me I reckoned I'd be able to bluff my way through it.

After a very quick rehearsal with Phillip, Lesley's pianist, on the afternoon of the show, with Lesley filling in all the tricky notes I couldn't hit, I prepared to make my operatic debut, not with steam inhalations and a vocal warm-up in the dressing room, but with a pint of cider and ten Lambert and Butler in the Artists' Bar.

Lesley went out first and sang a solo to a standing ovation, while I stood backstage and asked myself what I thought I was doing even attempting something like this, and wondering if I'd be missed if I made a run for it.

Once the applause had subsided, she introduced me as Dame Liliana Salvaggio, a diva from La Scala, and adopting all the elaborate affectations of the most monstrous of divas I sailed out to join her and together we sang the Cat Duet as it had never been heard before.

When the song ended both Lesley and I were completely overwhelmed at the reaction from the audience, who rose to their feet as one and shook the old building to its very foundations with their foot-stamping and cheering. The noise was deafening, and as I was with Lesley backstage waiting to go out and take another bow, shaking with relief that we'd got through it but also with shock at the uproar, Lesley, unaware that her mike was still live, turned to me and said, 'Listen to that! You can sod Covent Garden!' causing further pandemonium among the audience.

*Easter Sunday at the Palladium* and the Cat Duet at the Albert Hall with Lesley are two of the biggest highlights of my working life.

It wasn't just the thought of facing the Sunday slow train that prevented me from going back to London, it was more to do with me having such a good time in Blackpool. The show was going well, the weather was good and the social life was hectic with a seemingly endless stream of charity balls and after-show parties, not to mention the weekly shindig I used to throw back at North Park Drive each time a friend came up to see me from London.

When Ian McKellen arrived at Blackpool station, the taxi driver didn't wait for Ian to tell him his destination.

'North Park Drive?' he said. 'Thought so. They have all-night parties up there. They sent out for Kentucky Fried Chicken at ten o'clock this morning.'

Like me, Ian loved Blackpool. The local press reported on his visit, remarking that, 'Sir Ian was wearing black leather trousers.' Shocking.

At one of the many theatrical fundraisers, I ended up at a table with Keith Harris and Danny La Rue, both of whom were plastered. Danny could be a mean drunk with a nasty tongue, as Barbara Windsor and I discovered one night at my one and only Water Rats Ball when, for no apparent reason, he wiped the floor with the pair of us.

'Let's face it, Danny,' Keith Harris stated, staring morosely at a group of young dancers from *Summer Holiday* throwing themselves around energetically on the dance floor, 'this party is for the young folk and not for a pair of old has-beens like us.'

Danny sat motionless for a moment, his face a mask of slowly simmering fury, before turning with the speed of a cobra on poor unsuspecting Keith.

'A has-been? How dare you!' he roared. 'You might consider yourself a has-been but I'm still very much a star, darling.'

'Sorry, Dan,' Keith interjected, trying desperately to back-pedal, 'but you know what I mean. No offence intended.'

'No, I don't know what you mean.' Danny was in full flight by now. 'And offence has been taken. How dare you class me in the same category as yourself, you, who makes a living with his hand up a duck's arse. Fucking cheek.'

Murphy knew how to deal with Danny, as I found out at an afternoon party once at his little flat over Foyles book-shop.

As the party and the booze progressed, Danny slipped from being a charming host to loud, opinionated and angry. He was giving his critique of a musical he'd recently seen, viciously picking everyone involved in the production to bits and growing more vitriolic by the minute as he angrily wound himself up.

As he grew steadily worse we stood around in the tiny roof garden covered in astro turf staring at our feet as he ranted on, wishing we were miles away, waiting for the moment when he'd turn and start on one of us, which, in all probability, meant I'd be first in the queue.

Danny paused for breath and, seeing his chance, Murphy spoke up.

'You should direct, Danny,' he said calmly. 'You instinctively know what's right and what's wrong and with your years of

302

experience and formidable talent you would be an incredible director.'

'Thank God,' Danny said, gripping Murphy's arm dramatically. 'Someone at last who finally understands me. Who are you?'

They went off into the flat and had a lengthy discussion mainly about Danny, and with his ego well and truly massaged he emerged a different man, full of admiration and praise for Murphy.

'That's how to handle people like that,' Murphy bragged in the taxi on our way home. 'Do you know he asked me to represent him?'

'You're not seriously thinking about it, are you?' I said, panicked.

'Are you out of your tiny mind, Savage?' he answered incredulously. 'One monster is quite enough to deal with, thank you very much.'

I never rose to the bait when Danny had a pop at me. I not only respected him, I understood why he felt such animosity towards me. He saw me as an up-and-coming pretender to his throne and the ageing lion didn't like it.

Once the highest-paid and hardest-working entertainer in the country with his own night club and a string of hit West End shows to his credit, who could call the likes of Noël Coward and Judy Garland among his closest friends, he was now reduced to trailing around the country in old-time music hall playing to tiny houses. He mellowed towards me as he grew older and over the years I would receive the occasional card or letter from him full of praise and kind words. As with many of the other greats I got to meet and work with as I went about my business, I'm grateful that I got to know the old dragon.

*

Once the first night was over, Murphy never came up to Blackpool again, which was just as well as I wasn't exactly living like a monk, having shacked up with an ex-con who had been released from prison on the very morning that I arrived in Blackpool.

The gods were in a mischievous mood that morning for it seemed destined that we should meet, and inevitably end up in the sack. I've always had a penchant for the bad boys and this one was no exception, and despite being no Einstein he was good fun, handsome and a lot of trouble.

I suspected that he had designs on returning to London with me at the end of the season but I made it plain that our relationship was nothing more than an extended holiday fling, which probably sounds hard-hearted but it's best to lay your cards on the table at the start.

The illuminations supplied some welcome cheer to the town as the nights drew in and the end of our season drew close. The weather had turned nasty and on a stormy night we felt as if we were performing on a ship as the theatre rocked from the pounding of the waves.

There was a little tram to transport punters up and down the pier, although it was frequently not working. It made the Great Western service from London to Bristol look highly efficient. Towards the end of our run the damn thing packed up altogether and if the weather was really fierce, which in late October it always was, then a chain was strung along the centre of the pier for people to hang on to in case one of the bigger waves tried to carry them out to sea.

Perversely, I found hanging on to this chain as we made our way down the pier after a show, getting soaked and battered by wind and rain on a particularly vicious night, a lot of fun. So did Sonia, and we always seemed to be laughing whenever we had to do it.

We celebrated the end of our run with a few fireworks and a drink on the roof of the theatre. The pier management, as well as our company manager, strictly forbade this but we ignored them and let our rockets off into the cold November night sky and drank champagne as we said goodbye to this captivating town and our stint on Blackpool's very own Devil's Island, the North Pier Theatre. Despite the ups and downs I was going to miss Blackpool. I'd even considered moving there, I'd settled in so well. Pulling up at the traffic lights as we drove home down the Golden Mile I set eyes on a clump of illuminated toadstools swaying in the wind and a couple of lads undeterred by the foul weather singing drunkenly in the rain and wondered if I might find London dull and unfriendly in comparison.

The hour-long *Evening with Lily Savage* was broadcast just after I returned from Blackpool, my fling for the season having kindly driven me down in a rented car. I was a bag of nerves at the thought of the show going out. Preferring to pretend it wasn't happening, we went and sat in an empty pub round the corner with me constantly checking my watch to see if the hour was up yet and I could relax and breathe easy.

The Blackpool paramour went home for good and apart from a few people ringing me up to say they'd enjoyed the show it was all a bit of an anticlimax, confirming my suspicions that the *Absolutely Fabulous* special it was scheduled against had annihilated me, and with that thought in mind I slunk off to bed gloomier than Eeyore.

*

'Savage!' Murphy shouted from the end of my bed. 'Wake up, c'mon, get up!'

'What the hell's up with you?' I cried, coming out of a deep sleep and not quite sure who I was talking to. 'What's the matter?'

Shocked out of my stupor I recalled the previous night and the little matter of a doomed television programme.

'Do you want last night's viewing figures?' he asked, his face expressionless and not giving anything away.

'Go on then,' I sighed, propping myself up on the pillow and preparing for the worst.

'Are you sure?'

He could be so bloody irritating at times.

'Just tell me, Murphy, and stop pissing about.'

'Brace yourself then,' he said cautiously, as if he were just about to deliver the news to Hitler that the Russians had captured Berlin. 'You got . . .'

'Just tell me, will you, before I get out of this bed and rip your stupid head off and shit on your neck.'

As you've probably gathered from that eloquent if a tad scatological reprimand, my patience is extremely thin first thing, in fact it's anorexic, and I was in no mood for Murphy's teasing.

'All right then, you got over thirteen million.'

'What? Did you just say thirteen million?'

'No,' he said, maddeningly calm, 'I said *over* thirteen million. You blew *Ab Fab* and the other two channels out of the water. Now get dressed and we'll go and get something to eat.'

In the days long before Murdoch's Sky invaded our homes and gave us hundreds of channels to flick through in the vain hope that we might find something worth watching, we had only four channels at our disposal and consequently viewing figures were much higher than they are now. Even so, over 13 million wasn't bad and today the likes of *Britain's Got Talent* would be extremely lucky to come anywhere near that.

As we sat in the Cat and Cucumber Café on Tower Bridge Road among builders, lorry drivers and City boys waiting for the man behind the counter to call out our number to go and collect our full English, I noticed Murphy looked tired and drawn. I was also aware that he'd hardly touched his breakfast, and when I asked him if he was feeling OK he went on the defensive claiming that he was fine, just a bit tired, that's all.

Why is it good news always precedes the bad?

We were under the misapprehension that with viewing figures so high the network would be chomping at the bit to offer me something else. However, at a very unsuccessful meeting with them we were told that they had nothing available in the schedules for over a year, and would we mind waiting?

Well, we had no intention of hanging around for them as, like everyone else, we had a living to earn. So we went to the BBC, who offered me a series to be filmed as soon as I'd finished another four-month tour of *Prisoner*. ITV sulked and there were rumblings of 'disloyalty', but business is business and if they didn't want me then luckily there was someone who did.

If you're ever asked if you can get a big Christmas show together in less than a month, then don't do as I did. Instead, reply with a loud firm no and walk calmly away.

Following the success of the season on the pier, Murphy and

Martin Witts put their heads together and came up with the idea of going back to Blackpool and putting on a Christmas show at the Winter Gardens. It seemed like a good idea at the time and I was very enthusiastic about working in Blackpool again. Without giving it much thought I said yes.

A lot of material from previous shows at the Bloomsbury was dragged out, including the Mary Poppins opening, the Apache dance and the parodies of Christmas songs. Ten dancers were hired, as was MD Barry Robinson and seven musicians. Simon came on board as choreographer again, as did Mig Kimpton, who signed up as company manager/ director. Together with Brenda as Gayle Tuesday and Sean Maguire who, at the ripe old age of twenty, was already a household name from his roles in *Grange Hill* and *EastEnders* and had a string of chart hits under his belt, we prepared for a jolly Christmas in Blackpool. Ha.

As it was a Christmas show I thought it wouldn't do any harm to include some kids, and so Mig recruited a local children's dance school, who were going to perform 'It's A Hard Knock Life' from *Annie* and 'Goodnight, Farewell' from *The Sound of Music*. What possessed me? It was a complicated, not to mention expensive enough show to get together in less than a month without a troupe of kids to worry about, and though it hadn't dawned on me during rehearsals, it was also turning into a mess that didn't gel.

Murphy's health was slowly worsening. His weight had dropped alarmingly and his energy levels were in his boots. I nagged him endlessly to see a doctor and eventually, after me putting on the pressure, he gave in, only to return from the doc's crowing how it had been a waste of time as the doctor had been unable to make an accurate diagnosis and it was nothing that a bit of fasting wouldn't cure, blah, blah.

He was currently going through his alternative medicine phase, convinced that a cure for whatever was ailing him lay in Chinese medicine. After consulting a practitioner in Soho, he was diagnosed as having 'damp kidneys', whatever that is, and prescribed bags of herbs out of which he was to make a noxious infusion to drink three pints of a day. It tasted like sewer water that had been inhabited by alligators with dysentery, but he drank it religiously, believing it was doing him good. Judging by his appearance, I'd have said it was having the opposite effect.

'Go to the doctor, Murph, please!'

'I'm fine. There's nothing wrong with me.'

The night before I left for Blackpool he was so ill I had to virtually carry him up to bed. He couldn't make the stairs without assistance. I wanted to call an ambulance there and then but he was having none of it, adamant that he'd feel better after a good night's sleep and another pint of that poisonous potion that I had serious doubts about.

Working-class roots run deeper than Japanese knotweed and for a certain generation, like mine, you grew up listening to your older relatives and neighbours refusing to consult a doctor when they were ill. This fear and mistrust of all things medical is unconsciously absorbed and you may find in later years that you adopt the same attitude: not wanting to cause a fuss over nothing, preferring to suffer in silence and 'get on with it'.

'I'm not getting in no bloody ambulance . . .'

'They're not putting me in no hospital. Once they get their hands on you, you've had it . . .'

'What do I want to bother a doctor for? This pain in my chest is nothing more than a bit of indigestion . . .'

I grew up listening to protestations like this. Before the

NHS, a trip to a doctor cost money that many could barely afford, and hospitals meant death. Getting an ambulance, especially for yourself, was the last resort. It meant you'd given in. Asking a neighbour to run to the phone box to call for one meant accepting that whatever was wrong with you wouldn't be cured by Beechams Powders or a drop of Dr Collis Browne.

I'd inherited these traits and so had Murphy, and apart from being very annoying, this ridiculous behaviour can turn out to be life threatening.

I couldn't just waltz off to Blackpool and leave Murphy in this condition, but I had no choice. If I walked out of the show at this late stage a lot of people would be out of work, ticket sales would have to be refunded and the fallout would be enormous – not that Murphy would entertain the thought of me cancelling the show for one minute. So he made a deal with me. If I went to Blackpool, then he'd go to hospital – where not surprisingly he was admitted immediately.

'Don't worry about me, Savage,' he whispered in a barely audible voice from his hospital bed. 'This lot will sort me out and then I'll be up for opening night, so go on, hop it, I'm going to be fine.' Closing the door behind me, I was unable to speak for the lump in the back of my throat. I wished I could believe him.

Blackpool seafront in winter is grim. Torrential rain together with aggressive waves lashing the prom made the roads unsafe, while that ever-present bracing sea breeze had metamorphosed into a full-blown cyclone that it was impossible to walk into.

I'd been told over the phone that the house we'd rented for the fortnight wouldn't be ready for occupation until tomorrow, and as I seemed to have unconsciously gravitated towards

Talbot Square and the North Pier and was now trapped in a doorway sheltering from the weather with no hope of getting a taxi, I checked into the first bed and breakfast I saw.

The lady who ran it was exceptionally pleasant. She didn't mind dogs – quite the opposite. The first thing she did was to get a towel and enthusiastically rub Buster down. I wondered if I was next, but instead I got a cup of tea, a ham sarnie and a nice chat. Thankfully she did most of the talking as I was preoccupied with Murphy and the show. All that was required from me were a few sympathetic nods and grunts as she prattled on about the decline of the hotel business and Blackpool in general.

That night as I lay in the deep trench that had formed in the middle of the sponge that was masquerading as a mattress, I could hear a couple outside on the street arguing.

'Don't fucking come near me,' the woman was shouting. 'Christmas in Blackpool? Who comes to Blackpool for Christmas? I hope you drop dead.'

'No you don't,' I said out loud to the room. 'You really don't.'

Buster growled in agreement from the bottom of my bed, while I attempted to find a comfortable spot in the trench so I could forget my worries in sleep. I'd never felt so bloody desolate in my life.

I was on the end of a wire hanging thirty feet above the stage when Murphy rang me on my mobile, which normally I'd have turned off in rehearsals but I was desperate to hear the results of his tests.

'I'm fine,' he said not very convincingly when I asked him how he was feeling. 'I'm just a bit nauseous after the chemo, that's all.'

'Chemo?' The blood pounded in my ears at the mention of that word. Chemo meant one thing: Cancer.

'Oh, Sav,' Murphy sobbed. 'I didn't mean you to find out this way . . . over the phone. I wanted to tell you to your face . . . I've got cancer of the liver.'

The day just got worse. That morning at rehearsals I had nearly been killed or at the very least multiply fractured when the rope that was controlling the wire I was hanging from slipped and I plummeted thirty feet towards the stage like a sack of sand. I was saved by the wingman, Chris, who grabbed the rope in the nick of time, sustaining severe rope burns to both his hands in the process.

Now this, Murphy with cancer. I couldn't even bring myself to say the word.

Back in my dressing room, Mig told me the whole story. They'd known about the cancer for a few days but Murphy hadn't wanted me to find out. He wanted the chance to tell me himself. Suddenly everything seemed pointless. The struggle to get this stupid show in a reasonable state for opening night was no longer important. If Murphy died while I was stuck up here swinging on the end of a wire all dolled up as Mary soddin' Poppins, I'd never forgive myself.

However, in this game personal feelings have to be put aside. Tradition decrees that the show must go on, regardless of what's happening in real life. As I returned to the stage I wondered who it was that thought up that expression, 'the show must go on', and how I'd like to punch his lights out.

True to his word, Murphy arrived on opening night exactly ten minutes before the curtain went up. He was carried into my dressing room where he collapsed in the bathroom, vomiting and crying out in pain.

I don't know how I got through the show that night, but I did, even though it didn't take long for me to realize it was a turkey. There were too many different elements that clashed, and having children in it didn't help because the audience were confused over whether this was family entertainment or a raunchy Lily show – as indeed was I. Having kids around made me tone the act right down – no swearing, no filthy jokes, nothing untoward, and consequently no response from the audience.

I hated that show as much as the punters did.

There was no first-night party. I was out of that theatre as soon as the curtain came down. The slap was off and it was back to the rented house. Murphy was in bed and after a brief chat with Joan, who was also staying with us, I went directly up to see him. He was breathing hard and still awake so I lay down beside him on the bed, relieved that he was here.

'How was the show?' he asked in a voice so weak that it no longer sounded like him. It was the voice of a frail old man.

'Awful,' I said without any emotion. 'It died a death.'

I realized too late what I'd just said and started to gabble nervously in an attempt to cover up my unfortunate choice of words.

'We'll go on holiday as soon as you feel a bit better,' I said, hurriedly getting off any mention of death. 'We can go on the Orient Express. We've always wanted to do that.'

'You mean, you have,' he replied, smiling.

'No, you said you wanted to go on it as well,' I protested. 'Or perhaps we can go to Bangkok—'

'Savage . . .'

'D'ya fancy that? We can go to Hong Kong as well and the

Philippines.' I rattled these destinations off in a state of panic because I knew he was about to impart some information that I didn't want to hear.

'Savage . . .' He tried to raise his voice to stop me mid-flow but he didn't have the energy.

'Or we could just have a beach holiday and do nothing except lie in the sun and rest.'

'Savage, will you shut the fuck up and let me get a word in edgeways,' he finally snapped. 'We haven't much time.'

'How do you mean?' I said warily, dreading the reply.

'I'll be brief,' he went on with his usual directness. 'I'm not doing so well, sugar.'

'How well aren't you doing?' I hesitated, not daring to ask the question I didn't want to hear an answer to.

'They've given me three days to three weeks.'

On Christmas Day, Joan, Vera, Murphy and I gathered around the table for our lunch, pulling crackers amid an atmosphere of artificial joviality that fooled no one, least of all Murphy, who, slumped hollow-eyed and emaciated in his chair, resembled one of the living dead you see on documentaries about the liberation of Auschwitz.

I'm frequently asked by magazine journalists what my most memorable Christmas was, for the obligatory 'Celebs at Christmas' articles they always run at this time of year. Christmas 1996, in a rented house in Blackpool, spoon-feeding my dying man mashed roast potatoes, is the first image that comes to mind, but nobody wants to read that in a light-hearted article meant to reflect the Christmas spirit. That's why I always give them the 'finding a life-size Popeye in a pillowcase when I was a nipper' tale.

*

*Lily's Christmas Cracker* improved a great deal, as miraculously did Murphy, and by the time the show closed and we could finally go home he declared he was fit enough to drive, or at least part of the way. His determination to get well and not give in to this disease was staggering, and his powers of recuperation verged on the miraculous. I agreed to him driving – not that I had any choice – on the proviso that we broke the journey. He objected, claiming it was a waste of time, but when the light flurry of snow that had started to fall as we left Blackpool turned into a blizzard, he reluctantly agreed to us stopping off overnight at Armathwaite Hall Hotel in the Lakes. Here, seduced by the beautiful snow-covered vista, excellent food, comfortable rooms, log fires and the relaxing atmosphere of a grand country house, we didn't leave for three days.

Even though Murphy was improving by the day, albeit slowly, I refused to let my guard down, spending all of my time on tenterhooks in case this reprieve was only temporary and he'd have a relapse. Life without Murphy was unthinkable. I refused to even consider the eventuality of it ever happening. The sword of Damocles hung over our heads but I hid my feelings from him, trying to maintain a façade of always looking on the bright side (a song I loathe, by the way), while worrying myself sick. He was still underweight, though not as emaciated as he was at Christmas. Plead, beg and threaten as I did, I could not get the awkward swine to drink the protein shakes the hospital had given him. He claimed they were disgustingly sweet and undoubtedly full of chemicals. In the end I resorted to low cunning, mixing up smoothies laced with a flavourless weight-gain powder that I kept hidden under the kitchen sink. Then he found my stash one day and started making his own smoothies – 'Without the use of additives, Savage!'

Murphy was extremely positive about his illness every step of the way. With steely tenacity, he refused to let the cancer beat him. God help anyone who treated him like an invalid. He'd chew the face off them, and many an unfortunate nurse who ineptly jabbed him with a needle in an attempt to find a vein would be told in no uncertain terms exactly what he thought of them.

He'd long passed the three-days-to-three-weeks deadline that had chilled me to the bone, but even so, it was no time to become complacent. I'd lost too many friends over the last decade and I wasn't about to let Murphy go without a struggle. But all I could do was keep a vigilant yet surreptitious eye on him, try not to fuss and, even though I wasn't supposed to believe any more, light candles on a regular basis at Westminster Cathedral. I must've spent a bloody fortune on candles during Murphy's illness. I became quite a regular at the altar of the Virgin Mary, burning wax and making all sorts of wild promises in exchange for a complete cure for Murphy.

Around the corner from the Cathedral in Strutton Ground was a very good health food shop. After my session chewing the altar rails I'd drop in there to buy food beneficial for health that I knew Murphy would like: organic brown rice, alfalfa, mung beans and that unpalatable wheatgrass juice that repeats on me all day if I drink so much as a thimble full. The woman behind the counter became a confidante and would recommend supplements. She also prescribed a holiday, saying it would be beneficial for both of us because I looked like I'd been ridden hard and put away wet – a racing term, apparently, and not what I thought she'd meant at first.

I had four bank accounts at the time, personal, business, savings and one for tax and VAT. This last one always depressed me. I was now paying more tax than I ever thought I'd earn but as I didn't want those bastards from the Inland Revenue on my back I always set a large chunk of my earnings aside so when that demand fell on the hall mat, usually beautifully timed to arrive on Christmas Eve as a nice little surprise among your Christmas cards, I could pay it promptly and in full and then go off and sulk for a couple of days at the loss.

I'd made a few commercials: one was for a Ford Escort, and I did a long-running voiceover for the soft drink Oasis, which I'd drunk gallons of on *The Big Breakfast* because it wasn't fizzy and didn't make you belch. But perhaps one of the strangest jobs ever, especially for a man, was to be the leg model for Pretty Polly tights.

A magazine had run a competition to find the best 'celebrity' legs, showing an assortment of them, no faces, just the lallies, with Lily's among them, for the readers to decide the winner. Considering I wouldn't be caught dead wearing a pair of shorts in public and had always looked upon my skinny pins as being akin to two Park Drive hanging out of the packet, I thought Murphy was sending me up when he said that not only had I won, but Pretty Polly wanted my legs as the model for a new range of ladder-resistant tights called Resilience, the gag being that, like Lily, they were as hard as nails.

On being resuscitated after hearing of the disgusting amount of money they were offering, I duly turned up at the studio, put on three pairs of Resilience – I wasn't shaving my legs for any amount of money – posed with the knee bent in what is known as a stripper's dip for a confused photographer flown over especially from the States, then got changed and went home. There was no need for slap and wig as they only wanted me from the waist down, although at those prices I'd have shown the bloody lot if they'd asked, which thankfully for all concerned they didn't.

Still not knowing what the long-term prognosis of this cancer was, I raided the savings account and spent all the advert money on a holiday in the Far East. We started off in Langkawi for a week before moving on to Singapore, Bangkok via the Eastern and Oriental Express, and finally Bali.

It was quite a trip, and since this might be our last holiday together then the cost didn't come into it. We spoke openly about cancer these days. The word no longer scared us. Instead, we were angry that this disease had the temerity to invade our lives, and being of good Irish feuding stock we were not about to surrender without putting up a bloody good fight first.

I was ecstatic on the three-day journey on board the Eastern and Oriental Express. It was beyond any of my expectations and, along with its sister, the Venice Simplon Orient Express, has got to be the most beautiful train in the world.

We arrived at the end of our three-week journey in Bali, staying at an extremely flash hotel complex of private villas with plunge pools. One of the problems with this paradise, however, was the Balinese traditional music that was played on a loop tape. To the indigenous ear, Balinese music is probably a real foot-tapper, but to my untrained western ear it just sounded like people banging on hollow logs. There was no escape from this racket unless you left the hotel and hit the town, which looked like a scene out of *Good Morning, Vietnam* and was full of bars filled with drunken Aussies.

No, I couldn't warm to Bali at all, even though Murphy thought the opposite and couldn't understand why I disliked it so much.

In the end what drove me over the edge was something quite

trivial. The staff kept calling me 'Mr Murpee'. Each day I would be greeted by every one of these charming, efficient, hard-working staff with a cheery 'Good morning, Mr Murpee', and each day, despite my correcting them that I was in fact Mr O'Grady, they kept smiling and carrying on regardless, blissfully unaware that I was on a slow simmer and ready to go pop at any moment.

Despite all the travelling, or possibly because of it, Murphy's health had improved beyond both our expectations. While he was here in Bali he'd been having daily massages and treatments, and by the end of the week he looked like his old self.

'I'm ready for anything, Savage,' he said, and by that I knew he meant the next course of chemotherapy he had to face when we got back home.

It was on our last day that I cracked. We were woken up at 7.15 precisely by six members of staff bearing a trolley laden with fruit, champagne and a birthday cake.

'Happy birthday, Mr Murpee!' they chorused. I jumped out of my bed with the shock of it, forgetting about the voluminous folds of mosquito netting that surrounded it, bringing half of it down on top of me as I struggled like a frantic moth to escape.

'Happy birthday!' they sang again and, after watching me struggle to get out of the nets, one of them finally walked forward, still wearing the omnipresent grin, and lifted the netting off my head. At the same time his colleague presented me with the cake, complete with what looked like a hell of a lot of candles flickering in the breeze from the air con.

'It's not my birthday,' I protested. 'Is it? No, it can't be.' I was still groggy and confused from being woken from a deep sleep at this hour.

'Happy birthday!' they shouted again, ignoring everything

319

I'd just said and as per usual grinning like a group of Thermians from *Galaxy Quest*.

'Go, make a wish,' one of them said. 'Now, now, quickly.'

'I'll tell you what I wish, shall I?' I said menacingly, allowing Lily Savage to gurgle up from the depths and take control. I then enlightened them on my opinion of the island, the hotel, the music, the birthday and the annoyance of constantly being called Mr friggin' Murpee.

Now I'm normally very reserved in hotels, always courteous to the staff, tidy up after me in the room and very rarely complain, not even when the housekeeping staff appear to be hell bent on getting into my room at every conceivable moment of the day, or the steak that I ordered, despite my pleas for it to be cremated, arrives full of blood and perfectly able to get up off the plate, brush itself down and make a run for it.

This unexpected outburst therefore came as a shock to Murphy who, surprised by my eloquence at this hour of the morning, never mind my perfect command of the Queen's English, that's if the Queen swore like a trooper, broke down in laughter.

'Stop, Savage!' he hooted from his bed next to mine. 'Enough, enough, please,' and still cackling he rang reception to find out what was going on, while I stood bristling with rage in a froth of mozzie net refusing to blow out my candles.

It transpired that the special champagne birthday breakfast had been ordered for his wife by another Mr Murphy who happened to be staying at the hotel. The staff stopped grinning and went into overdrive with the apologies, to such an extent that it made me wonder if a mistake like that meant sixty lashes or demotion to toilet duty in one of the sleazier bars in Kuta.

Ashamed of my outburst, I joined in with the refrain, nodding, grinning and apologizing in unison with the group as they slowly backed out of the room.

'Sorry, Mr Murpee,' the last to leave said as he finally closed the door behind him, setting Murphy off guffawing again. God, it was good to see him laugh like a drain again. I was too energized after my rant to go back to bed and, despite the unexpected birthday party at such an unholy hour of the day, I was elated at seeing Murphy so trouble free and happy.

'Savage,' he sniggered, 'what I would've given for a tape-recorder just then. That was the best bit of comedy I've ever seen, and your rant, well, it was priceless. Galton and Simpson and the whole kit and caboodle of comedy writers couldn't have held a candle to that.'

I couldn't remember a word of what I'd said. It had just come pouring out like verbal diarrhoea, but whatever it was had tickled him.

Highly animated now, he walked around the room still laughing and I could see that he was either cooking something up or had lost the plot. It was both.

'I think it's about time you started giving it a go as yourself,' he said, bursting with enthusiasm. 'We both know you don't need the wig to be funny and you're forever wittering on about not wanting to do drag when you're ancient.'

'I've been on telly as myself,' I reminded him. 'On *That's Show Business* when I left my wig on the train that time and had no choice but to go on as me.'

'I know you did,' he said, 'but I'm talking about something bigger.'

'Like what? I can't really see me fronting one of those cheesy quiz shows. I can't stand them and I doubt if I could raise the enthusiasm,' I said, already picturing myself in a velvet jacket asking questions off a cue card.

'Savage, give over,' Murphy mocked. 'You'd raise the *Titanic* if the money was right and you know it. What you should be doing is this.'

'What? Kicking off in hotels?'

'Exactly,' he said, his eyes lighting up. 'What you need to be doing is a travel show and I'm going to get on to them as soon as we get back.'

'Like Judith Chalmers, you mean?' I scoffed. Just as I couldn't see myself hosting a prime-time game show, I certainly couldn't see myself in a lilac shell suit singing the praises of a child-friendly holiday resort.

'No, you fool,' he corrected me. 'One where you tell the truth about the countries you visit, and if you don't like them you give your honest opinion of the place. For example,' he went on, 'that little scene I've just witnessed would be television gold.'

'Murphy, nobody goes on telly and shows their true colours,' I pointed out. 'They wouldn't dare. All those presenters have a telly persona. It's not what they're really like. You don't hear Alan Whicker threatening to shove a cake up someone's arse, do you?'

'That's just it!' he cried. 'That's the gimmick, as you'd say. Nobody lets their guard down and says what they really think, so all you'll have to do is be yourself.'

'But what's that?' I asked warily. 'What is myself, actually?'

'I'll give you a clue, Savage,' he replied, smiling and picking up the phone again. 'It begins with C and ends in T and it's not Catherine the Great. Now, what do you want for breakfast?'

\*

I went on the road again for yet another tour of *Prisoner*, only this time with a slightly different cast a couple of whom I privately thought weren't a patch on the originals, but even so we played to packed houses again and enthusiastic audiences.

'It's like the bloody *Rocky Horror Show*,' Maggie remarked in the pub after a particularly lively show. 'They know the script better than us.'

It was when we were at the Bradford Alhambra that I came to eat my words about game shows. I'd rented a tiny terraced house in the Victorian village of Saltaire and became so enamoured with both the house and the village that I went out one morning to buy ciggies and milk and came back the proud owner of a flat in the newly converted mill instead. Property was an investment, I told myself to ease the guilt of such an impulse buy, and besides it was such a reasonable price.

During the run at the Alhambra, Murphy came to visit, bringing two producers from London up with him.

'How would you like to be the new presenter of *Blankety Blank*?' I was asked over tea in the front room of my terraced gaff.

Apart from *The Golden Shot*, *Blankety Blank* was the only game show I really enjoyed. Terry Wogan, with his car aerial microphone, made it his own, then the incomparable Les Dawson took over and, following the tradition, sent the whole thing up. That was the joy of *Blankety Blank*. It was designed to be gently mocked, with its star prizes of matching luggage and an up-to-the-minute hostess trolley and fondue set that would make you the envy of your friends and neighbours. More importantly it was a show that had lots of potential for a character like Lily in the driving seat, even if I did have big shoes to fill.

I gave it some thought before making my decision – about

three seconds to be exact, and happily agreed to start filming as soon as I'd finished the tour.

Learning the rules to a game is not my forte and so the rules of *Blankety Blank*, which I never really understood, and which I read out on every show I ever did, had to be written down on idiot boards and held up next to the camera by Buster's idol, my floor manager Quentin Mann.

Buster just loved the old BBC in Wood Lane and was more than capable of sneaking out of the scene dock when I wasn't looking and making his own way to the *Blue Peter* garden, where he once strolled on to the CBeebies' set as they were filming live and took over. He was obsessive about the *Blue Peter* garden because he once saw a squirrel there. Twelve years later he headed for the same spot to see if it had made a reappearance, but it hadn't. He grew up in that garden, just as I had really, when I think of the times I sat watching Valerie, John and Peter burying time capsules and dogs and hanging the fat balls that they'd made in the studio for the birds on a branch of a tree that Percy Thrower had planted all those years ago. After they sold Wood Lane, the garden ended up on a roof in Salford, an act akin to sacrilege, but I'm sure Buster's ghost is still chasing squirrels around what's left of the original.

The BBC had commissioned a series that I was busy writing as I was filming *Blankety Blank*. The show was a joy to do as it was all ad-lib, the only hard bit being thinking up twelve witty intros for the celeb guests as we filmed two shows a day. I was in the middle of thinking up something short but snappy, as the ad men say, for Sir Donald Sinden, a regular on the show, when Murphy walked into the dressing room. I spent most of my time in dressing rooms these days, although thankfully standards were much improved. Not only did I have my own lav, but I now had a sink with hot water and a tap, no less.

'Things are looking good, Sav,' Murphy said, unusually jolly. 'The Beeb are over the moon with the way the show's going and they can't wait for the series to start.' He stood behind me and checked himself in the mirror, running his hand through his fresh crop of hair, which was growing back less grey and more luxuriant than it had been before his chemo. His skin was glowing as well, and apart from looking extremely handsome, the bastard had shed ten years.

'If that's what chemo does for you then sign me up for a course,' I told him, talking to him through the mirror. 'You look more like Richard Gere every day.'

'No, Savage,' he corrected me. 'Richard Gere looks like me.'

As he rested his hands on my shoulders his mood turned suddenly grave. 'Speaking of chemo, I need to talk to you.'

I turned around in the chair to face him. 'What about?' I asked fearfully. I firmly believed that you had to pay for a run of good fortune with less than happy news.

'It's about the cancer,' he said quietly. 'I got my results back this morning.'

'Oh my good God.' I panicked. 'And what, what did they have to say?'

'Don't start kicking off.' He held his hand up to stop me. 'It's over, Savage,' he said calmly.

'What do you mean?' I was frantic now. 'You mean you're going to die?'

'No, you dozy plonk.' He laughed. 'It's gone. I'm not even in remission.'

'How do you mean?' It seemed incomprehensible that the

shadow that had hung over us for all this time, the spectre that had dominated my every waking moment, had finally given up, called a taxi and left the building to be out of our lives for good. No, it couldn't be. He was lying to protect me and I told him so.

'It's true, honestly it is,' he said, crying tears of happiness. 'Honestly, as unbelievable as it sounds, it's gone. The liver has completely healed itself. It's over, Sav, finished. Gone for good.'

The tension slipped from my body. I could feel it as I exhaled heavily, expelling it from me as if it were something physical that I'd been carrying around inside.

I leapt off the stool and hugged him, both of us crying now, but out of sheer relief.

Looking at our reflection in the mirror with our arms around each other, I mouthed a silent but heartfelt thank you to whatever entity wanted to claim it. Ever the drama queen with a cinematic eye, I also thought what a poignant picture we made: the brave soldier returning home from the front to his lover as the camera pans out to fade with a sweep of violins and into the closing credits.

'Now, then, Savage,' Murphy said, lifting his head from my shoulder and looking me straight in the eye determinedly, leading me to believe he was about to say something profoundly memorable that I would remember until my dying day.

'What, Murph?' I whispered in a tone that could be mistaken for tender.

'You'd better get your arse into gear,' he replied casually. 'It's nearly half past six and you haven't got your slap on yet. C'mon, chop chop, Sugar, you've got a show to do.'

# INDEX

**Paul O'Grady** first came to fame in the guise of Lily Savage, and was nominated for a Perrier Award at the Edinburgh Festival in 1991. Lily later became a regular on *This Morning*, took over the bed on *The Big Breakfast* and presented *Blankety Blank*, but has now retired (reportedly). Paul, of course, went on to further success presenting his chat shows on Channel 4 and ITV, *For the Love of Dogs* and *Animal Orphans* on ITV, and his weekly show on BBC Radio 2, inter alia. His three previous volumes of autobiography – *At My Mother's Knee*, *The Devil Rides Out* and *Still Standing* – were all *Sunday Times* bestsellers.

Paul has won numerous awards including a BAFTA for Best Entertainment Performance, National Television Awards for Most Popular Daytime Programme and Most Popular Entertainment Show, and a Comedy Award for Best Comedy Entertainment Personality. His show about Battersea Dogs and Cats Home, *Paul O'Grady: For the Love of Dogs*, has won two National Television Awards for Best Factual Entertainment and also received a BAFTA nomination.